If Home Is Not Here

THE AZRIELI SERIES OF HOLOCAUST SURVIVOR MEMOIRS: PREVIOUSLY PUBLISHED TITLES

If Home Is Not Here

Max Bornstein

THE AZRIELI FOUNDATION
www.azrielifoundation.org

Cover and book design by Mark Goldstein
Endpaper maps by Martin Gilbert
Maps on pages xxii–xxiii by François Blanc

LIBRARY AND ARCHIVES CANADA CATALOGUING IN PUBLICATION

Bornstein, Max, 1921–
   If home is not here/ Max Bornstein.

(The Azrieli series of Holocaust survivor memoirs. Series IV)
Includes bibliographical references and index.
ISBN 978-1-897470-27-5

1. Bornstein, Max, 1921– 2. Holocaust, Jewish (1939–1945) – Personal narratives.
3. Holocaust survivors – Canada – Biography. I. Azrieli Foundation II. Title. III.
Series: Azrieli series of Holocaust survivor memoirs. Series IV.

D804.196.B67A3 2012   940.53'18092   C2011-908479-1

PRINTED IN CANADA

The Azrieli Series of Holocaust Survivor Memoirs

Contents

Series Preface:
In their own words...

In telling these stories, the writers have liberated themselves. For so many years we did not speak about it, even when we became free people living in a free society. Now, when at last we are writing about what happened to us in this dark period of history, knowing that our stories will be read and live on, it is possible for us to feel truly free. These unique historical documents put a face on what was lost, and allow readers to grasp the enormity of what happened to six million Jews – one story at a time.

David J. Azrieli, C.M., C.Q., M.Arch
Holocaust survivor and founder, The Azrieli Foundation

Since the end of World War II, over 30,000 Jewish Holocaust survivors have immigrated to Canada. Who they are, where they came from, what they experienced and how they built new lives for themselves and their families are important parts of our Canadian heritage. The Azrieli Foundation's Holocaust Survivor Memoirs Program was established to preserve and share the memoirs written by those who survived the twentieth-century Nazi genocide of the Jews of Europe and later made their way to Canada. The program is guided by the conviction that each survivor of the Holocaust has a remarkable story to tell, and that such stories play an important role in education about tolerance and diversity.

Millions of individual stories are lost to us forever. By preserving the stories written by survivors and making them widely available to a broad audience, the Azrieli Foundation's Holocaust Survivor Memoirs Program seeks to sustain the memory of all those who perished at the hands of hatred, abetted by indifference and apathy. The personal accounts of those who survived against all odds are as different as the people who wrote them, but all demonstrate the courage, strength, wit and luck that it took to prevail and survive in such terrible adversity. The memoirs are also moving tributes to people – strangers and friends – who risked their lives to help others, and who, through acts of kindness and decency in the darkest of moments, frequently helped the persecuted maintain faith in humanity and courage to endure. These accounts offer inspiration to all, as does the survivors' desire to share their experiences so that new generations can learn from them.

The Holocaust Survivor Memoirs Program collects, archives and publishes these distinctive records and the print editions are available free of charge to libraries, educational institutions and Holocaust-education programs across Canada, and at Azrieli Foundation educational events. They are also available for sale to the general public at bookstores. All editions of the books are available for free download on our web site at: www.azrielifoundation.org.

The Azrieli Foundation would like to express appreciation to the following people for their invaluable efforts in producing this series: Simone Abrahamson, Florence Buathier, Jesse Cohoon, Darrel Dickson and Sherry Dodson (Maracle Press), Sir Martin Gilbert, Stan Greenspan, Robin Harp of the US Holocaust Memorial Museum, Richard Mozer, Arnaud Regnaud, Sylwia Szymańska-Smolkin, Keaton Taylor, Lise Viens, Margie Wolfe and Emma Rodgers of Second Story Press, Sylvia Vance and Piotr Wróbel.

About the Glossary

The following memoir contains a number of terms, concepts and historical references that may be unfamiliar to the reader. For information on major organizations; significant historical events and people; geographical locations; religious and cultural terms; and foreign-language words and expressions that will help give context and background to the events described in the text, please see the glossary beginning on page 251.

Introduction

Early in his memoir, Max Bornstein (then Mordechai Zalman) describes a seemingly banal incident at the Winnipeg orphanage where he and his younger sister, Clarice, lived for six years in the 1920s. At the time, Bornstein's father, Chiel, was a stateless refugee in Paris and his mother, Liba, was unable to care for her children due to ill health and a dearth of financial resources. While they played outside on the orphanage grounds, some of the older children invented a game of throwing the younger children into the air on a blanket held firmly at each of its four corners. When Bornstein, then six years old, took his turn, one of the older boys accidentally lost his grip on the blanket and Bornstein fell hard on the ground. Although he wasn't seriously injured, Bornstein recalls a deep sense of abandonment and aloneness in the aftermath: "the pain did make me cry and there was no one to comfort me."

In many ways, this childhood memory – and the deep loss and emotional pain it symbolizes – anticipates many of the central themes embedded in Bornstein's narrative: displacement, poverty, abandonment and institutionalization. Unlike many previously published survivor testimonies, Bornstein's account does not begin and end with the Holocaust. Instead, his story extends across more than twenty years of unfathomable suffering and is dominated by the two distinct but overlapping traumatic trajectories of domestic violence

and state violence. On the domestic front, Bornstein endured a de-
cade-long separation from a father who, once reunited with the family, was physically abusive to Bornstein's mother. Bornstein recalls
how he felt helpless to intervene and stop the violence and how the
constant clashes between his parents provoked in him tremendous
anxiety and worry. He writes, "In all the years I spent in Paris, nothing affected me so profoundly as having to constantly witness my parents fighting. It left me drained, confused, frightened and upset. For
children, nothing equals the pain of watching their parents exchange
violent blows." At the same time, the entire family was plagued by
their status as stateless refugees, and the Nazi threat loomed large in
a global climate of antisemitism and restrictive immigration policies.
What makes Bornstein's memoir truly striking, however, is the extent
to which he moved not only between countries but also between institutions. Over two decades, Bornstein found himself institutional-
ized in an orphanage in Canada, a homeless shelter in France, a concentration camp in Spain, and a psychiatric hospital in the United
Kingdom. In this sense, Bornstein offers us a Holocaust narrative that
differs from more familiar stories about surviving in hiding or living
through the horrors of the Nazi camps. Bornstein existed in a state
of nearly constant exile, fear and perpetual wandering before, during
and after the war.

Max Bornstein was born on November 12, 1921, into a poor
Jewish family in Warsaw, Poland. At the time, Poland was home to
2.8 million Jews, a number that would rise to more than 3.3 million
by 1938 due to immigration from the Russian and Ukrainian territories of the Soviet Union. Antisemitism was commonplace in Poland
during this period, stemming from hundreds of years of systemic
prejudice in the Catholic Church, persistent myths about Jews mur-
dering Christian children in acts of "blood libel" and a widespread
intolerance for linguistic, religious and cultural differences. Just as
Jews fled from pogroms in the Soviet republics to Poland, so Polish
Jews also emigrated westward in significant numbers. Bornstein's

family was among the thousands of Polish Jews who immigrated to France via Berlin in the early 1920s. Bornstein's father could not obtain a Polish passport because he had not completed his military service, so he arrived in France as a stateless and undocumented refugee. With Bornstein's father precariously employed and under the constant threat of expulsion, the family frequently relied on Jewish charities for subsistence. In the fall of 1923, Bornstein and his mother, then pregnant with Clarice, immigrated to Canada with the help of Bornstein's maternal aunts, leaving Bornstein's father behind with the promise that he could soon follow. In reality, the move to Canada was the beginning of a prolonged and painful separation for Bornstein's family.

That Max Bornstein and his mother could make the journey to Canada in the first place is remarkable. Between 1919 and 1923, Canadian immigration officials severely restricted the number of immigrants – particularly Jewish immigrants – allowed into the country. Harold Troper writes that in 1923, the same year that Bornstein arrived in Canada, "the government instituted several far-reaching administrative refinements clearly designed to block off most remaining avenues still open to Jewish immigration."[1] From that point onward, Jews required a special permit to enter Canada, and only a few were able to enter as immediate relatives of Canadian residents. In 1933, just as Hitler came to power in Germany and began to actualize his plan for a Nazi racial state, Bornstein's mother made the fateful decision to return to Paris with her children and reunite with her husband. Once they left Canada, it was nearly impossible to return. The Canadian government had further tightened immigration

1   Troper, Harold. "New Horizons in a New Land: Jewish Immigration to Canada," *From Immigration to Integration: The Canadian Jewish Experience.* (B'nai B'rith Canada and Government of Canada, 2000), http://www.bnaibrith.ca/institute/millennium/millennium01.html

restrictions for Jewish refugees; like most other nations at the time, Canada's doors were closed.

Yet, despite the restrictive policies of the government and widespread antisemitism in Canada, many Canadians were sympathetic to the plight of the European Jews. On November 20, 1938, for example, tens of thousands of Canadians across the country attended public demonstrations and rallies condemning the antisemitic violence of *Kristallnacht* and calling for Canada to assist Jewish refugees. Likewise, when Cuba refused to allow more than nine hundred Jewish refugees on board the MS *St. Louis* to land in Havana in the late spring of 1939, a group of prominent Canadians petitioned the Canadian government – to no avail – suggesting that Canada provide a safe haven for the desperate passengers. Canadian English-language newspapers also frequently admonished the antisemitic immigration policies of the Mackenzie King administration and demanded that Canada loosen its restrictions. Despite these vigorous interventions by the public and the press, Canada eventually earned the dubious distinction of admitting less than 5,000 European Jews between 1933 and 1945, which, Irving Abella and Harold Troper suggest, was "arguably the worst of all possible refugee-receiving states."[2]

Unable to return to Canada, Bornstein's family lived in Paris in abject poverty, surviving with very little food and money. In early 1938, at the age of sixteen, Max got a job as an office boy at the Oeuvre de Secours aux Enfants (OSE), a Jewish charity organization where his mother had sought financial assistance, and he suddenly became the primary breadwinner in the family. At the OSE, Bornstein came into contact with many Jewish refugees, who, like his own family, were struggling for basic survival. Bornstein was particularly struck

---

2   Abella, Irving, and Harold Troper. *None is Too Many: Canada and the Jews of Europe 1933–1948.* (Toronto: Key Porter Books, 2000), p.xxii

by the plight of Jewish refugees from Nazi-occupied territories, and his acute observations provide the reader with a unique glimpse into both their daily hardships in France and what they had left behind. Bornstein was both a victim and a witness. He writes, "Many of the refugees briefed me on the conditions that had led up to their flight – most had abandoned everything they had worked for. That part really horrified me, that so many of them had to leave all their possessions behind, including homes, successful businesses, law, medical and dental practices, and high-ranking civil service positions; many of the tradesmen had left good jobs. Some of them arrived in France absolutely destitute."

In the summer of 1938, after nearly five turbulent and impoverished years in France with his family, Bornstein's father was able to immigrate to the safe haven of Argentina. Bornstein's mother and sister soon followed him there. Living under Nazi occupation and unable to join his family in Argentina, Bornstein made a desperate attempt in 1940 to flee across the southern border of France into Spain, which remained neutral throughout the war. Francisco Franco, a right-wing nationalist dictator, had ruled Spain since the end of the Spanish Civil War in 1939, and he was sympathetic to both Hitler and Mussolini.

Spain's relationship to Jewish persecution fell along three axes: Spanish immigration restrictions for European Jews fleeing antisemitism and Nazi violence; the repatriation of Spanish Jews to Spain; and Spain's general diplomatic response, as a neutral nation, to Jewish deportations to Nazi concentration and death camps. According to Stanley Payne, Spanish policy in response to the Holocaust was "so dilatory and sometimes contradictory as to border on indifference."[3] During the war, Spain – like the rest of the world – had policies se-

---

3 Payne Stanley G., *Franco and Hitler: Spain, Germany, and World War II*. (New Haven: Yale University Press, 2008), p.234.

xviii IF HOME IS NOT HERE

verely restricting Jewish immigration. Still, approximately 20,000
to 35,000 Jewish refugees made their way into Spain, and many of
them continued on to safety in Portugal. Most of these refugees, like
Bornstein, entered the country illegally. As a general practice, Franco
did not expel undocumented Jewish refugees back to Nazi occupied
territories, but, instead, interned them in Miranda de Ebro, a Spanish
concentration camp.[4] Like most dictatorial or totalitarian leaders,
Franco relied on detention and forced labour to contain his political
enemies and solidify his power, and he established 188 concentration
camps across the country to serve this purpose.[5] Mirando de Ebro was
operational from 1940 to 1947, and it was the largest repository for
foreign prisoners in Spain, including significant numbers of Jewish,
French and British prisoners. Spanish Jews fared only slightly better than other Jewish refugees. Under pressure from the allies, Spain
repatriated approximately 1,000 Spanish Sephardic Jews, but the process was bureaucratically fraught and usually dependent upon third
party intervention that guaranteed eventual passage elsewhere. Spain
only showed serious concern for the general plight of European Jews
in the fall of 1944, when it joined several other countries in a diplomatic campaign to stop the deportation of the remaining Hungarian
Jews to Auschwitz-Birkenau.

While the handful of Jewish refugees who successfully fled into
Spain were free from Nazi terror, the millions who remained in the
Nazi-occupied territories were systematically starved and ghettoized;
interned in a network of transit camps and labour camps; killed
in mass shooting campaigns in the East; and, after the Wannsee
Conference on January 20, 1942, deported to six Nazi death camps:
Chełmno, Treblinka, Bełżec, Sobibór, Majdanek, and Auschwitz-

---

4 Payne, p.220
5 A. González-Ruibal, *The Archeology of Internment in Francoist Spain (1936-1952)*,
   Archeologies of Internment. A Myers and G. Moshenska, eds. (New York, Dor-
   drecht, Heidelberg, and London: Springer, 2011), p.65

Birkenau. Raul Hilberg suggests that the death camps were unique in human history: "The most striking fact about the killing center operations is that, unlike the earlier phases of the destruction process, they were unprecedented. Never before in history had people been killed on an assembly-line basis. The killing center ... has no prototype, no administrative ancestor."[6] In total, the Nazis murdered nearly six million Jews, two-thirds of the pre-war Jewish population of Europe.

Poland, Bornstein's birthplace, had the largest Jewish population and suffered the greatest number of deaths in both number and percentage. Polish Jews were forced into urban ghettos where they lived in horrific conditions, and beginning in 1942, they were deported to the death camps as part of Aktion Reinhard, the Nazis' plan to murder the entirety of Poland's Jews. Had Bornstein remained in Warsaw and survived ghettoization, he would almost certainly have been among the hundreds of thousands deported to Treblinka from the Warsaw ghetto and murdered in the gas chambers there. By 1945, the Nazis had succeeded in killing more than 90 per cent of Poland's 3.3 million Jews. In France, Bornstein's adopted home, the Vichy government notoriously collaborated with the Nazis, eventually deporting 76,000 of its population of 350,000 Jews to Nazi concentration and death camps between 1942 and 1944. Less than 3,000 of the deported French Jews survived the war. Among the victims in Poland and France were many of Bornstein's friends and family, and he frequently laments these losses in his memoir, highlighting the vulnerability wrought by Jewish statelessness.

Like all Holocaust survivors, Bornstein's story does not end with his liberation from Miranda de Ebro. The last third of his memoir provides detailed documentation of his continued frustration with

6   Raul Hilberg, *The Destruction of the European Jews.* (New York: Holmes and Meier Publishing, Inc., 1985), p.221

immigration restrictions, his isolation from friends and family, his descent into debilitating mental illness and suicidal thoughts, and, eventually, the solace he felt in the Zionist movement and the prospect of a Jewish state in Palestine. What Bornstein calls "a complete nervous breakdown" was clearly an acute post-traumatic response to both the harrowing personal events of his difficult childhood and the terror of living through state-sponsored Jewish persecution and Spanish internment. As a child, Bornstein felt abandoned by his parents and helpless in the face of domestic violence; as a Jew, he was abandoned by the world and helpless in the face of genocide. His post-liberation narrative provides a vivid account of repeated cycles of psychological crisis and recovery, including outpatient and institutional care, extensive treatment with both electroshock therapy and insulin shock therapy, and individual psychotherapy. As much as Bornstein attempted to stabilize his life through gainful employment and meaningful friendships, he could not shake his intense feelings of alienation. Lamenting his loneliness in the years immediately after the war, Bornstein saw his troubled mental state as a mirror of his past physical imprisonment. Once trapped by his circumstances, he was now trapped by his own mind. Unable to regulate his moods and emotions, Bornstein developed an obsessive – and seemingly unattainable – desire for emotional and sexual intimacy with a romantic partner.

As Bornstein details his struggle with anxiety, depression and fears about intimacy, we are reminded that Holocaust survivors are not one-dimensional figures who are wholly defined by wartime events, but fully realized human beings with complicated histories and layers of life experience. Bornstein's memoir is not simply a Holocaust testimony, but Bornstein's attempt to explain his past to himself, to give important context to his personal struggles by understanding the overlapping and interwoven traumas of his childhood and his young adulthood. There is tremendous bravery in Bornstein's storytelling, a refreshing honesty and candour in his disclosure about his father's abusive behaviour, as well as his internal psychological battles, his moments of deep debilitation and his extended periods of hospitalization. Bornstein is not defined by the Holocaust, nor is it the sole locus of his personal trauma. He bears witness to the collective traumatic memory of Jewish suffering in the Holocaust, while, at the same time, sharing a unique narrative that gestures towards deep memory and a very personal story of extended agony. Max Bornstein is real and we empathize with his pain. He ties the early twenty-first-century reader to his mid-twentieth-century experiences by openly exposing his vulnerabilities and limits. He reveals to us his traumatic scars, his overwhelming fears and, ultimately, his tremendous powers of resilience.

Amanda Grzyb, Ph.D.
University of Western Ontario
2012

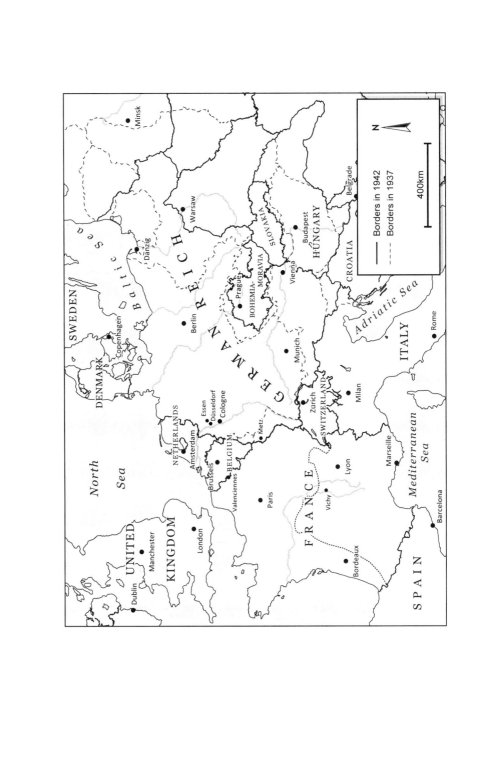

North
Sea

Dumfries

UNITED
York
Leeds
Dublin
Liverpool

IRELAND

KINGDOM
London
Epsom
Brussels

NETHERLANDS
Amsterdam

GERMAN

Cologne

BELGIUM

Valenciennes

REICH

Atlantic

Paris

Metz

Loire

FRANCE

Ocean

Moulins

SWITZERLAND

Vichy

Lyon

Allier

Bayonne
Hendaye
San Sebastian
Irun

Bordeaux

Miranda de Ebro

Toulouse

Ebro

Perpignan

Marseille

Figueres

Saragossa

PORTUGAL

Barcelona

Mediterranean

Madrid

Sea

Lisbon

SPAIN

Gibraltar

Borders in 1942
Borders in 1937
Demarcation Line
(1940-42)

N

400km

Max Bornstein's Family Tree*

MATERNAL GRANDPARENTS:
Mordechai Zalman Korman m. *Chayala Kahnneman*

AUNT:
Pola m. *Jacobson*
- *Jack*
- *Solomon*
- *Hélène* m. *Name Unknown*
  - *Paulette*
  - *Hilda*

AUNT:
Jennie

AUNT:
Sadie m. *Morris Kim* —— *Max*

AUNT:
Leah m. *Joseph*
- *Chaim Fishel (Philippe)*
- *Pierre* m. *Simone*
- *Chai Liba (Luba)*

MOTHER:
Liba m.

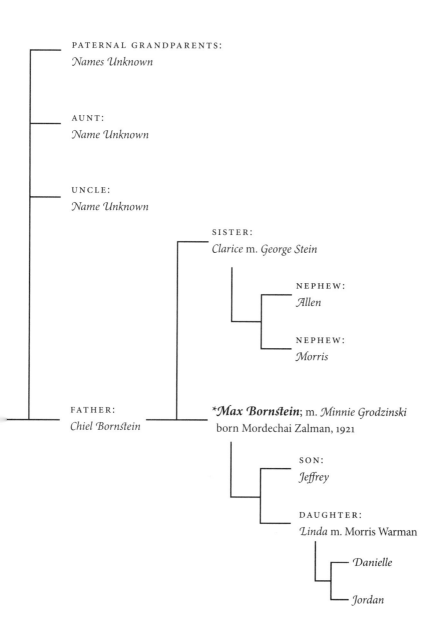

PATERNAL GRANDPARENTS:
Names Unknown

AUNT:
Name Unknown

UNCLE:
Name Unknown

SISTER:
Clarice m. *George Stein*

NEPHEW:
Allen

NEPHEW:
Morris

FATHER:
Chiel Bornstein

*Max Bornstein; m. *Minnie Grodzinski*
born Mordechai Zalman, 1921

SON:
Jeffrey

DAUGHTER:
Linda m. Morris Warman

Danielle

Jordan

In everlasting memory of my dearly beloved wife, Minnie, who, in her capacity as stenographer worked with tireless devotion and, as was inherent in her sweet nature, with infinite patience to type and retype every single word of my memoir – omissions and corrections included – and without whose dedication this project would never have seen the light of day.

With unbounded love for my exceptional daughter, Linda, for providing me with nourishing support and unfailing devotion.

With affectionate pride for my dearly beloved son, Jeffrey, who worked alongside me with supreme effort during the course of my successful import business.

I also dedicate this book in loving memory of the six million Jews who perished in the Holocaust, including my relatives and friends. Their spirits live on eternally in our hearts and minds as do their sacrifices, which shall remain an integral part of Jewish history. These noble souls were the innocent victims of a regime whose ideology identified the Nazis as the master race, and accorded them the power to decide who should live and who should die. In the name of that ideology, they tried to eliminate an entire people for no reason other than that they were Jews.

Acknowledgements

To David Azrieli;

I wish to express my profound admiration for his remarkable vision and benevolence in creating a foundation for Holocaust survivors wherein their unique experiences can be published for Canadians, for the world at large and for posterity. For his magnanimous gesture he is deserving of Judaism's highest honour. And though we have never met, he has my family's and my unending gratitude.

To Naomi Azrieli;

Ms. Azrieli has my heartfelt thanks for heading up the Foundation and for valuing her father's vision so highly that she lent it all of her support so that my book, and those of other survivors, may become a published reality.

To Andrea Knight;

All praise is due to my tireless, sympathetic and devoted editor for her spectacular achievement. She took my 867 page text and transformed it into its present abridgement so that it might take its place amongst the other Azrieli Foundation published memoirs.

To Arielle Berger;

I owe her much thanks for her quiet, competent and gracious contributions to my book as co-editor.

I would also like to acknowledge the contributions made by Jody Spiegel, Richard Mozer and Jesse Cohoon.

Author's Preface

As one of the Jewish survivors of the Holocaust, I have endured years of moral outrage, horror and revulsion toward the enemies who murdered so many of my fellow Jews. After years of suppressed emotion, I wanted to make some kind of personal contribution in honour of the victims. To that end, I decided to write my memoirs as a lasting tribute to their memory and through my writing send a message to their descendants about the crucial subject of Jewish survival – not only as a people but as a nation. I began to record my experiences as a young Jew in exile as a warning to subsequent generations that our future is indivisibly linked to the survival of our beloved state of Israel. Never again shall we become the unwanted aliens of some foreign land. Never again shall we find ourselves at the mercy of antisemites, begging for admission. Gone forever are the days of the helpless submissive Jews. We are a free people in our own land and masters over our own destinies.

Never will it be said that the victims of the Holocaust perished in vain or that Hitler and his murderous henchmen succeeded in carrying out the "Final Solution" of annihilating the Jewish people. Instead, we live on and thrive as a free and independent nation. It is our enemies who suffered a humiliating defeat and now find themselves relegated to historical infamy.

Jews of past generations, from the time of the Roman conquest of

4 IF HOME IS NOT HERE

Israel and Judea in the first century B C E well into the twentieth century were subjected to indignities and abuses that ranged from brutal assault, torture and death, to being dispossessed of their wealth and deprived of the means of earning a living, to being driven from their homes and expelled from the countries of their birth or in which they had lived for years. Present and future generations of Jews have inherited a sacred trust: to safeguard the State of Israel.

I offer this account of my struggles to make a point. My past experiences, along with those of millions of fellow Jews, tell me that the only salvation for us as a people lies in a secure abode in our very own Eretz Israel. To have witnessed the rebirth of our nation is to have known the ultimate feeling of pride and joy. Following the attainment of our statehood in 1948, I felt a reawakening of Jewish pride that had lain dormant for too long and restored my own sense of dignity. Above all, it fulfilled my greatest aspiration: being part of a people with our own sovereign state. It forever banished my feelings of insecurity, liberating my soul, allowing me to know a freedom that I had never before experienced.

In writing my memoirs, I wish first of all to pay homage to the fallen victims of the Nazis, to my aunt Leah, my cousins Philippe (Chaim Fishel) and Luba (Chai Liba), and my many friends, all of them innocent victims of the most diabolical persecution ever committed. I can't help but think about what might have been, a different reality in which I once again have conversations with them as I so often did in the past. To know these people was to admire their spirit and character, their positive attitude and cheerful disposition. They filled my life with happiness before their lives were cruelly cut short and I miss them dearly.

Leaving Poland

In the years after World War I, Central Europe had the largest concentration of Jews anywhere in the world. This is where my story begins, in Poland, where Jews trace their ancestry back a thousand years and where a highly developed Yiddish culture thrived.

I was born Mordechai Zalman on November 12, 1921, in the city of Warsaw. Like so many of my contemporaries, I was born into such abject poverty that basic survival was a daily struggle. My parents, Liba and Chiel, scarcely earned enough to make ends meet. But despite so much hardship, the large Jewish community of Warsaw displayed a remarkable resilience and energy. There were many communal associations and attractions that allowed people to find expression, warmth and comfort: synagogues, cultural institutions and Yiddish theatre and concert halls that presented vivacious Jewish songs and other performances. There were also a number of Zionist organizations affiliated with groups across the political spectrum.

I don't know very much about my paternal grandparents. My paternal grandfather – I don't know his name – passed away early in life, leaving my grandmother on her own. She remarried twice, having lost her second husband as well as her first. Her first marriage produced three children, the youngest of whom was my father. He was never able to get much formal education and throughout his life was never more than semi-literate. His first language was Yiddish and he learned to read it but not write it; he also acquired a smattering of Polish and taught himself to read some French. At the age of twelve, he was apprenticed to become a tailor but was never really able to master the skills of the craft.

As far as I know, my father's older sister was the first member of her family to immigrate to North America; she settled in New York City in 1912. In 1919, she sent for her mother and youngest brother – my father – having gotten permission for them to join her in New York. My father decided not to go, however, because by this time he was already engaged to my mother and didn't want to leave her behind. My father's older brother was already married with children and, for some reason, was denied entry into the United States.

My maternal grandfather, Max, died in 1910, before I was born. By all accounts he was a dignified scholar who was strictly Orthodox and spent much of his time studying the Torah. A man with a distinctive white beard, he was a hatter by trade and counted some members of royalty amongst his customers. The honour of serving them, however, did not provide him with an adequate living and when he passed away, my grandmother was left destitute with five daughters to support. Not one to give in, my grandmother became a fresh-fruit merchant, selling her wares on the streets of the Jewish neighbourhoods of Warsaw. Despite all her efforts, she barely earned enough to meet her family's daily needs. Nonetheless, she maintained her dignity and her independence. A devout woman who found inner strength in her religious convictions, she was determined to succeed and rented a store in the hopes of increasing her income.

My mother was only nine years old when her father passed away and the desperate new family circumstances also deprived her of the opportunity for any formal education. Like my father, she grew up illiterate, something that was a source of embarrassment to her throughout her life. When she was twelve, she was sent away to work for her mother's sister as a domestic. These were the difficult years of food shortages during World War I and working for her aunt spared my mother from going hungry.

My mother's aunt was married to a lumber merchant of considerable means and they had a large household that employed a number of domestics. My mother later told me that throughout the years she worked for her aunt she had great difficulty accepting the inequities that provided her with ample food while her mother went hungry. Her conscience finally got the better of her and, although it meant going against her mother's strict religious values, she decided to take some food from her aunt's house to her mother, believing that her aunt would not object. After all, her aunt and uncle's kitchen larders were always overflowing.

When my mother arrived home with the food, her mother was very disapproving because she knew where it had come from. In addition to her conviction that stealing was wrong, her pride would not allow her to accept any charity, even from her own sister. Indignant, she reprimanded my mother and made her promise that she would never take food from her aunt again. She also insisted that my mother return what she had brought.

My maternal grandmother had six children in total, one of whom unfortunately died during World War I. Her five surviving daughters in order of seniority were Pola, Jennie, Leah, Sadie and my mother, Liba. Jennie was the first member of the family to immigrate to North America, settling in New York City in the early twentieth century and then moving to Winnipeg, Manitoba. Sadie was sponsored by her sister Jennie as a young girl of sixteen in 1912 and, during the approximately two years that she stayed in New York City, Sadie met and married her husband, Morris; shortly thereafter they moved to Canada as well. Morris was a furrier and the couple decided to settle in western Canada, taking up residence in Winnipeg, where, just prior to the outbreak of World War I, my uncle founded what would become a thriving fur-coat manufacturing business.

Our story took an unexpected turn in 1920 when Sadie sent her mother a telegram telling her that she and other members of the family, including my mother, had been granted entry permits to Canada. Needless to say, my grandmother was overjoyed by her sudden good fortune. To everyone's delight, Aunt Jennie arrived in Warsaw not long after the telegram. For eastern European Jews of that era, going to America – the land of opportunity and freedom – was the greatest ambition. As far as my family was concerned, Jews were barely tolerated in Poland. They certainly didn't want to raise a family there.

My family's plans to leave for Canada did not proceed quickly, however, because bringing her relatives to Canada was not Aunt Jennie's only reason for being in Europe. I was never sure exactly what her business was, but she seemed to deal in jewellery and international currency and her primary objective in coming to Europe was actually to conduct some business in Germany. Only after her business was concluded would she turn her attention to her relatives' emigration.

By the time Aunt Jennie arrived in Warsaw, my mother and father were already engaged. Both families were apparently very happy about the engagement and plans were already underway for my parents' wedding. My paternal grandmother was very fond of my mother and pleased that her son was marrying a girl who had her wholehearted approval. As for my maternal grandmother, whose health had greatly deteriorated, she gave thanks to the Almighty that she could depart this life knowing that her remaining unmarried daughter would not be left alone to fend for herself.

While Aunt Jennie was away on business, my paternal grandmother left for New York City to join her daughter, reluctantly leaving my father behind, but vowing to make every effort to bring him and his bride over to join her. In fact, it would be thirty long years before she saw her son and daughter-in-law again.

When Aunt Jennie returned to Warsaw some weeks later, in late 1920, she was shocked to find her mother lying gravely ill in hospital.

After consulting my grandmother's physician, my aunt learned that her mother only had a short time left to live. There was no longer any question of bringing my grandmother to Canada, but at her hospital bedside Aunt Jennie promised to fulfill her dying wish to see her youngest daughter married. Jennie immediately set about making the arrangements for the wedding to take place that same week. The ceremony was held at the home of my grandmother's rabbi and the reception was held in my aunt Leah's apartment. Right after the wedding, the newlywed couple went straight to my grandmother's bedside. My mother told me that she arrived at the hospital still draped in her white wedding gown and my grandmother beamed at the sight of her married daughter. Unfortunately, my grandmother only lived for another eight days; she died peacefully in her sleep.

After my grandmother's funeral and shiva – the seven-day period of mourning – life went somewhat back to normal. My father continued to work in the tailoring trade while my mother started work in a chocolate factory. Having fulfilled her obligations to her mother, Aunt Jennie left on yet another business trip, promising this time to return shortly and take my parents with her to Canada. While she was away, my mother's oldest sister, Pola, decided to move to Berlin with her family, planning eventually to go from there to set up a dressmaking business in Paris.

Waiting for Aunt Jennie's return was anything but easy for my parents, who were living in Aunt Leah's very cramped quarters. The small apartment soon became even more congested and their financial situation more difficult since my mother was now pregnant with me and forced to give up her job. Aunt Jennie didn't return until several months after my birth on November 12, 1921. It was a welcome relief when she finally did show up, but to everyone's dismay, she confessed that she had suffered a substantial business loss and would once again have to delay my parents' immigration to Canada. She had lost all the money that Aunt Sadie had given her to pay for the travel expenses.

My parents weren't sure whether to wait in Poland for Aunt Jennie to take us all to Canada or ask her to help us get to Berlin to join Aunt Pola. The latter would require smuggling my dad into Germany without any papers – he couldn't get a Polish passport without first doing his mandatory military service. My mother had no problem in securing a Polish passport with me included on it, so was free to legally travel anywhere. After much debate, the family decided that Aunt Leah should write to Aunt Sadie and tell her what had happened, asking her to send more money.

When the long-awaited response from Aunt Sadie finally arrived, everyone gathered around Aunt Leah to hear her read the letter written in Yiddish. To everyone's disappointment, Aunt Sadie wrote that she was too upset by Aunt Jennie's behaviour to do anything further; she said that it would take her at least a year to get over the shock. In the meantime, she wrote a separate letter to Aunt Jennie asking her to help my mother, father and me join Aunt Pola in Berlin before going on to Paris.

With the idea of going to North America temporarily laid to rest, preparations began for our departure for Berlin as soon as Aunt Jennie returned to Warsaw. The arrangements to get my father safely out of Poland and into Germany entailed a series of complex negotiations. Aunt Jennie, with her worldly experience and business know-how, organized everything, presenting my parents with a fait accompli. She had apparently come to some agreement with her business partners to cover all our expenses until we safely reached Berlin. My parents apparently didn't ask too many questions, but gratefully accepted Jennie's help.

On the eve of our departure I was three months old. Like so many of our predecessors over the past two thousand years, I too became a wandering Jew.

To Paris

On the eve of our departure for Germany, family and friends came together to bid us farewell and convey their blessings for a safe journey. My father's farewell to his brother would turn out to be the last; they never saw each other again. I don't know much about what happened, but according to his family, my uncle was fatally kicked by a horse while performing his military service in the Polish army. My father only learned of his brother's death from his widow several years later. The news came as a blow – he was counting on his brother to join him later in Paris.

We left on a cold, sunny winter day in February 1922. My parents apparently weren't at all sad to be leaving our native Poland despite the fact that their ancestors had lived there for hundreds of years. My mother's only regret was leaving her sister Leah. According to what my mother later told me, they could hardly let go of each other as they embraced on the train station platform in tears, consoling each other that they would see each other soon in Paris. The whole family gathered at the station and waved to us until the train was out of sight. Along with my mother, my father and me, Aunt Jennie and her two business associates were also on the trip to Germany.

When we arrived in Berlin the following day, Aunt Pola met us at the station and then prepared a wonderful meal in her small apartment. The discussion around the table centred on the issue of smuggling us across the border into France. My parents got up the next morning to find that Aunt Jennie and her associates had left to conduct some business, promising to return soon. We were left stranded for a few weeks with Aunt Pola, who did everything she could to look after us. For their part, my parents did what they could to help her with her dressmaking business. But just as my parents began to adapt to life in Berlin, Aunt Jennie resurfaced with everything necessary for our next move, telling them to be ready to catch a train for Essen the following morning. Aunt Pola accompanied us on our trip with plans to stay in France and everything went according to schedule. Her friends met us at the station in Essen and took us to their home. We spent several days there until it was time to leave for Düsseldorf. We spent another week in Düsseldorf and then went on to Cologne. This would be our last stop in Germany before undertaking the risky border crossing into France.

While we were in Cologne, Aunt Jennie told my parents and Aunt Pola that she was again running out of funds – she only had enough to pay for a hotel and food for another week. She left on yet another business venture, leaving us to fend for ourselves in a strange city where we didn't know a soul. Aunt Pola knew her sister only too well and didn't rely on her promise to return before the week was up, however well intentioned it may have been. Fortunately, there was a sizeable Jewish community in Cologne with a number of well-organized institutions, including some that catered to needy Jewish immigrants and travellers.

Aunt Pola turned out to be quite correct in doubting Aunt Jennie's reliability. Even though Aunt Pola didn't speak a word of German, she walked to the business section of the city to look for a store with a Jewish-sounding name. She eventually chose a menswear store and went in, hoping that someone there spoke Yiddish. The woman behind the counter greeted her in German and, when my aunt responded in Yiddish, she went to the back of the store and returned with her husband. He addressed Aunt Pola in perfect Yiddish – it turned out that he was also a Polish Jew.

When he learned of my aunt's situation, the good-natured gentleman personally escorted her to a Jewish relief organization. Thanks to that Jewish organization, we managed to sustain ourselves for the next month or so, that is, until Aunt Jennie showed up again. She arrived with her associates, prepared to get us across the French border.

~

When we crossed the border into France in late March 1922, our first stop was the mining town of Valenciennes. Miners were apparently in such demand there that my father was able to obtain a job without any difficulty. The employers' only criterion was a person's willingness to work – all my father needed to do was state that he was born in Poland and wished to live and work in France.

Aunt Jennie and her associates arranged for hotel accommodations, paid a month in advance and left us with enough money to carry us over for that period. We didn't stay longer than that in Valenciennes – Aunt Pola had her sights set on a big city where she could pursue her trade as a dressmaker. At the end of April 1922, Aunt Jennie returned from her latest business trip, arranged transportation to the northeastern French city of Metz in the Lorraine region and stayed long enough to put us up in a hotel where we spent the next three months. There was a fair-sized Jewish population in Metz and Aunt Pola had no problem setting herself up as a dressmaker. It was more difficult for my father to find work – he needed a work permit in Metz and, as an illegal immigrant, was afraid to approach the authorities to apply for one. He did manage to find work as a ladies' garment presser, but the trade was seasonal and the job barely lasted six weeks. He looked for other work, accepting anything he could find, but working without a permit was risky both for him and for an employer.

When Aunt Jennie returned to Metz at the end of three months, she announced that she would take all of us as far as Paris before she herself left for Canada. She told my parents and Aunt Pola that they would find lots of opportunities for employment there and, in the midst of a large Jewish community, be able to obtain assistance from various Jewish agencies. According to my mother, she painted an almost fairytale vision of what my parents' life would be like in Paris.

We left for Paris the next day. On the train, Aunt Pola broached the sensitive issue of our immigrating to Canada. With a mixture of guilt and embarrassment, Aunt Jennie said that she could not take us with her – she confessed that she didn't have the money to buy our fares and there was the additional problem that I was not included in the original sponsorship papers. She assured everyone that once she was back in Canada she would make every effort to speed up the immigration process and would guarantee all the financial arrangements. By this time, however, no one took her promises seriously; she had let everyone down too many times.

When the train arrived in Paris in the heat of summer 1922 – it was almost July by this time – Aunt Jennie put us in a cab and instructed the driver to take us to a hotel she had booked. Our accommodations turned out to be a room in a working-class hotel in Montmartre that contained a round stove for both cooking and heating. We were once again deserted by Aunt Jennie, this time in the beautiful French capital, with very limited resources and unable to speak any French. My father's status as an illegal immigrant meant that he couldn't apply for a work permit. Yet despite the obvious difficulties, Paris still had an appeal that grew with the passage of time. People who remain there for any considerable period become so enamoured with the French way of life that they develop a deep attachment to the city. As a Yiddish expression common among Polish Jews living in Paris put it, anyone who had ever tasted meat in Paris was certain to leave his own bones.

Aunt Jennie had prepaid our hotel for two weeks and left my family with enough money to buy food for the same period. Again, she had promised to return to Paris in the not-too-distant future and take us back with her to Canada. In the meantime, my parents were left to fend for themselves in a foreign country with the constant fear that my father would be expelled from France because of his illegal status. After many futile attempts to find work, my father was hired as a presser in a small ladies' garment factory. My mother was also able to find work in a glove factory through her sister Pola. With both my parents working, I was taken every day to a *crèche*, a French day care centre.

Just as things were beginning to look up, disaster struck in the fall of 1922. Without any warning, in my father's twelfth week of work, the police raided the factory and demanded to see everyone's identity cards. My father was arrested and taken to the Prefecture of Police, where he was interrogated with the help of a Polish interpreter. At the end, a police official handed him an expulsion notice, telling him that he had thirty days to leave the country. He was in a terrible situation – he could no longer return to Poland, nor would he if he could, and they knew of no other country that was willing to provide asylum to a stateless Jew.

Pandemonium apparently set in when my mother and Aunt Pola learned the news. Aunt Pola tried to calm everyone down and proposed that they all go to the office of the Jewish Colonization Association (JCA), an immigrant aid agency, the following morning. There, my parents were assured that the organization would do everything possible to extend the date of my father's expulsion and were told where they could get temporary financial help. Fortunately, just before my father was due to be expelled from the country in November 1922, the aid official gave him the good news that they had managed to secure him a month's extension, to be followed by further monthly extensions until they could find a country willing to take him in.

My father couldn't return to work for his previous employer, but he eventually found a new job as a ladies' garment presser. By this time it was February 1923 and about seven months had slipped by without a word from Aunt Jennie.

Our lives went on fairly uneventfully for quite a while. The threat of my father's expulsion was still hanging over my parents' heads and there were numerous problems getting the required monthly renewals. The aid agency had to keep offering proof that they were trying to secure an entry permit to another country for my father. The organization knew that my parents intended to emigrate to Canada, but the officials had to satisfy the prefecture that they were making applications to countries that would take my father as soon as possible.

Things began to change toward the summer of 1923, the beginning of our second year in Paris. My father's employer had second thoughts about employing people without work permits and dismissed him. My mother was afraid to return to her job after what had happened to my father and after two weeks my parents ran out of money, forcing them to apply for assistance. Five weeks passed before my father landed another job. The ladies' garment industry operated on a seasonal basis – steady employment lasted anywhere between ten and twelve weeks, followed by a slack period of similar duration. Under the circumstances, one had to earn enough money during the busy season to carry over what was referred to as "la morte-saison" (the dead season). The disruptive conditions of the trade often made it difficult to work a full season and my parents faced many weeks of economic hardship. Somehow they managed to survive, eating well when money was available, doing with little or without when it was not.

In the fall of 1923, while my father was again unemployed between seasons, Aunt Jennie unexpectedly arrived from Canada and announced our imminent departure for Canada. According to my mother, my parents' mood instantly changed from one of hopelessness to jubilation.

It didn't last long. My mother told me much later that as soon as she arrived, Aunt Jennie began to malign my father at every opportunity. She accused him of being incapable of providing for his family and implied that he ran around with other women. Unbeknownst to my mother, Aunt Jennie only intended to secure passage to Canada for my mother and me, excluding my father. She adamantly refused to pay for the forged documents he would need for immigration to Canada. She had been criticizing my father to convince my mother to leave Paris without him, telling her that she managed on her own and my mother could do the same. Of course, what Jennie neglected to take into consideration was that she didn't have to care for a child. My mother confided in me years later that she had never wanted to leave France without my father – she never stopped loving him and he in turn loved her dearly. As I write this memoir in 1980, it is with mixed feelings that I think about the crucial role that Aunt Jennie – who passed away in 1963 – played in my life. I owe her a significant debt for taking me to Canada, my home and the country that I truly love, but she was also instrumental in breaking up my family.

When Aunt Jennie arrived in Paris, my father had been out of work for the better part of two months and our family was in desperate financial straits. Once again one of the Jewish agencies had had to come to our assistance. Both my aunts Jennie and Pola worked together to convince my mother, against her better judgment, to leave my father behind, telling her that she would face a life of misery if she stayed with him. In a moment of weakness, my mother gave in to them, a decision she never ceased to regret.

In my opinion, what my aunt did was tantamount to kidnapping. My father had absolutely no idea what was about to happen. One evening, during the secret preparations for their departure to Canada, he arrived home exhausted from yet another lengthy search for work and announced with pride that he had landed a job and had just put in his first nine hours. My mother told me later that she was overcome with joy at the news and suddenly realized that she didn't want to leave him. She told her sister that she would only agree to go to Canada if my father was included; if he wasn't, she would stay with him in Paris.

Confronted with my mother's strong opposition, Aunt Jennie

took a different approach. She told my mother that they had to leave at once, that if there were any further delays, the Jamaican and Cuban visas she had acquired for the first leg of the journey would expire. She also admitted that she didn't have enough money to both procure false travel documents for my father and pay his passage. She promised my mother that if she agreed to travel as planned, she would bring my father over as soon as she was in a financial position to do so.

Aunt Jennie and Aunt Pola finally succeeded in convincing my mother to leave without my father. My mother was three or four months pregnant with her second child at the time and her sisters argued that she would face increased hardships in Paris with two children in a small hotel room and my father's precarious situation. My unsuspecting father, on the other hand, had no idea what was coming – he was at work when my mother and I left with Aunt Jennie. When he returned home later that evening he found a note on the kitchen table, written in Yiddish by one of my aunts on my mother's behalf, saying only, "My beloved Chiel, my sister Jennie is taking us to Canada and will in due course send for you. Love, Liba." Years later, when my mother told me this story, she confessed that she had no idea what her sister had written – she had no idea that the note was completely devoid of any explanation.

We left Paris on a train to Marseille to board a vessel that would sail to Jamaica. After that, we were to go on to Cuba, then the United States and then, finally, Canada.

Even after all these years, it is hard to imagine how my poor father must have felt when he learned that his family was gone. My aunt's deception was outrageous and would have repercussions for all of us for years to come.

Beginning Life in Canada

We arrived in Marseille on a balmy fall Sunday morning in 1923 and boarded our ship the same afternoon. I was not yet two, so my account of the voyage comes from what my mother told me when I was older. We set sail during the early hours of the morning and the crossing was generally pleasant, although there were several days of rough seas, causing most of the passengers to suffer seasickness.

When the ship docked in Kingston, Jamaica a week or so later, we were greeted cordially by several black businessmen who were associates of Aunt Jennie. They drove us to a spacious residence that belonged to one of them, where we spent the next two weeks as their guests. When Aunt Jennie had concluded her business, she made preparations for our journey to Cuba. We bid farewell to our host and boarded a smaller vessel for the short voyage to our next destination. Before long we were approaching the beautiful port of Havana, where we went ashore and found our hotel.

Unfortunately, Aunt Jennie had once again run out of money and had to send a cable to Aunt Sadie urgently requesting immediate funds. My mother was very upset and only calmed down when Aunt Jennie pawned some of her jewels to get cash to see us through until the funds arrived less than forty-eight hours later.

We finally completed our journey to North America, first to the United States and then on to Canada. Our ship landed at the port of

New York, where we were checked through US customs and immigration. When we finally met up with Aunt Sadie and Uncle Morris, they greeted us enthusiastically and my uncle found a porter to carry our luggage to their huge black Studebaker. Surprisingly, Aunt Sadie drove the car instead of Uncle Morris – for some reason he had never shown an interest in learning to drive. I would hazard a guess that in 1923, my aunt Sadie may have been the first Jewish woman driver in Winnipeg.

We drove west from New York, covering a considerable distance in several days, finally approaching the Canadian border and seeing our adopted country for the first time. We had to clear customs and immigration again at the border, then continued on to our new home in Winnipeg, capital of the province of Manitoba. In December 1923, our long journey that had started in Poland and taken us through several European countries and eventually across the Atlantic Ocean had come to an end. A new era of freedom and security had dawned for us. As new immigrants, this was the very stuff of dreams.

At the time of our arrival in Winnipeg, Aunt Sadie lived in a huge exquisitely furnished and decorated four-bedroom apartment. She was a social climber who possessed many other attributes such as intelligence, a good business sense and an immense capacity for gossip and storytelling, as well as being able to express herself with utmost ease while simultaneously attracting everyone's attention. She was not well educated; she had attended English classes at night school and learned enough to read English but not write it. Unlike my mother, however, she had learned to read and write Yiddish in Warsaw. My aunt's nature was somewhat complex – she could be very generous one moment and then the very next day deny you the most trivial thing. She was a very strong-willed woman who could often be egotistical, cold, detached and inconsiderate.

Uncle Morris, on the other hand, was a benevolent, compassionate, loveable gentleman. He was an observant Jew and student of the

Talmud, a member of the Orthodox Beth Tzedec congregation and an outstanding member of many Jewish organizations that he generously supported. Last but not least he was a strong Zionist. He was a true son of Israel who lived his life in the best Jewish tradition, a Galitzianer Yid through whom I discovered my Jewish heritage and the meaning of our great Jewish traditions. He made a deep impression on me, shaping my morals and ethics and passing on an invaluable legacy of treasured memories. In particular, I remember the wonderful Passover seders he held at his home when I was a child. Happy as the occasion was, the long hours seemed to drag on endlessly and I would get hungrier and hungrier just thinking about the meal ahead. Considering that I was unaccustomed to eating so late, I would get more than a little fidgety. Despite my restlessness and hunger, however, my uncle would make every moment a great event. This applied to all the relatively few Jewish holidays I was privileged to share with him. To my profound regret, his holiday celebrations were the only traditional ones I would ever experience.

My mother hadn't seen her sister Sadie for years and had barely recognized her. She now found her to be mature and sophisticated, if a trifle snobbish, which made her a little uneasy. Sadie's dazzling appearance in the latest American fashions with an array of glittering jewels made my mother embarrassed about her own shabby appearance. My aunt's luxurious apartment only increased my mother's discomfort with her sister's obvious wealth and the reality of her new circumstances.

Following a wonderful meal prepared for our arrival, everyone retired to the living room to discuss family matters. My mother told me that when the discussions turned toward my mother's predicament, Uncle Morris was surprised to learn that she was pregnant and furious with Aunt Jennie for not bringing my father with us. He took her to task for placing such a burden of responsibility on them and being so heartless as to separate a wife from her husband and the children from their father.

Since Uncle Morris, as an important fur manufacturer, was a man of substantial means, Aunt Sadie had climbed into social prominence and now participated in many important functions. Her busy social schedule often left my mother on her own, unable to communicate with maids who only spoke English.

My sister, Clarice, was born on April 15, 1924, and my father was informed of her birth by telegram. Another message was sent to my paternal grandmother in New York City. She was so delighted by the news that she sent my mother a gift of one hundred dollars, quite a handsome sum in those days, especially to my grandmother, who had so little herself.

Soon after giving birth to my sister, however, my mother returned from the hospital to an uncertain welcome. The tension that had developed between the two sisters grew with each passing day. There were now three children living in the apartment – including Aunt Sadie and Uncle Morris's son, Max – making it too crowded from Aunt Sadie's point of view. With a two-and-a-half-year-old and a newborn, my mother was completely at my aunt's mercy and it became increasingly difficult for her to cope with her sister's constant reproaches. The situation went from bad to worse until it reached a climax. In the heat of an argument, Aunt Sadie told my mother to get the hell out of her house with her two brats, knowing full well that she had nowhere else to go. My mother was too proud not to comply and prepared to leave immediately.

My mother had met a lovely family named Morantz at some of the lavish social events that my aunt frequently held at her home. Having nowhere else to turn, she decided to contact them and ask their advice. As soon as the Morantzes heard of the falling out, they invited us into their large home. The Morantzes were by no means rich but were, rather, an average Canadian middle-class family. They had four daughters, all of whom worked. But they welcomed us into their home with open arms, offering us their large spare room without asking for a penny from my mother.

I only have a vague recollection of the senior Morantzes, but I remember their daughters vividly, two of them in particular – Clara and Rose. Rose's married name was Pinchuk. She and Clara often played games with me and were always hugging and kissing me. Mr. and Mrs. Morantz suggested that my mother take me to a day nursery and let Mrs. Morantz look after my baby sister while my mother went out to work. My mother agreed and the Morantzes helped her get her first job in Canada, as a seamstress for the Jacob-Crowley company.

After several weeks, my mother asked for a raise and got it. She now earned enough to fend for herself and asked the Morantzes to help her find accommodations in a nice Jewish home, preferably where someone was willing to look after my sister for a fee. Although they were reluctant to see us go, they respected my mother's wish to be independent. We settled into our first independent residence with a family named Abramovitch, who had five children of their own. They were a very loving couple who genuinely enjoyed children.

Our lives settled into a normal routine for several months until, in 1925, my mother became seriously ill and was rushed to hospital. Aunt Sadie was away in California at the time, Aunt Jennie was on one of her frequent business trips, and Uncle Morris was extremely preoccupied with running his factory. Under the circumstances, my mother had only her friends the Morantzes for support.

When the Morantzes consulted the doctor regarding my mother's condition, he told them that she required stomach surgery. When she heard that, my mother's main concern was her children. Who would take care of us? Once again, the Morantzes came to the rescue, assuring her that they would arrange to have us looked after. At the time, there were approximately 18,000 Jews living in Winnipeg, a relatively small but progressive Jewish community that had established a large orphanage that could accommodate hundreds of Jewish boys and girls. My sister and I were placed there; I was three years old and Clarice was only seven months.

Considering that we still had both a mother and father, it was very unusual that Clarice and I were designated orphans, but we ended up living as orphans for the better part of six years. When you live in an institution where you must adhere to strict rules, with no one to turn to in moments of distress, you feel abandoned and unloved. In this milieu children learn to adapt and become hardened. I experienced one such incident in the orphanage, which I have never forgotten. Lunch was being served in the huge dining hall when I suddenly heard a loud pitiful cry that sounded like it was coming from a baby. It continued for a long time, intermittently turning from sobs to screams. The incident was not unusual in itself, but this time the baby crying was my sister. I was so upset by her distress that I started to rush over to comfort her when I was intercepted by one of the supervisors, who scolded me for leaving the table. My poor little baby sister was left alone to cry it out, without so much as a human voice to comfort her or someone to pick her up and soothe her.

Another incident also stands out in my mind. I couldn't have been more than six and was playing outdoors on the playground when a group of older boys somehow got hold of an old blanket and decided to play a game of tossing youngsters up and down in it, all in the spirit of good fun, of course. When my turn came, the four boys holding each corner of the blanket tossed me up and down over and over again until the blanket inadvertently slipped from one of the boy's hands and I came crashing down to the ground. Fortunately I wasn't seriously injured, but the pain did make me cry and there was no one to comfort me. I firmly believe that children raised in these conditions are bound to be psychologically scarred for life, although there may be other benefits – they often become more self-reliant because they have no one but themselves to depend on. There's no room for the faint-hearted in this environment; you have to be tough, both physically and mentally, since you have to fight your own battles.

After a three-week convalescence, my mother regained enough strength to begin visiting us every week. She would have visited us every day, but the regulations permitted only one visit a week. I don't remember much about her visits when I was only three, but I do have vivid recollections of them by the time I was five or six years old. What stands out most in my memory are the lengthy walks we took along Main Street, always stopping in front of our favourite bakery to look through the window with delight and select one of the mouth-watering French pastries. The orphanage didn't allow any sweets, so it was a thrill for me and my sister to have my mother indulge us with such delectable treats.

On one of my mother's weekly visits, I remember asking her when she would be taking us home to live with her. Holding back tears, she told me that she didn't yet have the means to support us. She promised that as soon as she could afford to make a home for us, we would all be together again. Finding a job was very difficult for her. Uncle Morris would gladly have given her a chance to learn the fur trade if she had been on speaking terms with my aunt. This situation with Aunt Sadie lasted much longer than my mother had ever anticipated and it was actually Mrs. Morantz who finally resolved the situation after five years. She apparently appealed to my aunt's conscience, reproaching her for callously allowing my mother to remain penniless. This had the desired effect – Aunt Sadie approached my mother to ask that they both let bygones be bygones and made amends by getting my uncle to employ her. They both agreed to make a fresh start.

Given my aunt's affluence, it's difficult to understand why she hadn't been willing to help her sister and her children in such a time of hardship, why she had let her own sister's children spend years in an orphanage. We were not her responsibility, but out of basic moral decency, she might have shown us some compassion. Unfortunately, my most perplexing questions about my aunt's behaviour will never be answered.

In the end, almost six years passed before my mother could afford to take us out of the orphanage. She continued paying us regular weekly visits while she saved every penny she could. In the interim, our lives at the orphanage followed a regular routine: we rose early in the morning, got washed and dressed, ate breakfast in the dining hall, and then went off to attend cheder – Jewish elementary school – classes on the lower floor. After school we played games outdoors until the bell rang for supper and after dinner we played until bedtime, something we never looked forward to since it always seemed to come too soon.

At long last, in the spring of 1930, my mother was finally able to take us out of the orphanage. It was one of the happiest moments of my childhood. The ever-dependable Morantzes had helped her with the search for suitable accommodation and found us a place to live: two large rooms in a four-storey building on Main Street called St. John's Block. The owner, a Jewish gentleman by the name of Dr. Moss, ran his medical practice on the first floor.

I was eight and a half years old when the day finally arrived for my mother to take us out of the orphanage and knowing that I was going to live with her, free from the institution, was like a fairytale come true. Aunt Sadie and Uncle Morris brought my mother to the orphanage in their big black Studebaker to drive us to our new home. By coincidence, a friend of mine from the orphanage, a young Jewish boy roughly my age by the name of Sammy Cohen, also left the institution within weeks of my own departure and his mother happened to rent a room in the same block of flats. Sammy's parents were divorced. I was delighted to find that I would have a friend from the orphanage to play with.

It was the beginning of the next chapter of my life.

Happy Days

I look back on the years after Clarice and I left the orphanage as among the best years of my life. They were the years in which I enjoyed the greatest sense of security, being back with my mother. The days were filled with fun and games and the carefree feeling of adventure that should be part of a young child's life. During that time, I was a happy child.

Free from the strict regulations of the orphanage, it was easy to adapt to my new environment and daily routine. However, while I was happy to be back with my mother, the reality that, unlike most of the other children, I didn't have a father at home was beginning to sink in. My mother explained that my father was living in a far-off land called France, in the city of Paris. I had no idea where that was and it was hard not to feel envious whenever my friends boasted about their own fathers. Still, I told myself, I had a father, even though he lived so far away. Whenever conversations concerning fathers arose, I told my friends that my father would be joining us soon – even though I knew that it wasn't true. I began fantasizing that my father had just come home from work to play with me, to take me by the hand to go for a walk, to protect me from bullies, to buy me toys and tuck me into bed at night. Not having my father with me became a source of constant heartbreak.

When Clarice and I left the orphanage in the spring of 1930, Aunt

Sadie invited us to spend the entire eight days of Passover at her new home at 256 Garfield Street. It was a beautiful home, a mansion. I've mentioned before that Aunt Sadie was very conscious of her social status – everything she undertook had to stand out and bear a special mark of distinction. In 1928, she went to California expressly to find an architect willing to draw up plans for a home built to her exact specifications. After spending almost three months in California, where she looked at countless homes, she finally came home with a set of plans that met her every requirement. Her dream home, completed in 1929, was the nicest in the neighbourhood and possibly one of the nicest in all of Winnipeg.

The first time I saw the magnificent structure I was awestruck. A beautiful sprawling two-storey home about twenty-three metres wide, it had an emerald-green stucco exterior sprinkled with little stones, the effect of which was dazzling. Half a dozen front steps led to a wide platform and the front entrance. Both the front door and side door had electric bells that registered on a gadget hanging in the kitchen, indicating the front entrance bell as Number 1 and the side entrance bell as Number 2. This was a most unusual feature in 1929.

The foyer led to a centre hall and immediately to the right of it were glazed French doors with sparkling crystal knobs leading into an exquisitely furnished dining room; at the far end there was a swinging door into the kitchen. On the opposite side of the hall was another set of French doors that led into an equally beautiful living room with an unusual brick fireplace. Yet another set of French doors led from the living room to the sun room. There was a separate brightly lit eating area in the kitchen that overlooked a back garden with a half dozen fruit trees. A little way up the hallway adjoining the kitchen was my cousin Max's bedroom. Further up the hall was a little square hallway and off that was the huge master bedroom with a spectacular modern adjoining bathroom with a built-in bathtub and shower, toilet and sink, all decorated with coloured ceramic Italian tiles. A circular stairway from the hall led upstairs to three more bedrooms, including maids' quarters and a large bedroom for guests with a separate washroom, and a huge storage room. In the basement, along with a laundry room and a children's playroom, was a room I never did get to see since it was always kept locked. The family referred to it as the mystery room – for reasons only known to my aunt, no one was ever permitted to enter it. For a poor boy from Winnipeg's north end, spending an entire week in such luxurious surroundings was like living in a Hollywood movie.

My cousin Max was five years older than me and, given that we had the same name, both being named after our maternal grandfather, we were referred to as big Maxie and little Maxie. He was a tall handsome boy full of vitality and fun to be with, a brilliant student who was always near the top of his class. Despite our age difference, we got along splendidly. It was Max who first took me along to a swimming pool and taught me to play miniature golf. He let me hang around whenever he invited his friends over and always seemed to go out of his way to please me, taking me to shows, playing baseball with me or buying me treats. He was so good-natured that he would have gladly given me toys or sports equipment that he had outgrown if only his mother had allowed him to. Unfortunately she had a habit of hoarding everything and would rather let things rot than allow her poor sister's children to benefit from them.

I remember a specific incident that really illustrates my aunt's behaviour. During the late 1920s and early 1930s there were a variety of chocolate drinks that were popular with people who could afford them. One in particular, Vi-Tone, came packed in an attractive tin container. One day when I was visiting, Max began preparing himself a snack of Vi-Tone and cookies. The powdered chocolate drink had to be mixed in a special tall glass container with a metal cap with a hole in the centre through which you pushed a metal object up and down to get the effect of an electric milk shaker. I had never tasted Vi-Tone and Max told me what a treat he had in store for me. I so enjoyed that foamy chocolate drink that I ran to my mother and asked her to buy me a tin of Vi-Tone. Aunt Sadie, who happened to be within earshot, interjected, saying, "Now, Maxie, you know your mother can't afford such luxury." I was mortified, as was my mother.

For the first evening of Passover in Aunt Sadie's new house we sat at her beautiful dining-room table covered with a white linen table-cloth and laid with glittering silver and the finest porcelain china. As I've mentioned before, Uncle Morris conducted the full seder without omitting any part of it, complying with strict Jewish tradition. I vividly remember him raising his silver goblet to say Kiddush over the wine at the beginning of the seder, but the service went on so long that by the time dinner was served, I was half asleep. It was a great occasion for me nonetheless – as the youngest person at the seder I was given the privilege of asking the Four Questions, which gave me a sense of importance when all eyes were focused on me.

I also remember attending my cousin Max's extremely lavish bar mitzvah in Winnipeg's Talmud Torah Synagogue in 1930. Aunt Sadie spared no expense to make her son's bar mitzvah one of the largest affairs ever held in the city. There must have been well over five hundred people in attendance and I can still see all the guests seated at long tables around the four corners of the huge hall. Max received so many gifts that they had to be carried away in a panel truck. To this day, I have never attended such an opulent affair.

～

My earliest school recollections go back to Grade 3 at the David Livingstone School in Winnipeg. Amazingly enough, I still recall my grades 4 and 5 teachers' names – Miss Shager and Miss Cavanaugh. I have very fond memories of Miss Shager, who was very pretty; I was a top student in her class. Miss Cavanaugh was also an excellent teacher, even though I was only in her class for three months. Like all the other Jewish children, I also attended the Hebrew Free School after my regular public school classes. My Hebrew teacher, whom I remember with affection as well, was Mr. Klein.

In those days, strapping a child for bad behaviour was part of the school system and I recall being strapped by the principal on two separate occasions. I don't remember what my offences were, but the punishment was very convincing – I remember not being able to turn the doorknob when I left the principal's office because my hand was so sore. The strap consisted of a thick piece of leather and, depending upon the seriousness of the offence, we were given five or more lashes on each hand.

Winters on the rugged Western prairies were long and severe. At the school lunch break, a gang of us boys would get together to play on an ice rink that we had improvised. We slid on the ice with our moccasins because in those early Depression years most of us couldn't afford skates. We also had fun with snowball fights. At four o'clock, when school was out, we went home for a snack and then back outside to trek through the crispy white snow to Hebrew school. That ended at six and we all went home for dinner. No sooner had we finished eating than our gang reassembled, playing cowboys and Indians, imitating the great movie cowboy idols of our day, performing daring feats such as climbing trees and jumping off into snow that was over one metre deep, swinging from the trees to rooftops and then leaping back into the snow below. One friend of mine owned a huge sleigh that his father had built for him. It had leather reins and we attached it to a huge Belgian Shepherd dog that pulled us when we took turns riding in it, giving us the thrill of our lives.

One fun-filled day followed the next. The kids I hung around with were either poor or extremely poor – we had no televisions, very few of us had radios and fewer still could afford sports equipment, so we had to be resourceful. We participated in all the outdoor sports that didn't require expensive equipment and we made up our own games. I remember one time when a boy, with the help of his friend's father, made snowshoes that proved to be quite effective. Our whole gang then tried snowshoeing, venturing far out into the deep snow. The sensation of keeping aloft on snow without sinking to the ground was exciting. We also tried "skating" with our moccasins on the frozen surface of the Red River, ever leery of cracks in the ice.

One of my school friends was a Jewish boy by the name of Nathan Streifler. He was a very recent immigrant from Poland and didn't speak a word of English. Although I understood Yiddish quite well, I spoke very little, but Nathan and I somehow managed to communicate with each other. He was a very bright child and it wasn't long before he had a fair command of English. I don't remember exactly how our friendship began, but I am proud of myself for having enough compassion at nine years of age to befriend a young boy whom nobody would play with, let alone talk to.

Many decades later this reminded me of my own plight when I found myself in a foreign land in a similar situation, unable to speak the language and with no one to help me. It is impossible for anyone who hasn't had the experience of being a child living in a foreign land to understand how frustrating it is not to be able to express himself in a new language. Before his second year in Canada, Nathan became so proficient in English that he could use slang words as well as any native-born Canadian. Nathan and I became very good friends, so much so that his parents insisted on having me over for Shabbat dinner every Friday evening. They lived in a quaint little red wooden house built on one level.

When spring arrived, we had a whole new set of diversions. The mounds of snow melted away, leaving mud puddles everywhere, allowing new green grass and dandelions to grow in the open fields and on the front and back lawns of the houses. The arrival of spring on the prairies is a spectacular event – everything suddenly comes alive in the warm sun and the scent of blooming flowers fills the air along with the sound of chirping birds, humming bees and insects. Spring beckoned us outdoors to play and tumble on the grass.

On one such day my friend Sammy Cohen invited me to join him and his father on a ride into the country. What was so special about this event was the fact that Sammy's father owned a truck – no small possession in those days; hardly anyone I knew owned a vehicle except my rich aunt. Sammy's father was a plumber and owned a little shop where he kept all his tools. Before setting out on our drive that morning he took us to his shop, where Sammy and I were allowed to look at some of the equipment. Soon we were on our way to the countryside. I was struck by the wide open spaces that seemed to stretch to the horizon. After driving for several hours we turned off the main road onto rough gravel and stopped at a farmhouse owned by friends of Sammy's father. The farmer greeted us cordially and invited us in for lunch, after which we spent the remainder of the afternoon exploring the farm. It was a perfect day.

Another exciting event in those early years was the arrival of the circus. Each year it opened with great fanfare to the thrill of the children, who flocked to it with their parents. My mother took my sister and me to the circus for the first time in 1930. It was eye-opening and thrilling and we went every year after that. Everything we saw was fascinating and introduced us to a whole new world of unforgettable wonders – performing monkeys riding around a near-vertical slanted wall on tiny motorcycles; someone diving from a great height into a small pool of water; hair-raising aerial acts. Adding to the fun were children's rides – the rollercoaster, the Ferris wheel and the merry-go-round – and the fun houses, some with mirrors that completely distorted your appearance. Last but not least were the clowns, candy floss, taffy apples and other magical attractions. These were the happy days that I treasure when I look back on my childhood.

Our celebrations of the Jewish high holidays were another beautiful part of that era. Before Rosh Hashanah, the Jewish New Year, Aunt Sadie indulged us with gifts of new clothing to be worn at the Yom Kippur, Sukkoth and Simchat Torah services.

My deep-rooted passion for my religion and people and my early pride in being Jewish can be attributed in large part to the teachings of my Hebrew teacher, Mr. Klein. He kept his students mesmerized with his descriptions of historical events. I most enjoyed learning

about Jewish history from him and we were rewarded for good behaviour by his readings from a Jewish history text in Yiddish. He was
an exceptional teacher who took the trouble to explain every detail
and imbued us with a deep sense of our heritage; we were fortunate
to have had a teacher of his calibre. Unfortunately, I was only able to
study with Mr. Klein long enough to learn to read and write Yiddish
and learn just enough Hebrew to enable me to pray, though I couldn't
really understand the words.

In this time of security and contentment, a crisis was looming at
Uncle Morris's factory. My mother was working as hard as she could
at her job as well as taking care of me and my sister. Despite this,
in the fall of 1931, she learned that she was about to be laid off and
her whole world fell apart. The Depression was upon us and she was
about to join the multitude of unemployed people. Poverty and unemployment were widespread and every family that suffered these
setbacks had to devise some way to fend for themselves. Some sought
part-time jobs while others had to resort to relying on charity and
welfare.

My mother had confided in our neighbour, a widow by the name of
Tillie, about our circumstances, sometimes crying her heart out. After
several weeks of unemployment, we were completely penniless and
Tillie became concerned that we had no food in the house. Without
consulting my mother, she contacted the municipal Department of
Public Welfare on our behalf, explaining the urgency of coming to the
assistance of a mother with two small children who were facing starvation. A bright, forthright and educated woman, Tillie succeeded
in arranging an appointment with officials at the welfare office who
promised to send out a social worker that very same day.

My mother's English still wasn't very good so she asked Tillie to
act as her interpreter. It didn't take the social worker long to understand the seriousness of our situation and approve our application for
relief. After her interview with the welfare department, however, my
mother learned that the allocation for rent was so low that we would

have to move out of our apartment and rent a single room. A proud and independent person, she abhorred the idea of having to be on welfare and when Tillie first told her that she had contacted the welfare office, my mother insisted that she wouldn't accept charity and would find another job. When Tillie explained that there just weren't any jobs available, my mother's independence and self-confidence both came to an end. We moved out of St. John's Block and into one room in a house on Selkirk Avenue.

By a stroke of good fortune, the room we found was in a house owned by a Jewish family whose warmth and hospitality overwhelmed us. If I live to be a hundred the memory of their kindness will never fade away. Our landlords, the Strikers, were a middle-aged couple, Russian immigrants with four children. One of their sons was married and was a newspaper vendor on Portage Avenue near the Winnipeg Piano Company building; the other children, two boys and a girl, were much younger and lived at home. I became good friends with the youngest of the brothers, Louie, who was close to my age. His sister, Sarah, was several years younger than him and his older brother, whose name I forget, was four or five years older.

Mr. Striker made his living as a painter and also earned income from another house he owned. Mrs. Striker ran the household and looked after her husband and children as well as the tenants. Her expertise in the art of cooking and baking, as well as her other talents for preserving fruits and vegetables, could have won her first-class honours in any competition. She was a truly loving woman with a wonderful temperament who taught my mother to become a fairly good cook as well as how to bake. My mother's illiteracy was always a handicap in this – she had to memorize recipes instead of taking notes. Despite the hard times, we never went hungry because the welfare food vouchers provided us with enough to eat. But there was never any money for the little extras, such as candy or toys. We improvised our own bats from wood that we found lying around on the ground after the long cold winter, but they were a poor substitute for the real thing. I confess that, like many other kids during the Depression, I sometimes snuck into shows without paying. On the rare occasions that my aunt and uncle visited, they would casually slip my mother a dollar bill, which she would use to buy goodies and allow me a nickel for the show.

In those days, most homes were constructed of wood, especially in working-class areas. I remember fondly the two-storey white wooden-frame house in which we occupied a room on the upper floor. Fifty years later I can still remember clear as day a frosty January morning when I went out the front door to get the two quarts of milk delivered daily by the milkman to discover the snow piled high enough to block the four or five steps from the enclosed veranda to the front pavement. The milkman hadn't been able to deliver the milk that morning because the snow was so high. Mr. Striker and others soon appeared and began to clear a path to the roadway leading to the milkman's horse-drawn sleigh. This was not an uncommon occurrence in the winter, when everyone had to clear their front porches and sidewalks for the milkman.

When the snow was this deep we went tobogganing in a nearby park that had specially built elevated slides that twisted and turned. Half a dozen kids shared the same toboggan and, as it made its descent with ever-increasing speed, held on to the fellow in front, experiencing a queasy sensation along with the fun and excitement. Some of the slides were built on such extreme sloping angles that, given the speed of descent, you had the sensation that you were about to tumble over. It was a thrilling ride.

My mother assumed her new role of homemaker reluctantly and never got used to being a welfare recipient. Only in her late twenties, she was extremely lonely and, as Clarice and I got older, we were beginning to ask questions about our father. We wanted to know where he was, why he was there and why we couldn't be with him. For some reason, there was never any serious attempt to bring my father to Canada. There were some vague references to the fact that he still didn't have the necessary documents required for immigration and comments that Canada wasn't allowing any more Polish Jewish immigrants into the country. I don't know if either of these were really the reason for my father not coming to Canada. Perhaps neither of my aunts were willing to sponsor him, although it's also true that the Canadian immigration policies of the Mackenzie King government were antisemitic. Whatever the cause, it was inhumane to prevent a father from joining his wife and children.

My cousin Jack, Aunt Pola's oldest son, had arrived in Canada in 1927 and it still mystifies me as to why Aunt Sadie chose to bring over my cousin, who was still a bachelor, before my father, who already had a wife and two children in Canada. It's true that Jack had the proper documents, but in the 1920s it was fairly easy to obtain documents as long as someone was able to pay for it. The true motives for not bringing my father to Canada continue to elude me.

None of this is meant to show any disrespect for my cousin Jack, who is a fine gentleman. In 1932 he married a lovely girl named Luba and their wedding, paid for by Aunt Sadie, was the first I ever attended. I was unexpectedly made the centre of attention when I was asked to perform a solo Russian-style dance that I had learned from some of my friends. It was the kind of dance in which you bend your knees all the way down, then cross your arms, kicking out your feet back and forth. The wedding was a very successful affair attended by quite a few people. It was held in a large hall and a band played continuously while people danced. What I looked forward to most that evening was having a big chunk of the beautiful wedding cake.

Jack eventually became the proud father of three children and eight grandchildren. He started out working for Uncle Morris, where he established his career as a cutter and fur designer. His oldest son, Dave, was a professor of mathematics and his younger son, Max, is a lawyer. He also had one daughter, Pearl.

～

When we moved to the Strikers' house in the late fall of 1931, I was just turning ten. Life once again began to follow a regular routine, with the exception of the occasional special event. I especially remember having my first birthday party. My mother and Mrs. Striker prepared all sorts of goodies, and the best was a surprise birthday cake that consisted of a huge chocolate layer covered with white icing sugar and topped with blue candles. Many of our friends joined in the celebration, including the entire Striker clan. Toward the end of the party, I unwrapped the first birthday gifts I had ever received. Then we played games and sang songs to the accompaniment of an old piano.

The following spring, in 1932, we spent another delightful Passover at my aunt's home. It ended all too soon and we returned to our room on Selkirk Avenue. Leaving our brief stay in the lap of luxury was made easier by the fact that three months later I was due to leave for my very first summer vacation at the B'nai Brith Fresh Air Camp for underprivileged children in Gimli, a resort area on Lake Winnipeg, about seventy-five kilometres north of the city.

The summer arrived in no time and a large crowd of children assembled at the railway station to board the train to Gimli. After a lot of hugging, kissing and waving, the train left. My mother made a hopeless attempt at holding back tears. I had a wonderful time at the camp. On the train ride to Gimli, we sang songs at the top of our voices, chatting and taking in the country scenery. When we reached our destination, we were split up into different groups and assigned to dormitories. My dormitory, which accommodated about thirty boys, was large and airy, screened in with wide windows all along the length of the room.

Soon after our arrival, we met the counsellors who prepared us for the day's activities – the one we looked forward to most was swimming. All the meals were a treat for poor kids like us. Everything was of course strictly kosher with a *Yiddishe tam* (Jewish flavour). I vividly recall our early morning dips in the lake that built up a ravenous appetite for breakfast. After breakfast on our first morning at the camp we also took part in a treasure hunt. The trail led through a thick forest where we were supposed to detect clues posted on tree trunks. It was a bit scary at first but wound up being lots of fun. Prizes were hidden throughout the dense forest and the objective was to be the first to find them. Certain trees contained messages with arrows pointing in the direction one should take, a number of them tricky and confusing if you weren't smart enough to decipher them. It was a great adventure that was part of teaching us to become self-reliant.

I loved the huge bonfires at night on the sandy shores of Lake Winnipeg, where we all gathered around to sing old songs and learn new ones, telling stories and eating a variety of goodies. The camp had so much to offer and I took part in all of its activities, playing volleyball, basketball and table tennis, and learning how to swim and dive. Other special events included running races, sack races and a "horseback" game that involved four boys, two on the backs of the other two, trying to be the first to pull the other fellow off in order to become the winner. On rainy days we did indoor activities such as checkers, dominoes and a variety of card games. I wrote my very first letter to my mother from the camp – which Mrs. Striker read to her – with the style and skill of a ten-year-old.

My exhilarating holiday ended all too quickly and we were all reluctant to depart. Within weeks of my return from camp, however, I had a little surprise waiting for me: my aunt, uncle and cousin had arranged to take me and Clarice on an outing that included a visit to the zoo in Winnipeg's Assiniboine Park. I was so curious about all the wild animals that I could hardly tear myself away. I especially loved watching the antics of the monkeys swinging to and fro, and the enormous bears standing upright, begging for peanuts and then retreating to a huge pond where they splashed around. Seeing the elephants, the ferocious lions and roaring tigers, the spotted leopards and other wild animals and birds filled me with delight.

At midday we took a break for a picnic. My uncle spread a colour-

ful tablecloth over the grass and opened a picnic basket containing
a variety of sandwiches and fruits. Cousin Max had brought along a
baseball and two mitts and we began tossing the ball back and forth,
as well as playing all sorts of games. By the time we stopped playing we were exhausted and very thirsty. Sure enough, to quench our
thirsts and top off a perfect day, we were treated to Cokes and ice
cream, followed by another visit to the animals.

I have other wonderful memories of my childhood in Winnipeg.
Most important were my friends with whom I played and went to
public and Hebrew school. We went to the movies together, mainly to
see cowboy pictures, where our favourite stars were the ever-popular
cowboys Tom Mix, Ken Maynard and Buck Jones. We enjoyed the
Tarzan movies as well, not to mention such hilarious comedians as
Laurel and Hardy, Charlie Chaplin, Harold Lloyd, Buster Keaton, Slim
Summerville and Joey Brown. In a more serious vein, we admired actors such as Wallace Beery, Jackie Cooper and the pretty little Shirley
Temple, as well as a host of others. There were great programs on
the radio, too, although we didn't have one; I could only listen to the
Sunday evening programs with Eddie Cantor, Jack Benny and Amos
'n' Andy when visiting my aunt. My friends and I also loved reading
comics and playing with marbles.

When I think back to the clothing I wore in those days, it brings
a smile to my face, especially my two pairs of breeches, held up with
suspenders, that were full of patches. Tree climbing and other wild es-
capades were the main reasons for the holes in my pants. During the
winter I wore thick combinations (long underwear), as well as several
pairs of heavy wool socks and regular Indian moccasins. My pièce de
resistance and proudest possession was my aviator cap, which resembled the ones pilots wore in those days. Made of leather and fur-lined,
it had flaps over the ears and buttoned under the chin, with the added
special feature of attached goggles that could be pulled over my eyes
during severe winter storms.

By late 1932 more and more of our family discussions centred around the issue of my mother, Clarice and I joining my father. Being only eleven years old and never having known my father, I became obsessed with the prospect of seeing him and spent almost all my time wondering what he was like. All I could think about was having a real father of my own.

Unbeknownst to me, Aunt Sadie and Uncle Morris had already decided to suggest that I remain behind to live with them in Winnipeg while my mother and Clarice went to join my father in Paris. It might have been that they felt guilty about sending us off to France instead of bringing my father over to Canada, but it also could have been that they didn't want to interrupt my education. Whatever their reason, I'm sure that it was well-intentioned. When I was actually presented with the idea, however, it caused quite a furor. I couldn't believe that they had the temerity to even suggest such a possibility. Nothing was more important to me than seeing my father. My mother took a neutral stance, but told me later that she hoped that I could be persuaded to stay to protect my future, even though it would mean a painful sacrifice for her.

While these discussions were going on, Aunt Sadie received letters from my aunts Pola and Leah in France. They contained news about my father's desperate state of affairs and strongly advised against sending us over there. I'm not sure how much my mother knew about any of this. Many years later I learned from my aunts in Paris that they had repeatedly warned my aunts in Winnipeg to dissuade us from leaving Canada. Why Aunt Sadie and Aunt Jennie didn't try harder to stop their own sister and her children from embarking on a journey with such obviously bleak prospects will forever remain a mystery to me.

The Striker family were fully aware of my mother's intention to join my father in Paris and Mrs. Striker made every attempt to convince my mother that leaving the American continent for Europe would be a grave mistake. It was to no avail – my mother simply could not be persuaded of the risks. There is no way that she could have known that ominous clouds were gathering on the European horizon in 1933. Her only response to Mrs. Striker was that if she didn't go, her children would grow up to hate her when they discovered that she had taken them away from their father.

~

It is by now evident that when I describe my childhood in Winnipeg, I have made few references to Aunt Jennie, who was so instrumental in bringing us to Canada. The truth is that she hadn't changed much over the years – she was frequently out of the country on business and we didn't see her very often. One of her rare visits was during our last summer in Canada, when she arrived accompanied by her business partner to take us on an outing in his car, a picnic at a huge electric-generating plant on a river. Apparently this was a very popular picnic site and I remember it being fairly crowded.

My main association with this occasion is, of all things, Kraft cheese, the soft velvety type that came packed in a long narrow box wrapped in silver paper. I'd never tasted it before. When it was time to have lunch, my aunt prepared these delicious cheese sandwiches for us and to say that I enjoyed them would be an understatement – I kept asking her for more. Sitting on the bank overlooking the river, my main preoccupation was to ensure that I got enough of those cheese sandwiches. In my memory, it was the high point of the day.

Sometime during that summer of 1933, when I was eleven, I had my first encounter with antisemitism. Many of my Jewish friends and I regularly played in Stella Park and one day we were taken by surprise and attacked by a bunch of young hooligans carrying sticks. They lashed out at us with fury, calling us dirty Jews and other equally offensive names. We were completely unprepared and had nothing to use to strike back; as a consequence some of us were left severely bruised and bleeding, running for dear life to the safety of our homes. We later learned that we were attacked mainly by immigrant boys from Galicia, though others were involved in that gang as well.

The injuries I personally sustained were one cut to my forehead that required stitches, leaving me with a permanent scar, other facial cuts and a bruised leg. The incident did not pass without revenge. As soon as we recovered from our injuries, my friends all rallied to do battle with our antisemitic foes. Somehow the word got around that we were planning to meet our attackers in Stella Park. This time, however, we came prepared, sticks and all, ready to teach them a lesson they would not soon forget. Our group made its way to the park, half of us entering from one end and the rest coming in from the other. When those of us at the main entrance confronted the hooligans, they were surprised to see how few of us there were, though obviously pleased that they were not outnumbered. They charged at us with sticks and whatever else they had, but before they knew what was happening, the rest of our group rushed at them from the rear. Between us we gave them the thrashing of their lives and they never repeated their cowardly attack.

～

As my last glorious summer in Canada drew to an end, I returned to school to enter Grade 5. At the time, I didn't realize my school career would end for good at the age of twelve, which affected me tremendously in later years. Whatever additional knowledge I acquired came from life experience, which in my particular case was the school of hard knocks.

My friends and my teachers – Miss Shager from Grade 4 and Miss Cavanaugh, my new Grade 5 teacher – soon became aware of my impending departure for Paris, France, which turned me into something of a celebrity. I became the envy of the neighbourhood. I had two reasons for feeling proud and boasting to my friends about my impending journey: I would be going on a train trip followed by a long ocean voyage and, best of all, I was finally going to see my dad. I basked in all my glory, enjoying every moment of the preparations with ever-increasing anticipation.

A few months before we left, Mrs. Striker got together with the Morantzes to try to persuade my mother one last time to change her mind. Sadly, despite all their pleadings, my mother couldn't be dissuaded from rejoining her husband. She didn't want to spend the rest of her life alone, raising two children without a father. Whatever the risks, she was convinced that we belonged with our father and she with her husband. Events would prove what a travesty it was, particularly for a Jew, to have exchanged the secure refuge of North America for the insecurity of Europe in 1933.

Aunt Jennie, the first of our family to set foot on the North American continent and directly responsible for bringing us to Canada, was now, together with Aunt Sadie, instrumental in reversing the process. They both financed our trip, with Aunt Sadie contributing the major portion of the fares. I cannot help but wonder what went through their minds at that particular time, whether they worried about our future welfare. It's likely that my aunts were somewhat relieved; we weren't just poor relatives, we were something of an embarrassment by being on welfare.

The months faded into weeks and then to our last few days in Canada. All too soon I found myself saying goodbye to all my friends, my schoolteachers and my wonderful Hebrew teacher, Mr. Klein. When the day of our departure finally arrived, no child could have been happier or more excited than I was.

Into the Eye of the Storm

We left on a bitterly cold, bleak day in December 1933, just weeks after my twelfth birthday. We drove to the railway station in my aunt's black Studebaker and our sendoff was truly memorable – countless friends and relatives showed up to wish us well. My aunt and uncle kissed and hugged me and the Morantzes and Strikers gave us their best wishes. Aunt Sadie's last goodwill gesture was to slip my mother a fifty-dollar bill; Aunt Jennie gave her twenty-five dollars.

As we set off on our journey, members of the Nazi Hitler Youth were already training for war and the atmosphere in Europe was becoming increasingly menacing. Jews in Nazi Germany were fleeing the country in droves while their possessions were seized. Harassed, beaten and vilified, their stores were looted. The arrogant Nazis stormed into their homes and arrested innocent Jews. Life for German Jews was becoming a nightmare, although most of them still thought that the situation was only temporary.

It was at this moment in history that we set sail for Europe. As far as anyone knew in 1933, the Nazi menace was strictly confined to Germany – we thought we were headed for a safe and prosperous country. With its Maginot Line, France was considered impregnable, a world power second to none, safe and unbeatable. We were confident that this was true, that we had no reason to worry about our safety.

Our train pulled out of the Winnipeg railway station en route to Montreal, where we would board the ship to France. My mother prepared the upper sleeping berth for me and the lower one for her and Clarice, then we all retired for the night. Settling into my berth, with my head on the pillow, I listened to the clicketty-clack of the train as it sped along the tracks and the rocking motion soon put me to sleep.

When I awoke the next morning, I jumped down to the lower berth and woke up my mother and Clarice so we could go to breakfast. Once we were dressed, we went on what seemed like a long walk to the dining car. Eating on board the train was a new experience for all of us – my mother had to depend on me to read the menu and allowed me to order all my favourite things. After breakfast we returned to our car and sat near the window, peering out at the beautiful countryside until we got bored and decided to unwrap some of our gifts. Amongst them were some games that my sister and I played.

The train trip, more than three thousand kilometres, took two nights and three full days. When we disembarked in Montreal, we took a taxi from the station to the Carlton Hotel, where we were met by the steamship company's agent. He told us that we unfortunately wouldn't be able to board our ship on the following day because of a sudden freeze up in the harbour. The company was anticipating a delay of several days but would put us up at the Carlton at their expense for the entire time, including all our meals.

We passed the time enjoying all the tall skyscrapers and walking up Mount Royal. When we got to the top, we discovered that we could pay for a horse-and-buggy tour. Seeing how eager we were, my mother ordered one for the three of us. We climbed into our seats and looked at all the splendid sights of Montreal while the horse trotted along the road. These few days turned into a really nice holiday, especially for my mother, who had never had one before. We spent most of the time sightseeing and took in at least one show every day. In the middle of the Great Depression, it was a dreamlike adventure in one of Canada's largest cities and we savoured every moment of it.

After several days there was another announcement that because of the ongoing weather conditions, we would have to travel to Quebec City to board our ship. We were really excited at getting the chance to see yet another city. The next day, we caught a train to Quebec City, where we were taken to the docks. During the drive, we got a glimpse of the city's picturesque sights. Wonderful as it all was, though, I started to feel a bit homesick, thinking about the friends I had left behind, perhaps forever. The possibility of never again returning to Winnipeg, the only place I had ever known and loved, was overwhelming. Still, I forced myself to focus on the far more important reason for this journey: my desire to get to know my father.

We arrived at the docks, boarded the SS *Aurania* and set sail that same evening, slowly heading up the St. Lawrence River and out to the open sea. Our cabin had three beds, with dressers and closets, as well as a washroom. For some reason, I found the round porthole window very amusing. The ship also had a recreation room, where we could play all kinds of games, including table tennis, and there was a theatre where we could watch movies. One of my favourite pastimes was running around the ship's three decks. I didn't want to miss out on anything. The dining room served delicious meals – the best part of all, of course, were the desserts. I can only remember being seasick once, during a very intense storm. Otherwise, the whole trip was exciting. There were hundreds of people on board, each and every one of them with a different story and reason for travelling.

Passengers travelling on ocean liners in the 1930s were divided into three categories: first, second and third class, according to their ability to pay. Needless to say, we were in the last category. First-class passengers occupied the top deck and, I believe, had their own private dining room. Only first-class passengers were permitted on the upper deck, but I always managed to sneak up there without any interference from anyone. From the upper deck I had a clear view of the ocean and could see ships at a considerable distance. I made a point of inspecting the whole ship, making new discoveries that amazed me.

After ten days at sea, we approached the port of Le Havre. On the day of our arrival I was so excited that I woke up earlier than usual and went on deck. In the hazy distance I could make out the French coastline. What a truly momentous occasion – I wanted to stay on deck until the ship docked. Other passengers began crowding the decks, eager to catch sight of land. When we heard that the landing would not actually take place for many hours, my mother persuaded me to join her and my sister for breakfast. It was to be my last hearty Canadian breakfast for quite a while. I had become used to a breakfast of orange juice and cereal with sweet cream, followed by eggs or pancakes, toast and milk; in France, breakfast consisted of only coffee and a croissant.

When our ship docked in Le Havre, the tension and excitement was almost unbearable. We would soon be setting foot on French soil, our new home, and years of separation from my father would be part of the past. My parents' years of loneliness and frustration would finally come to an end and my father would see his nine-year-old daughter for the very first time. I had long imagined what my father would be like, picturing him to be like my movie idols, the hero types, tall, strong, confident and courageous.

We disembarked and went straight to the railway station to catch a train for Paris. All of a sudden I was in strange and unfamiliar surroundings, with new and unrecognizable customs, the sounds of a foreign language all around me. I couldn't understand a word people were saying, nor could I speak to them. Nonetheless, the closer we got to Paris, the more my heart pounded with excitement. When our train pulled into the Saint-Lazare railway station in Paris, before it came to a complete stop, we saw someone running along the platform, waving to attract our attention, shouting at the top of his voice, "Liba! Liba!" My mother turned to us excitedly and said, "Children, that's your father!" I was dumbfounded when I realized that all my preconceived ideas about my father were completely different from reality. What I saw was a pitiful sight, a man who was only about five foot three, frail and sickly looking. I did my best to disguise my disappointment – I didn't want to offend my dad.

When the train came to a complete stop, Clarice was the first to get off. My father rushed toward us, clasping my sister in his arms; then he hugged me, smothering me with kisses. Finally, he threw his arms around my mother, her eyes filling with tears as they embraced for the longest time. Aunt Leah and Uncle Joseph were also at the station, as was Aunt Pola. When all the kissing and hugging subsided, we hailed a cab to take us to my aunt and uncle's place.

It was night as we drove along many grand boulevards through the city, so I couldn't see much. After a relatively short time, we turned into a narrow passageway and stopped about three-quarters of the way down. We got out of the taxi in pitch darkness to find ourselves facing a huge door; we rang the bell and, when the door opened, went across a small courtyard to a stairway. Still in the dark, except for the three or four matches that my dad used to light our way, we climbed to the second floor. We entered Aunt Leah's place and I couldn't believe the scene of abject poverty in front of me. When my aunt lit a miniature gas lamp hanging from the ceiling that gave off a dim shadowy light, I could see only two rooms, one was the kitchen and the other a bedroom. Five people – my aunt, uncle and their three children, Philippe, Pierre and Luba – lived in the confines of this small area. There was no electricity and no sink or washroom. One toilet out in the hall served two flats housing a total of eleven people – my uncle's brother lived across the hall with his wife and four children in a similar two-room apartment. The toilet had no seat, just two foot stands, and flushed with a pull-chain. To obtain light in the apartment you had to pull a metal chain attached to a handle suspended from the ceiling that started the flow of gas into a tiny white net bag that had to be lit with a match. To turn the light off, you pulled a second chain on the opposite side of the gas bag. Since there was no sink, you had to wash in a basin using a pitcher filled with water from a tap in the hall. We would have to go to the municipal public baths to shower. The kitchen contained a small coal-burning stove, an old second-hand table and chairs, and two metal folding beds. The bedroom had a double bed, an armoire and an additional folding bed.

Accustomed to the Canadian way of life, with modern amenities and sanitation, I was shocked to see such primitive conditions, but I had to adapt to my new situation. We spent our first night in Paris bedded down on Aunt Leah's kitchen floor, having just learned that my father was penniless, homeless, without a job and still under an expulsion order for being an undocumented alien. He had never managed to get a French residency permit despite the fact that he had lived in the country for eleven years.

I think of that first painful night in my aunt's dismal two-room flat in Paris with deep sadness. My dad did everything he could to gain my affection, untying and pulling off my boots as if I were still the little baby who had been taken away from him some ten years before. But I was returning to him as a twelve-year-old, somewhat embarrassed by someone taking off my boots for me.

The next morning I was cold in the dreary room until my aunt started the stove. I had my first French breakfast of coffee, served in a bowl in the French custom, with only a piece of bread known as *fendu* because the loaf was scored, or split. The meal left me very hungry. Several days later I was introduced to a different type of French bread called *fantaisie*, a crusty bread that was more expensive than *fendu*. It became my favourite bread for breakfast, but my aunt served us the *fendu* with a little butter more often because it was cheaper.

After our first uncomfortable night's sleep on the floor of my aunt's kitchen, my mother started looking for accommodations and rented a room in an inexpensive hotel in the 18th Arrondissement. Like my aunt's flat our room had a double bed, a coal-burning stove used both for heating and cooking, a tap out in the hall for our water and a toilet a little further down the hallway. We finally began to live together as a family for the first time in ten years.

The day after our move to the hotel, Clarice and I were registered in the appropriate public schools. In France in those days, girls and boys attended separate schools. I never actually ended up getting much schooling in France – it ended almost as soon as it began. There were many reasons for that, but the primary one was the difficulty I had with the language. I had always been with my own age group in Canadian schools, but here I was placed with children who were just learning to read and write, in the equivalent of a Canadian Grade 2 or 3 class. It was very embarrassing to be such a big kid amongst much smaller children and many of the other students made fun of me.

I was also made a laughingstock by my own teacher, who seemed to get satisfaction from whipping me over the knuckles with a long pointed stick for the flimsiest reasons. He shouted at me at the top of his voice, fully aware that I didn't understand a word he was saying, exaggerating my foreign-sounding Jewish name, loudly calling out, "Bornstein! Bornstein!" When I didn't answer, the rest of the children would burst out laughing. Looking at me with a big grin on his face, the teacher would come to my desk and slam me over the knuckles repeatedly with his stick. I don't know for sure that the source of his behaviour was antisemitism, but he certainly didn't show me any compassion.

My sister's school experience was quite different from mine. She had the good fortune to be placed in a classroom where the female teacher treated her with utmost respect and kindness, and even went further, taking the trouble to translate what she was saying into English word by word to help Clarice learn French. My one and only French teacher not only frequently hit me over the knuckles but followed that punishment by making me put both my hands on my head and holding them there for at least a half hour. These humiliating experiences were further aggravated when the children were let out for recess and I found myself all alone, unable to communicate with anyone.

All of these experiences made me quite homesick. As the days gradually turned into months with no prospect of my father finding a job, our situation deteriorated. The seventy-five dollars my mother had brought with her from Canada was quickly running out. It had been enough to feed and house us, but the money would soon be gone. It got to the point that our resources would only last another two weeks at most. My father made repeated attempts every day to find work, but none of the manufacturers he knew were willing to take the risk of hiring him without a work permit or a residency permit. My mother had a residency permit but not a work permit, so she was also forbidden to work.

At the end of the two weeks, my mother turned in desperation to her oldest sister, Pola. Aunt Pola, who herself was barely scraping by working as a dressmaker, nonetheless offered my mother her last few francs. To paraphrase a Yiddish saying, "Zie hot gehat a hartz fin gold, undt kenner hot nisht gekent shtar-ben far ihr cent." (She had a heart of gold and no one would die for want of her money.) Naturally my mother wouldn't think of accepting Pola's last few francs, so Aunt Pola suggested that she approach a Jewish welfare organization. Applying for charity was still an anathema to my mother but there didn't seem to be any other alternative. The Jewish agency my mother appealed to arranged for us to move into a large shelter for destitute Jewish families. The residence, known as an *asile*, or shelter, provided sleeping accommodations in dormitories, three meals a day in a huge dining hall and clothing.

Since this was the beginning of the Nazi actions against Jews in Germany, there was a huge exodus of German Jews and some found refuge in France and ended up in the *asile*. Consequently, there were a considerable number of destitute German Jewish refugees living there while HICEM, an acronym of three different immigrant aid organizations, one of which was the Jewish Colonization Association, searched for countries prepared to offer them asylum. Most of these German Jewish refugees were not allowed to take up permanent residence in France, nor were they permitted to work or practice their professions. It was no easy task for HICEM to obtain immigration permits for Jewish refugees in those difficult years of the 1930s – Jews were barred from many countries and accepted by few.

We weren't able to move into the *asile* for another week because there wasn't any room. In the interim, the HICEM officials gave us money for food that we had to use to pay our rent. All we had left in the house were a few potatoes and some rice and by the third day we had nothing left to eat and no money. My parents decided that my mother would pawn her gold ring, for which they received a quarter of its value. I had never before known what it was like to be this hungry, and my mouth watered and my stomach rumbled whenever I saw a *boulangerie* or *pâtisserie* with delicious breads, cakes and pastries. More than anything else, I craved the long crusty *fantaisie* bread. Moments like these made me so homesick for Canada that I would try to pretend that my present situation was only a nightmare, that tomorrow I would wake up to find myself back home in Winnipeg. The further removed I got from my life in Canada, the more the possibility of ever seeing it again seemed remote.

A Young Apprentice

On our last night at the hotel I had trouble falling asleep, wondering what our new place would be like. My answer was not long in coming; the following day we assembled our belongings and headed straight for the *asile*. When we arrived we found ourselves standing in front of two buildings surrounded by a high brick wall. The first building was three or four storeys high and contained offices as well as a large all-purpose hall on the main floor and dormitories on the upper floors. The smaller building housed the kitchen and an extremely large dining hall.

There was some limited schooling at the *asile* to teach the children French, since most of us were recent arrivals. I could finally learn French – without being whipped and humiliated – from a Jewish teacher who translated each word into Yiddish or German. What a contrast to my cruel public school teacher. Being referred to as "salle Juif" (dirty Jew) was in no way uncommon in France in that era and far worse derogatory remarks were thrown around on a regular basis. It was not unusual in Paris to see virulent antisemitic slogans written on public walls such as "Morts aux Juifs" (Death to Jews) and "Salle Jupains" (Dirty Jews), and a slew of other vituperative comments that translate as "Dirty Jews, get out of our country," "Jews are taking away Frenchmen's jobs" and "Most of the two hundred richest families of France are Jews." Antisemitism was everywhere in the 1930s, with foreign Jews bearing the brunt of it. Of course, not all of the French people were antisemitic – I had the great pleasure of associating with many who were decent and courteous to everyone.

The *asile* ended up being our home for the next nine months. Our days were pretty routine, with strict rules designating when we rose in the morning, when we had our meals and when lights went out at night. But there was a constant flow of new faces and I soon made a number of friends amongst the refugees. In particular, I became friends with a girl about my own age from Germany who had a younger brother and sister. As German Jews they had been forced to flee the country, leaving behind most of their possessions, including a stately house. These people were from an affluent background – the father was an architect – but the Nazis had left them with only enough money for their fares out of the country. Our friendship lasted about six months. She spoke to me in German and I responded in Yiddish. Sadly, one day she told me that HICEM had gotten them a visa to immigrate to Montevideo in Uruguay. I was very disappointed to lose such a good friend, but I remember that she gave me a kiss on the cheek, making her the first girl to ever kiss me. Unfortunately, I don't remember her name.

I also made friends with a number of boys, one of whom was about my own age and showed me how to make a little money by buying packages of cigarettes and selling individual cigarettes to the residents of the *asile*. It was my first lesson in business and before long I branched out on my own. I had no money to buy my first package, so I managed to convince my father to give me one of his, as long as I promised to replace it later. Before too long, I became quite adept at selling the cigarettes and even expanded my sales to include chocolate bars. My newfound venture resulted in some profit, which in turn allowed me to treat my sister and me to the occasional chocolate bar or candy and even provided my dad with the odd cigarette whenever he ran out of money from his sporadic part-time work.

As the months passed, it became abundantly clear to my mother that she had placed the three of us in a precarious situation by bringing us to France and that she urgently needed a solution to our problems. Knowing that a number of refugees had been able to secure visas to South American countries through HICEM, she decided to ask for their help. Because of our extreme destitution, the ever-present threat of my father's expulsion from the country and his inability to earn a living in France, the agency officials agreed to do everything they could to help us. At the same time, however, they told us how difficult it was to obtain visas for unskilled workers and their families. Tailors, in particular, were way down on the list of desirable immigrants.

As time passed, near the end of the summer of 1934, our hopes began to wane. The people at HICEM informed us that it was becoming next to impossible to obtain permits anywhere because most countries had a closed-door policy toward Jews. This didn't necessarily mean that they wouldn't get us settled somewhere eventually, but it did mean that nothing would happen quickly – we might have to wait several years. So our immediate objective became getting out of the *asile* and setting up house again as a family. There was no privacy in the *asile* and we were becoming increasingly demoralized – dependent on charity we felt as though our lives had no purpose, no challenges or stimulation of any kind. The only way to carry out this plan was for my father to find a full-time job. Luckily, within weeks of making the decision to leave the *asile*, my father was offered not one but two jobs. The ladies' garment industry was gearing up for the new season and two firms needed his services for four or five hours a day. This meant my father would actually be employed full-time as long as the season lasted. Even though the work might only last from eight to twelve weeks, it was possible to make enough during the season to carry over into the slack time.

While we were waiting for our plans to take shape, there was another matter that needed my family's attention: I would be turning thirteen in only three months and it was time to arrange for my bar mitzvah. Not being part of any congregation, we had no rabbi to prepare me for the momentous occasion. My mother appealed to the head of the *asile*, who arranged for us to get help from one of their philanthropic supporters, an elderly devout Jewish woman named Mme. Bleustein. I believe that she was a member of the family that owned the huge furniture conglomerate Lévitan. This extremely Orthodox woman was committed to ensuring that no Jewish boy was deprived of having a bar mitzvah simply because his parents couldn't afford it. When we met Mme. Bleustein, she was very warm and immediately put us at ease. She came straight to the point, advising us that she would arrange for a rabbi to begin giving me private lessons right away and, when the lessons were completed, perform the ceremony in the synagogue she belonged to. She also surprised us with an invitation to have dinner at her luxurious home after my bar mitzvah service. After a thoroughly enjoyable meal, she presented me with a most remarkable gift: a *tallis*, *tefillin* and a *siddur*, and gave my mother a one-hundred-franc note. Mme. Bleustein's generosity did not end with giving me such a memorable bar mitzvah: she told my mother not to hesitate to call on her if she encountered any financial difficulties in getting settled in our own living quarters.

The *asile* was in the district of Montmartre, so it was easier to begin searching for a place to live in that area, especially since it was also close to my aunts Pola and Leah. My parents eventually found an affordable one-room flat. It was on the fourth floor of a dilapidated old building, with no running water or toilet facilities – the one available toilet, shared with several other tenants, was on the fifth floor. The toilet had no seat and one had to relieve oneself standing up. Water also had to be hauled from a tap on the same floor. Our flat was rectangular, rather small, and furnished with a table and four chairs, a coal stove and two single metal fold-up beds. My mother and father's sleeping accommodations consisted of a mattress on the floor. The only light was a petrol lamp and we had to use an enamel basin to wash ourselves. The dirty water was emptied into a pail and poured into the toilet on the fifth floor.

Instead of improving our lot, things became even worse – two growing children, one thirteen and the other ten, were put in the position of sharing a one-room flat with two adults, without the slightest bit of privacy. The conditions were made more difficult by the fact that my father was a chain smoker. In choosing such grim living conditions I can only assume that my mother saw it as a temporary arrangement, a stepping stone until we could afford better accommodations. But as a sensitive young teenager, I felt embarrassed to have my friends see our abominable living conditions and tell their parents what an appalling space the four of us shared.

In reality, we had little choice in the matter. My father had already been working steadily for two weeks and we had an obligation to leave the *asile* and make room for other destitute people. Moving out of the *asile* and into our new room took only a matter of days. We bought the few odds and ends that we still needed, such as second-hand furniture, pots and pans, and dishes, a good many of them supplied through the generosity of Mme. Bleustein.

Our new Paris address was 11, passage Kracher in the 18th Arrondissement of Montmartre. Almost immediately after the move I argued with my mother over the issue of returning to school. In view of my past experiences, I was insistent that I would not be ridiculed again. I told her that instead I wanted to be apprenticed to learn a trade, even though at thirteen I was still too young and didn't have a work permit. Going back to school would have been the easier option, but I was adamant. Once my mother understood that the very thought of being put into a classroom with smaller children and being poked fun at was repugnant to me, she agreed to comply with my wishes.

On one of our frequent visits to Aunt Pola, my mother told her about my desire to work. Among Aunt Pola's friends was a couple who were long-time residents of France. The husband, whom she jokingly called "the Balagula" – someone who drove a horse-drawn wagon – because that's what he did when he still lived in Russia, was a vest contractor in the men's ready-to-wear trade. Most of these small-time contractors worked in their apartments, converting the largest room into a workshop. Every tailor, in both men's and ladies' garment manufacturing, had their own clients – one or more department stores or a combination of small and large retail outlets. Every season, the contractors would contact their clients, who in turn prepared bundles of cloth in a variety of styles that were cut and ready to be assembled into complete garments by the contractors. The tailors took home the unassembled garments, made them up and then returned the completed garments to their respective clients by taxi. Earnings were based on the amount of production according to a fixed rate for each individual style. By and large, most tailors made a comfortable living, depending on the length of the season.

Aunt Pola spoke to her vest-manufacturing friend about hiring me and he told her that he could likely help but first had to discuss it with his son-in-law. His French-born daughter had recently married a young Polish Jew named Bernard Kujawski, a recent immigrant from Poland in his late twenties who was a tailor specializing in mass production. After Mr. Kujawski married the Balagula's daughter, the Balagula offered his son-in-law his contracting business. A newly arrived immigrant like myself, Mr. Kujawski had no work permit but his status changed when he married a French citizen and he was able to obtain a residency permit that allowed him to run a business in France. Mr. Kujawski and his wife rented a fairly large apartment at 19, rue Labat with the intention of setting up a factory in their front room. As he had promised, the Balagula soon contacted Aunt Pola to give her the good news that his son-in-law had agreed to take me on as an apprentice. This is how I came to land my first job at the unusually early age of thirteen.

Several weeks later Aunt Pola told me that she had arranged for me to meet with the Balagula. Our meeting was a rather strange experience, for the man was extremely funny, keeping my aunt and me laughing, and he took his time before speaking seriously. He told me that I would meet his son-in-law the next day to discuss my apprenticeship. I felt euphoric about the prospect of taking on my very first job. Aunt Pola deserved all the credit for making it happen and I shall always be grateful to her. My mother was also grateful and had come to the conclusion that working would be good for my morale and keep me busy.

Hoping to make a good impression on my first employer, I arrived right at the appointed hour to meet Mr. Kujawski. He welcomed me into his apartment, greeted me with a hearty handshake and a broad smile and spoke to me in Yiddish because he, like myself, only knew a little French. Roughly five foot nine with an athletic build, light brown hair and a fair complexion, he was a friendly, intelligent man and I took an instant liking to him. During our interview, he explained how apprenticeships used to work in Poland: an apprentice might be asked to perform all manner of jobs including sweeping the floor. After a number of years of apprenticeship, one could qualify as a full-fledged tailor, but during the process of reaching that goal, an apprentice was not paid. In reality, an apprentice was actually paying for the privilege of learning a trade. Be that as it may, Mr. Kujawski was familiar with our circumstances and offered to speed up the process so that he would find it profitable to give me a weekly allowance. It would take at least six months before I was skilled enough to be paid. Mr. Kujawski was so convincing and his attitude so reassuring, however, that he won me over completely and I readily consented to start work the following week.

From the very first day that I started work, I was surrounded by hilarious Polish-Jewish expressions that I was hearing for the first time. My workplace was a treasure trove of Yiddish culture, including songs sung with such heart that they brought tears to my eyes. The stories and funny Yiddish expressions cheered me up and contributed to my knowledge of Jewish life. I owe a great deal to Kujawski and his Polish-Jewish immigrant workers for smoothing over a time in my life that was filled with so much misery, pain and frustration.

When I started my first day's work, it wasn't anything like I had imagined it would be – the menial work I was given was boring and repetitious. I had to rub a huge brown bar of soap onto the tapes sewn on the front edges of the vest to stiffen the garment. I also had to press the seams of the vests with an automatic gas iron. The iron had a holder that was approximately five to ten centimetres deep and in the centre a piece of metal protruded so that when you put the iron in the holder, forcing the metal downward, the gas lit up from the pilot light, heating the iron. Being barely five foot three and quite thin, manipulating an iron weighing between eleven and thirteen kilograms was a heavy load, especially when the pressing had to be done for about four hours at a time. Despite this, I don't remember finding the job too difficult to handle because of the happy environment. Every day offered something new and different and I soaked it all up. For most of my youth I had only been exposed to Western Jewish culture, so learning about my Eastern European Jewish roots was a revelation.

Contrary to our expectations, my father's jobs didn't last long. One of his bosses was inspected by the police so he had to let my father go. The season at his second job only lasted ten weeks, leaving him barely enough money to last us a month. There was no counting on me for any financial contribution for the time being. My prospects seemed good though, since Kujawski intended to start me on the sewing machine within six months. Once I mastered those operations he would start paying me a weekly allowance. But I would still have to work for at least a year and a half before I would be qualified enough to receive a reasonable wage. Given our present circumstances, that seemed like an awfully long time to wait.

More Ups and Downs

During my first year at 11, passage Kracher, when I was not yet fully fluent in French, I led a very lonely existence. I wrote a letter to Aunt Sadie, describing our extreme poverty, telling her how lonely I was, how much I missed my old buddies and begging her to help us get back home. Appealing to her conscience was futile, however. Aunt Sadie never even had the common courtesy to reply. She did write to us – occasionally sending a money order for five to ten dollars – but there wasn't so much as a mention of my desperate plea to return home.

Sometime after this, I met a young Jewish boy named Henri Bruckner and developed a long-lasting friendship with him. We got to know one another while attending the Patronage, a Jewish organization that brought Jewish children together every Thursday, the afternoon off for French schools, to meet new friends, play games and do crafts. We were also given a snack. Henri's parents were Polish-Jewish immigrants and his father made a living as a men's custom tailor. There were five children in the family and although they were poor by French standards, they were better off than we were. They had a two-bedroom apartment, in which their largest room served as both a workshop and my friend's bedroom. Their circumstances were also better than ours because three of their children were born in Paris, which automatically entitled the father to get a work permit. Henri, for reasons of necessity, quit school at the age of fourteen to work for his father as an apprentice men's custom tailor.

By this time, in the summer of 1935, my father had been out of work for three months and we no longer had the means to support ourselves; we didn't even have a penny left to buy food. For several weeks our suppers had consisted of bread and butter and coffee and for the last two nights it had been bread with no butter and coffee. Our larders were now completely bare; all we had left was coffee and we all went to bed very hungry. Aunt Pola suggested that we go to a Jewish welfare agency on rue des Rosiers in the 4th Arrondissement, where they provided poor Jewish families with a parcel of food and sixty francs in cash every three months.

The agency was a considerable distance from where we lived and, having no money to take the métro, my parents had to get up early in the morning to walk there. At least they wouldn't have to walk all the way back because they would have their sixty-franc allotment that would, at best, only feed us for another two weeks. As if things weren't bad enough, we were also subjected to an infestation of big brown bedbugs that kept us from getting a good night's sleep. The only remedy was to fumigate our room, even though this only provided temporary relief.

My father was beginning to show signs of stress, overwhelmed by the pressures of his new role as breadwinner for a family of four. Ten years of separation had not equipped him for that responsibility and the long lonely interval contributed to an emotional state that frequently erupted in fits of violence. My mother didn't understand that the lonely years he had spent by himself had contributed so significantly to his disturbed mental state, causing him to act irrationally, which in turn created tension between them and caused bitter arguments and terrible physical fighting. In all the years I spent in Paris, nothing affected me so profoundly as having to constantly witness my parents fighting. It left me drained, confused, frightened and upset. For children, nothing equals the pain of watching their parents exchange violent blows.

As time passed, my father's mental health worsened and his eruptions became more frequent. The turmoil was sometimes so bad that I developed severe anxiety and began to really resent him. I didn't even want to call him Papa, and our relationship became very cool and detached. If I needed anything from him, I communicated it through my mother.

~

I had been laid off work for a spell of eight weeks in the summer of 1935, but when the season resumed, Mr. Kujawski would begin teaching me to use the sewing machine. Until then, nothing had happened to improve our lot and conditions remained as bad as they ever were. We still didn't have enough to eat, even though my mother had pawned anything she had of value. We went to bed hungry on many nights, having had little or no supper, and my mother was always giving up her own portion of bread to feed us.

When I think about those terrible days, I never cease to be amazed at how one learns to live with hunger as though it were a natural state of affairs. You know that you would jump at the chance to eat if food were offered, but you somehow develop a kind of discipline that allows you to block out the feeling when you have no other choice.

Since my father had been out of work for so long, he decided to look for some other employment. Although it was still illegal because he had no business permit, he wanted to try his luck at being a peddler, buying up scraps of iron and other metals and selling them by weight to a variety of wholesalers. His first problem, however, was that he didn't have any startup money. He placed his hopes on our next charity allotment of sixty francs from the Jewish welfare agency to get himself launched. All he needed to start was a hand-cart and an area that looked promising. Peddlers had to ring a bell at the front entrance of each building along their chosen street to gain access to the inside courtyard and be admitted by the concierge. Once inside, the custom was to shout, "Second-hand clothing and scrap-metal merchant," hoping to attract someone's attention from the many apartments. They, in turn, would call back to the peddler through the window to sell whatever they wished to get rid of.

If my father was caught in this enterprise, it would definitely spell disaster – he would be arrested and escorted to the border by the police within twenty-four hours. It boiled down to a choice between starving or taking the risk, and in our desperate situation, he opted for the latter. Without the means to buy a hand-cart, my father settled for using a sack to collect his purchases and carrying the heavy load on his back.

In the meantime, my mother was also looking for work as a fur finisher. Some of the retail fur stores responded positively, asking her to come back as soon as the season started. Unfortunately, the beginning of the season was quite some time away, so the job offers did nothing to help us out of our present circumstances.

When the season finally did start, it felt good to get back to work. More than anything else, it meant being back in good company, listening to my boss's amusing tales and antics. I was able to spend hours in a normal environment filled with laughter and camaraderie, away from my miserable home life. Working there also significantly improved my Yiddish to the point that I was just as proficient as I was in English. As an added bonus, Kujawski informed me that my work had improved so much that he was seriously considering putting me on a salary at the start of the next season. I was so overwhelmed by the news that I couldn't wait to get home to tell my folks. It wouldn't be long before I was in a position to contribute to the family income.

Almost a year had slipped by since I first started work and as we approached the end of another season my expectations rose with the prospect of earning a salary when the new one resumed. At long last, I would be in a position to treat myself to a show once a week, to enjoy attractions such as the circus and the outdoor fêtes, and occasionally play billiards or belote, a card game. Like my friends, I would also have some spending money. A whole new world was about to open for me, allowing me to escape the daily tensions at home. It was getting close to the end of my second year in France and I now had a good command of the French language, without even a trace of an accent, which gave me more opportunities to make friends.

As the weeks passed, my father persevered as a scrap-metal peddler. Every night, he would return home exhausted, soaked with sweat from carrying the heavy loads on his back – at least on the days that he was fortunate enough to get customers. His work kept us afloat for a while, until his purchasing funds ran out. The problem was that he never had enough money to buy the bigger loads offered to him, nor did he have any way to transport them. The earnings he got from the smaller loads was less than the amount we needed for our living expenses, which meant that our funds were gradually exhausted.

Fortunately, one of the fur retailers was now prepared to offer my mother work finishing fur coats, new ones as well as remodelled ones. She had to do the work at home because the storeowner didn't want to risk his licence by taking on someone without a work permit. This particular storeowner turned out to be a fine, upstanding person who never exploited my mother simply because she didn't have a work permit. Quite the opposite – he offered her at least the going rate and in many instances more. I remember my mother working right through the night with nothing but a petrol lamp for light, hurrying to meet her employer's commitments to his customers.

When my father was eventually forced to give up the scrap-metal enterprise, neither he nor I worked for months and I anxiously awaited the start of the 1936 season. In the meantime we did all we could to help my mother by picking up and delivering her work. It was a haphazard way to live, but we didn't have much choice. We were grateful to accept any opportunity to put food on the table. We wanted to avoid the embarrassment of resorting to charity if at all possible. My mother worked away feverishly for two solid months until the season gave out, never complaining or letting on how terribly overworked she was. For the first time there seemed to be a bright spot on the horizon, breaking our cycle of bad luck. We had enjoyed three square meals a day for the past three months and life was happier for all of us. I also returned to work and from here on in earned a weekly salary of seventy-five francs. Out of that, I would get an allowance of ten francs a week.

My mother had promised me that I could buy a bike as soon as we could afford it and our newly improved circumstances now made it possible. Buying a new one was out of the question, but a second-hand bike could be purchased quite reasonably at the Saint-Ouen flea market. Within two months of earning a salary, I bought a bright orange light-weight racing bike with three-speed derailleurs, wooden-framed wheels, two front brakes, a pump, front and back lights, and a drink holder. My newfound freedom to go on distant outings with my friends gave me immense pleasure.

It was at about this time in 1936 that we received some shocking news from Aunt Jennie in Winnipeg: my dear cousin Max had passed away from leukemia at the age of nineteen. Poor Max suffered a terrible, lingering death. Our attachment was so strong that, even on his deathbed, he thought of me, making his mother promise to send me his entire savings of thirty-five dollars. What a pity that such a gentle, good-natured soul had his life cut so short. He had a brilliant mind, about to enter his second year of university and planning to become a doctor. His funeral was attended by throngs of people, many who were students from the University of Manitoba. Beloved by one and all, and by me in particular, I shall always carry a special place in my heart for him.

Aunt Sadie and Uncle Morris, now left childless, were so devastated by grief that, according to Aunt Jennie, they had both contemplated suicide. The only thing that consoled them was a first cousin in New York City, Tzivia, who, when she learned of Max's tragic death, asked them to take in one of her five sons and teach him the fur trade. David, about Max's age, was a tall, handsome boy with barely a high school education who was eager to learn a trade. After much persuasion, Aunt Sadie and Uncle Morris accepted Tzivia's benevolent gesture. David soon arrived in Winnipeg to live with my aunt and uncle and take an active part in their fur business. The arrangement proved to be ideal. For my aunt and uncle, having David join their family filled a sorrowful vacuum in their lives. For David, it was a golden opportunity to lead a life of affluence with all the advantages that entailed.

~

In the 1930s, when there was so much poverty and unemployment, it wasn't surprising to find most working people looking for political solutions to their situation. The only political organization that appeared to offer answers to the needs of the poverty-stricken workers was the Communist Party, with their promise of jobs, good wages and decent living conditions. The Communists also promised to provide work permits to foreign residents, a commitment that no other party dared make. Who but the Communist Party would show compassion to someone like my father, threatened with expulsion and prevented from legally providing for his family? At the age of fifteen, I knew little or nothing about politics, but the appeal of a party that showed understanding toward people like us persuaded me to join the Jewish Communist Youth League. I made a number of new friends there whose parents were also facing expulsion from France.

Maurice Thorez, head of the French Communist Party at the time, had repeatedly stressed the urgent need to come to the assistance of Jews who were being expelled from France with no other country willing to accept them. Only one other party in France had the courage or decency to make an appeal on our behalf: the Socialist Party under the leadership of Léon Blum. Although my only association with communism was my brief membership in the Youth League, I am unapologetic in supporting them at a time when hardly anyone else had the human decency to show concern for our plight.

Every member of the Jewish Communist Youth League had to perform some volunteer work and I was assigned the task of selling the Communist Youth newspaper called *L'Avant-Garde*. Every day during the *morte-saison*, I stood on my assigned corner on rue Ordener and shouted at the top of my voice, "Demandez, lisez L'Avant-Garde, organe centrale de la jeunesse communistes, organe de défenses de tous les travailleurs!" (Read L'Avant-Garde, the central organ of the Communist youth, defender of all workers!) and tried to sell as many newspapers as possible. Had the French police asked me for identification, as an undesirable alien, I would probably have been arrested.

Throughout this period, our home life continued to erupt into terrible turmoil on a regular basis. In fact, it seemed to be getting worse. Hardly a week went by without horrific fighting and I could barely take any more. In the face of the ongoing physical violence, my deepseated hatred for my father grew; I wished that he would vanish from our lives for good. My mother understandably refused to submit to my father's irrational outbursts, which further aggravated an already tense situation. She came out of each confrontation terribly battered and bruised. The embarrassing scenes, over which I had no control, tore me apart. I couldn't bear to see my poor mother being brutally beaten and wanted to rush to her aid, though I didn't dare intervene.

I realize now that my father was a very emotionally disturbed person who needed psychiatric treatment. Of course, none was sought or even known to be available. In those days, no one was ever considered moderately mentally unstable – if you displayed any symptoms of irrational behaviour you were declared "abnormal" and often put into a lunatic asylum for life. As a rule, my parents made up after their stormy sessions when my father begged for forgiveness, but these were just temporary lulls between eruptions.

⁓

After the season ran its course, I was once again laid off for a lengthy period, which further worsened our home situation. No one else in the family was working and we only had enough reserves for a couple of days. Without food or money, it became necessary to again ask for charity from a number of Jewish agencies. The problem with charities was that some people abused them, which led them to strictly screen applicants to weed out the cheaters, which made it much more difficult for people like us, who were genuinely in dire need, to prove our case. This was particularly true when we applied to a new charity that didn't know us. Fortunately, the staff who interviewed my mother were quick to recognize how desperate she was. They calmed her down and assured her that she would not go home empty-handed.

Meanwhile, some of my father's friends helped him get started in another new enterprise: selling second-hand American blue jeans, pants, jackets and overalls in the flea market. One acquaintance who was an antique dealer at the market agreed to let him use a small part of his space and another friend loaned him a treadle sewing machine, necessary for repairing the clothing, until he was in a position to buy one of his own.

The blue jeans all came from the USA, worn and discarded by workers and collected by an American wholesaler who had all the clothing cleaned before shipping them off to a client wholesaler in Paris. Garments were accepted in any condition, which meant that most of them had to be repaired. The French wholesaler had the clothes dyed to conform to their original blue jean colour, then resold them by weight to dealers like my father. My father purchased his first load of jeans with money loaned to him by his friend, then took them home to make the necessary repairs on the sewing machine. When they were ready, he took them to his space at the flea market to sell.

This period was a very positive interlude in our lives and provided me with a rare opportunity to get close to my dad when he took me with him to the flea market every day to help him. He was so proud when I sold my first few pairs of jeans to a couple of Algerians. While we worked together he was concerned that I had enough to eat, so he treated me to crêpes and grenadine, which he knew I loved. Although he had a hard time showing affection, he managed to let me know

how much he cared for me. These precious moments we spent together at the flea market stand out as the only time I felt close to my
father.

This business definitely had its drawbacks – the blue jean im-
porter often ran out of stock at the very time we desperately needed
his goods. His shipments came in irregularly, making this a haphazard way to earn a living. In fact, our blue jean business came to a
sudden end after only eight weeks when we were no longer able to
get any further supplies. It ended up being another in a series of futile enterprises through which my father struggled to make a living.
Nonetheless, it served its purpose for a time – we had managed to
build up a reserve fund that was enough to carry us over for a month,
almost until I was recalled to work for a new season.

At the age of fifteen, I had mastered my trade to become a full-
fledged vest-maker earning 150 francs a week, more than enough to
buy us food. The whole family was now dependent on me alone to
keep us afloat. It was fortunate that I was able to learn my trade even
faster than my boss had anticipated, making it possible for me to earn
an almost adult wage.

Now that I was earning more money, my mother agreed to increase my allowance to twenty-five francs a week. My friend Henri
and I, together with a half dozen or so other Jewish male friends,
would meet every Saturday evening at our favourite café to play billiards and belote. Whoever lost had to pay for all the drinks, be it
coffee or panache, a mixture of beer and lemonade. At about eleven-
thirty at night, we all left the café to go to the movies. We mainly
based our choice of films on our favourite actors and actresses, with
a preference for the musicals that were the rage in the 1930s. Since we
overwhelmingly favoured American productions, with the dialogue
in English with French subtitles, I had a distinct advantage over my
friends, who didn't understand a word of English. In those days, all
the movies were double features with a cartoon, world newsreel and
travelogue, so it was close to three in the morning by the time we

came out. I still remember with nostalgia the sound of our voices, singing as we strolled home, harmonizing at the top of our lungs, with some of my friends tap dancing to the music in an effort to imitate the great talents of our time.

Even though we all came from extremely poor backgrounds, when we spent these magical hours together everything bad was temporarily obliterated and we lost ourselves in pure enjoyment. Paris was a spectacular city that had so much to offer. The times I spent in the company of my friends in Paris are memories that I shall always treasure.

~

Whenever my father was out of work, he spent time in a café with his friends. One day, when the French police carried out surprise raids in parts of Paris where they might find undocumented aliens, he was unexpectedly picked up by the authorities. They rode around in closed paddy wagons, stopping in front of certain cafés and asking everyone to produce their identification. The actions were usually carried out so swiftly that there wasn't time for people to escape. If people were already under an expulsion order, they were given twenty-four hours' notice to leave the country. In this particular instance, my father and his friends were trapped. Since they were all already under expulsion notices, they were shoved into the paddy wagon and taken to the Prefecture de Police. They were detained for a short period of time and then released with an order to leave the country within the next twenty-four hours.

This was the disaster that we had feared most. My father came straight home and told us what had happened. When the initial shock wore off, we contacted HICEM, who urged us to come down to their office without delay. Since my father was still on their list as a potential immigrant destined for a South American country, this proved to be enough to convince the French police that everything possible was being done to arrange for his departure. HICEM had once again succeeded in having the twenty-four-hour expulsion notice rescinded and replaced with one that gave him a thirty-day extension. HICEM also now considered the situation to be grave enough to step up their efforts on my father's behalf – his situation had become precarious enough for them to give him top priority on their list of immigrants seeking an entry permit to a South American country. It would no longer be possible to keep extending my father's expulsion orders without arousing the suspicion of the French authorities.

~

During our turbulent time in France, we confronted a host of intolerable situations, but none more humiliating than an experience my mother and I had riding the Paris subway. Since my mother couldn't read and didn't speak much French, it was difficult for her to ride to new and distant locations on her own, especially when it involved making transfers, and whenever she had to go to the HICEM office, I accompanied her.

Whenever my mother spoke Yiddish, she always spoke loudly and clearly. As we were riding the subway one day, because she didn't understand much French, she was unaware that about a half dozen Frenchmen sitting near us had started making antisemitic remarks aimed at us, calling us "dirty Jews" and becoming increasingly abusive. I tried to ignore them and asked my mother to please stop speaking Yiddish in front of all the passengers. I quietly explained to her that the men had called us "dirty Jews" and had said that if we wanted to speak Yiddish we should get the hell out of France and go to Palestine. When my mother heard what they had said, she gave them a dirty look and a piece of her mind, coming out with the only French expression she knew: "Fermez la!" (Shut it!) This so incensed the men that they then began using the most foul antisemitic invectives imaginable. I took the abuse without responding and was even unfairly annoyed at my mother for making things worse, imploring her to stop speaking Yiddish. My mother, however, refused to be quiet. If there was ever a time to extricate oneself from a difficult situation, this had to be it; I resolved the matter by telling my mother that the next stop was ours even though it wasn't, which put an end to a very offensive encounter.

Following that episode, I made my mother promise not to speak Yiddish to me in public in the future; if she absolutely had to, then she should only speak quietly so no one could hear her. I have felt really guilty ever since for not defending myself against such antisemitic intimidation. In retrospect, I'm very proud of my mother for challenging this unjustified verbal attack.

~

In the early summer of 1936, France was undergoing significant political change. Working people across the country were celebrating the June 4 election of a new Socialist government headed by Jewish prime minister Léon Blum. The Socialist and Communist parties had formed a coalition, the Front Populaire, inspiring great expectations amongst foreign Jews. We hoped that with a new Popular Front government, there would no longer be any need for us to emigrate. In the euphoria of the event, I remember a crowd of thousands of working people gathering at either the Bois de Vincennes or Bois de Boulogne to celebrate the Popular Front victory. The subway trains were filled to capacity as we rode to participate in the celebration.

In the crowd, along with the working people, were also the petits commerçants (small shop owners), jubilant over the anticipated new era. No one at the rally could have possibly foreseen the untimely demise of the Popular Front government in just over a year. As a result of their downfall, none of their policies for foreigners were ever put into place. Any hopes of finding an opportunity to remedy our own status were dashed. Our status remained unchanged, so we had to map out our next move with the help of HICEM.

In May 1937, before the demise of the Socialist government, we saw the opening of the Exposition Internationale des Arts et Techniques dans la Vie Moderne (the International Exposition dedicated to Art and Technology in Modern Life), where I saw television for the first time, along with many other futuristic products that today are part of everyday life. We were also honoured with a visit from Aunt Jennie, who came to Paris for the spectacular event. Fortunately, her stay was rather brief; no one was sad to see her leave.

During the six months or so that I was working, we were able to put food on the table, but the rest of the time my mother had to apply to the Jewish charities. From time to time, either my mother or father found part-time employment, but these odd jobs never lasted long enough to meet our needs. In spite of every effort to keep the wolf from the door, we often had neither money nor food.

During one of those desperate periods, in the fall of 1937, my parents contacted a new Jewish agency that did not seem like the others that simply provided food. The Oeuvre de secours aux enfants (OSE) was an organization to help Jewish orphans and ran an orphanage. At the OSE my parents met an accountant named Mme. Klatchka, who was fluent in Yiddish. With tears streaming down her face, my mother poured her heart out to her, telling her how destitute we were, how we were faced with starvation and threatened with eviction for being a year behind in our rent. This warm-hearted woman was so empathetic that she had to use a handkerchief to dry her own tears. Mme. Klatchka then said that she had to talk to one of the directors, M. Millner, and asked my mother to wait for her.

When Mme. Klatchka returned she had a broad smile on her face and to my mother's surprise, handed her a one-hundred-franc note. She also told my mother that further assistance would be forthcoming if no one in the family found employment. This was the beginning of a relationship that eventually led me to change my career. My mother ended up having to apply to Mme. Klatchka for help a second time and during the interview asked whether the OSE could help me find a permanent job. My mother explained that I had a job but could only work six months of the year. Mme. Klatchka promised to look into it.

We all soon returned to the OSE office and were thrilled to learn from Mme. Klatchka that, in conjunction with the directors Dr. Gurevitch and M. Millner, they had decided to hire me as their office boy and receptionist. My duties were also to include other functions that required a good deal of training. I was almost delirious about this unexpected opportunity. Working full-time was a dream come true. My mother was so happy that she kissed Mme. Klatchka and thanked her profusely.

As soon as I started my new job I experienced a greater sense of security. The work also gave me a unique opportunity to learn about the various aspects of the Jewish refugee problem and, to a lesser extent, the conditions for Jews in general around the world. In my capacity as an office boy/receptionist, I came into daily contact with Jewish refugees from the countries controlled by the Nazis who had been forced to flee their homes – in addition to Germany itself, these soon included Austria and the Sudetenland region of Czechoslovakia. For the first time, my eyes were opened to the serious nature of their ordeal. I got to know many of them when they applied to our office for help in being relocated to the few countries still willing to receive them. Many of the refugees briefed me on the conditions that had led up to their flight – most had abandoned everything they had worked for. That part really horrified me, that so many of them had to leave all their possessions behind, including homes, successful businesses, law, medical and dental practices, and high-ranking civil service positions; many of the tradesmen had left good jobs. Some of them arrived in France absolutely destitute. Whole families came to our office with as many as three, four and five children without the wherewithal to see them through another day. I identified strongly with them and my heart went out to them.

My new workplace was on the most famous boulevard in Paris, the Avenue des Champs-Élysées, at No. 92, I believe. My immediate superiors were two charming ladies – unmarried sisters – by the name of Levine, who were the personal secretaries of Dr. Gurevitch and M. Millner. They initiated me into the job with a good deal of patience, first instructing me on how to use the telephone switch-board, which was quite primitive by present-day standards. I mas-tered it fairly quickly and was then given a typewriter to practise on and within a few months I had developed enough skill at two-finger typing to be able to type lists of names to be pasted onto the organiza-tion's monthly review and distributed to their supporters. My work area was in the middle of a long narrow corridor half-way down from the entrance. I was the first contact for anyone entering the premises.

Most of the staff, including the directors, were of Russian-Jewish descent and very cultured. They were accustomed to having after-noon tea and biscuits at three o'clock and it was part of my job to prepare and serve it. After awhile I became quite proficient at it, to the point where the director often complimented me on both the tea and the service. Another one of my jobs involved hand delivering sealed letters – under no circumstances was I to give them to anyone but the person to whom they were addressed. I carried out their instructions carefully, always eager to fulfill my missions to their satisfaction.

Among the many high-profile philanthropists who supported our organization was Édouard de Rothschild and one day, to my aston-ishment, I was instructed to hand deliver a very important envelope to him. He lived on Avenue de Marigny, in a house that was sur-rounded by a tall brick wall and while I was there I had the privilege of meeting him face to face. A servant appeared shortly after I rang the bell and inquired as to the nature of my business. I replied that I had a confidential message from la société O S E and the servant asked me to follow him inside. He ushered me into a huge foyer that led into a well-ornamented room and asked me to wait. After what seemed like an eternity but was probably no more than ten minutes, a tall, dignified man appeared and greeted me in a business-like manner. I handed him the sealed envelope and was shown out. On my return home, I excitedly related the incident to my parents and later that evening boasted to my friends that I had personally met and spoken to Édouard de Rothschild. To a sixteen-year-old of my background, this was truly an extraordinary occurrence.

Throughout the time that I worked for OSE I met a number of distinguished people, including the Baroness de Gunzburg and the wealthy socialite Mme. Praeger. There were many more but I have long since forgotten their names. Despite the fact that my position was fairly inconsequential, it gave me the opportunity to meet some of the most renowned and wealthiest Jews in France. It gave me a sense of importance and dignity and, at the same time, I earned the respect of my superiors and benefactors. The fact that I was doing this job without a work permit didn't seem to present a problem. OSE had apparently identified me as a volunteer and the employment regulations didn't apply to volunteers in charitable organizations.

At this stage in my life, my friendships had become extremely meaningful to me, serving as a counterbalance to my home life. My friends and I found solace in one another and our friendships gave us the strength to view life from a healthy perspective. I often visited my friend Henri's apartment – I was actually there so often that whenever I entered Henri's father would declare in Yiddish, "Ot gait de kallah!" (Here comes the bride!) I considered Henri my closest friend; he was considerate, gentle and honest, and was never at a loss for words. We also had a great deal in common, especially a shared appreciation for music. Above all, he was a loyal son to his parents, helping to supplement the family income by spending long hours working with his father in the custom tailoring trade, much of which involved laborious and eye-straining hand-sewing.

No one except the wealthy had telephones in the 1930s, so all our activities were arranged in person. I would call on Henri first and we would then meet our other friends at our favourite café. As I've already described, we would usually start with a game or two of billiards, followed by belote, but on Saturday nights we always played cards at the home of one of our friends, Abramovitch, who was the most affluent among us. His family lived in a huge apartment – considering that there were as many as fifteen of us, the place had to be large enough to accommodate us all. Fortunately, our friend's parents were very hospitable and always served us tea and cake. At one point, we showed our appreciation by pitching in and buying my friend's mother a beautiful gift.

Throughout the spring and summer we often walked through the various parks in Paris, where we had our first experiences chasing girls. Those of us who were less inhibited managed to persuade the girls to let us walk them home. I was extremely shy with girls, mainly, I think, because I had so little self-confidence. Henri and I also took long subway rides to the Bois de Boulogne or the Bois de Vincennes parks, where we spent leisurely days doing things like renting a rowboat and gliding along the various lakes. After the exertion of rowing, we were ravenous and, more often than not, couldn't resist indulging ourselves in gourmet foods that we couldn't afford.

It's painful for me to write about these beloved friends, most of whom were murdered in the Holocaust. They were brilliant young men whose lives had barely begun to shine, who had so much to live for and so much to offer. I shared some of my most precious moments with them.

We were all very proud of being Jewish despite the fact that most of us had had very little in the way of Jewish education. In 1937, I remember one antisemitic incident that happened on France's most important annual holiday, Bastille Day, celebrated on July 14. On this festive holiday, people danced in the streets of Paris. Some of our group had, like me, spent four years or less in France, but we were all looking forward to entering into the spirit of the celebrations. When some of us approached some girls to ask them to dance, however, they flatly turned us down, calling us dirty Jews and inciting a chorus of insults from the crowd around us. We had to leave the café we were in, although not before retaliating with our own remarks. Every one of us stood our ground as long as we could. We didn't want to let the episode ruin our evening, so we moved on to a larger café in the hope of finding more congenial people. Fortunately we found a place where people were only concerned with enjoying themselves and we spent the rest of the evening dancing with different girls. Music, song and dance all combined to make it a happy event and it would have been hard to not get caught up in the joie de vivre all around us.

Music played an important role in our lives in those days and we zealously keep abreast of all the new songs. Among our favourite singers were Tino Rossi, Mistinguett, Charles Trenet and Maurice Chevalier and we took great pleasure in emulating them. Unfortunately, I failed miserably the time we took dancing lessons together – after ten lessons, I had learned absolutely nothing.

The security that came with my new job helped build my self-esteem, alleviating some of the anxiety that came from my home situation and our financial problems. Things were already looking up when we received word from HICEM that they had finally succeeded in securing my father a permit to live in Buenos Aires, Argentina. We were so overjoyed by the news that we celebrated by dining out at a kosher restaurant. Despite the wonderful news, however, things didn't proceed as quickly as we hoped; there was a delay of nine months before the Argentinean foreign ministry officially sanctioned my father's entry permit. My mother was ecstatic that my father had finally found a safe haven, but my father remained reluctant. He had never really wanted to leave Paris, even though doing so would be the key to his salvation. Nonetheless, he accepted the fact that immigrating to Argentina would give him an opportunity to make good for the first time in his life, and he started making the necessary preparations.

As the date of my father's departure drew nearer, my parents discussed the prospects for a new life in a new land. For the first time, we would all be able to work without restrictions. It seemed almost too good to be true. The promise of our immigration to Argentina gave us a new sense of purpose and hope and our spirits soared. My father was going ahead to Argentina alone because HICEM had secured his visa by presenting him as a businessman. He would have to travel first class with a fund set up by HICEM. Once settled with a job and a *cédula de identidad*, or identity card, he would apply to the

Argentinean ministry of external affairs for permission to bring over
his wife and children.

~

Ever since the German annexation of Austria on March 12, 1938, the
inflow of Jewish refugees had been increasing at an alarming rate,
most of them arriving in France without legal permits. As a result,
many Jewish organizations, including OSE, worked at a furious pace
to help them. Since OSE funding was mostly directed toward Jewish
orphans and destitute families, the ones who didn't fall into those
categories were redirected to the proper sources. We spared no effort
in helping those who qualified to emigrate to the few countries that
would accept them, such as Argentina, Brazil, Chile, Bolivia and the
Dominican Republic. As a last resort, some of them even opted to go
to Shanghai, China.

As a former employee I can testify to OSE's outstanding contribution to saving so many of the refugees who sought their assistance.
Though I only played a minor role, I am nevertheless proud to have
been part of an organization that did so much to rescue Jews who
found themselves destitute. It was a privilege to have worked with
such fine people and to have been treated with decency and respect.
I also deeply appreciate their help in smoothing over a beleaguered
part of my own life, for making it possible for my family to survive.

From what I was told, my superiors were planning to help me rise
in the ranks of the OSE, particularly because I spoke English well. I
don't know this for sure, but I think that they intended to groom me
for a fundraising position in North America. The impending war and
my prospective immigration to Argentina, however, brought what
might have been an encouraging career to a close. Nonetheless, OSE
remained my guardian angel and I was committed to doing anything
I could to justify their hiring me. With each passing day, surrounded
as I was by highly educated people, I was learning more and more
about people and places and world events. It made me long for a
proper education.

Hope, Peace and War

In the spring of 1938 all the daily newspapers were filled with rumours about the prospect of war. The Nazis continued to maintain
that their only interest in moving into countries such as Austria and
Czechoslovakia was the liberation of ethnic Germans living there,
not territorial expansion. It was, of course, all lies; they would soon
invade more countries, occupying them and creating a climate of fear
over the entire European continent.

As if the situation were not bad enough, I was further disheartened by the defeat of the second Léon Blum government on April 10,
1938, leaving the country in chaos. The opposition had defeated them
with loud demands for substantial expenditures to prepare for war
with Germany. From that point on, there was evidence that a German
"fifth column" was infiltrating various parts of French society, including the government. For some inexplicable reason, the response from
the French government and people was one of laissez faire – there
weren't any organized efforts to eliminate the German influence before it took firm hold. Evidently there was a vast network of fascists
and Nazi sympathizers in France.

The French and British governments followed a policy of making
compromises with the Germans in an effort to avoid war, even to
the extent of later acceding to the occupation of a peaceful demo-
cratic country like Czechoslovakia, whose president, Edvard Beneš,
was forced to resign and surrender his country to the Germans. In

hindsight, it's beyond comprehension that two of the most powerful nations in Europe stood by while Germany built up a mighty war machine.

There was a ray of light amidst all the gloom in the late spring of 1938: my father's documents for his immigration to Argentina came through. Unfortunately, we still had to figure out a way to get him a passport. It turned out that HICEM had overlooked the fact that he was ineligible for a Polish passport – because he had left Poland without doing his military service, the Polish government had revoked his citizenship. Under international law, though, the French authorities had to issue him a Nansen passport, an internationally recognized document for stateless people. Once the document was issued, all my father had to do was present himself to the Argentinean embassy to receive his visa. After sixteen years of being harassed by the French police, my father finally became a free man. It would only be a matter of weeks until my father left and, whatever his future prospects, he would at last find some degree of security with both legal residency and the right to work.

Both my sister and I were hugely relieved that my father would be leaving so soon – that tells you how traumatic living with my father had been over the past five and a half years. His disturbed mental state made him so difficult to live with and we never knew how he might react at any given moment. Although we were careful not to show it, I wonder if he knew how deeply we resented him. My attitude toward him has changed drastically over the years as I matured enough to realize what a difficult life he had. I grieve that he departed this world unloved by either his wife or his children.

Shortly before my father's departure for Argentina, we were served with an eviction notice. This was not completely unexpected – we hadn't been able to pay our rent for well over a year. Our sole source of income were my earnings, which were barely sufficient to feed a family of four; there simply wasn't enough left over to pay the rent. This put us in the very difficult position of having to look for a new place to live without any money to pay the first three month's rent. Fortunately, Uncle Joseph, Aunt Leah's husband, had become well established in men's shoe manufacturing and offered to lend us the money.

It is interesting to note how my aunt and uncle's fortunes were just beginning to rise after many years of hardship. With determination and hard work, my uncle, along with his youngest son, Pierre, had managed to build up a shoe manufacturing business. Pierre was an exceptionally brilliant student who, if given the opportunity to go to university, no doubt would have become a renowned intellectual. His father didn't want him to continue his education beyond high school, however, so Pierre directed all his energy and his brilliant mind to his father's business. In the spring of 1938 they had been able to move out of their dingy two-room flat into a large three-bedroom apartment with a living room, dining room, kitchen, three-piece washroom with a shower stall, and a separate toilet room. They left Montmartre and moved to 5 rue du Soleil, just off rue de Belleville. By the time World War II broke out, Uncle Joseph was considered a wealthy man.

On the eve of my father's departure, in June 1938, we all assembled for a farewell party at Aunt Leah and Uncle Joseph's apartment. It was the first party I'd gone to since my return to Paris and it was a truly memorable occasion. My father wore a brand-new tailored suit specifically made for his trip. He looked wonderful and enjoyed being the centre of attention, probably for the first time in his life. The following day the whole family gathered at the railway station to see my father off to Marseille, the first leg of his journey. As I kissed my dad goodbye and wished him a safe journey, little did we realize that we wouldn't see each other for another ten years. My feelings for him were anything but love, but he was still family. We also needed each other: he needed our moral support and we were depending on him to help us reach a new land.

My mother was able to keep her composure until the final few moments and then burst into tears. My mother and father embraced, followed by my sister and me. My mother's last words to my father were to remind him to contact HICEM as soon as he arrived in Buenos Aires and urge them to speed up our permits so that we could join him as soon as possible. I often wonder how my father felt as the train pulled out, what he thought about finding himself alone again, separated from his family.

~

With my father gone, our lives changed drastically. We enjoyed a peaceful calm that we hadn't known since we left Winnipeg and I now looked forward to coming home at the end of the day. We followed our usual routine, but with a marked difference in attitude. I continued working at OSE, returning home to a loving mother and a satisfying meal, then meeting up with my friends for a couple of hours of pleasant distraction.

In this carefree environment, however, it was impossible to ignore the signs of the coming war. The daily reports in the newspapers were bad – there was nothing but talk of war and how the Germans were preparing for new invasions, with Poland possibly being the next target. War jitters became all-consuming and people's morale began to drop. These were troubled times for all the free democracies in Europe. No one questioned the inevitability of war – it was simply a matter of when it would break out. At the same time, though, everyone remained optimistic that the French and the British together would defeat Germany.

In the early part of 1939, my beloved Aunt Pola was rushed to a hospital with a very serious condition and passed away within a month or so. She was an intelligent and refined woman with a wonderful nature and a remarkable personality. She was the kind of person who would give all and seek nothing in return. While she was in hospital, she displayed unusual courage. Even though she was very weak, she completed two beautifully tailored dresses for my mother and sister. She realized that she didn't have long to live and wanted my mother and sister to have a going-away present to take to Argentina. I still have a photograph of my mother and sister wearing the dresses she made for them. She also managed to complete a whole wardrobe for her daughter, Hélène, hand-sewing the clothes on her deathbed.

It wasn't long before we got the first letter from my father. He reported that he had arrived safely in Buenos Aires after an enjoyable ocean crossing. True to his promise to my mother, he had already contacted HICEM, which had helped him get settled and find a job as a ladies' garment presser within a week. He had even met up with a couple of friends, one of them another recent immigrant from Paris. HICEM was also helping him secure a *cédula de identidad*, which would allow him to apply for entry permits on our behalf. Our prospects had never looked better, although our excitement was somewhat overshadowed by the reports in the daily newspapers about Germany's harassment of Jews, many of whom were doing their best to flee. Rescue efforts were underway to save as many children as possible, most of them going to England.

Rumours were now rampant that the Germans planned to invade France. The French based all their hopes for security on the impregnability of the Maginot Line and people continued to go about their daily business in the optimistic belief that France was invincible. During this time, we received another letter from my father, this time expressing a desire to return to Paris. We were all perturbed by the irrationality of such a suggestion, especially considering what everyone had done to secure him a safe haven. We were so concerned that we began to press HICEM to speed up our visas. We had to be discreet about why there was a sudden urgency, but we told them that my father's loneliness was making him ill. The HICEM officials sent a letter to their branch in Buenos Aires, describing my father's deteriorating condition and asking them to give our case top priority.

Several more months passed before we got a reply informing us that our entry permits had been processed and not long after, HICEM received a cable telling them that our permits would be arriving within a matter of weeks. The news left us utterly breathless – we had a lot to do in the roughly three months before we left. We had to give notice to our landlord and dispose of our few pieces of furniture and other possessions to get some extra money. When we had attended to all these things, we were faced with the problem of not having anywhere to live for an indefinite period of time. Since we didn't want anything to interfere with our departure, my mother decided to approach her dearest childhood friend, Sarah Silberstein.

Sarah was married to a fine gentleman named Favel and had two beautiful children. They were long-time residents of Paris and since both their children were born in France, they had been granted work permits. Consequently, both Sarah and her husband had good jobs, earning a comfortable living and occupying a nice-sized apartment. When they learned about my mother's departure for Argentina, they were very happy for us, especially since they knew all about our financial problems. Sarah was sad to be seeing us go, but she was genuinely glad that we had an opportunity to improve our lives. When she heard that we had no place to stay in Paris, she insisted on putting us up until we left France. She not only let us share her apartment for our last six weeks in Paris, but also fed us without letting us pay for anything.

This wonderful couple, along with their daughter, Esther, were to become victims of the Holocaust, tragically perishing in Auschwitz. Their son, Yosele, survived and is now living in Switzerland.

~

We had to vacate our rooms in the middle of August 1939 and moved in with the Silbersteins just two weeks before the war broke out. Our permits had still not come through, though we were assured that they were on their way.

On September 1, 1939, Nazi Germany invaded Poland, which was followed by Britain and France declaring war on Germany on September 3. As the war moved into its second week, the news we waited for so desperately at last arrived. HICEM notified us that they had our permits to immigrate to Argentina, so, just as my father had, we now had to get passports in order to obtain the visas from the Argentinean embassy. We were refused passports at the Polish embassy, however, because according to legislation passed by the Polish government in March and October 1938, Poland no longer recognized us as citizens, despite the fact that both my mother and I were born there.

HICEM helped us apply for Nansen passports from the French authorities, but when the documents were ready and we were asked to go to the prefecture to pick them up, we were in for a rude shock. We had assumed that because we were undocumented aliens, the French authorities would be only too pleased to be rid of us. Instead, unbelievably, they had decided to deny me an exit permit so they could detain me for military service. I was only seventeen years old, still a minor by international law, a stateless individual who was not permitted to legally live or work in France, yet they refused to let me leave for Argentina with my mother and sister. As far as the French authorities were concerned, as stateless Jews we were at the mercy of whatever policies they chose to implement, without regard for human compassion or the rights of individuals.

In October 1939, shortly before my mother and sister left for Argentina, I volunteered for a new temporary project. With most of the young men being called up into the armed services, there was a shortage of labour that particularly affected farmers who had no one to harvest their crops. Jewish organizations responded to the government's appeal for young volunteers by arranging for Jewish boys to spend two weeks helping farmers with the harvest. I was sent to a farm in a northern part of France to hand-pick potatoes. Needless to say, the work was strenuous, particularly for someone unaccustomed to physical labour. Despite that, we developed a spirit of camaraderie, singing our way through the gruelling hours that culminated in a rewarding meal, followed by a couple of leisurely hours after which we retired to the barn, where, exhausted, we spent the night bedded down on soft hay. Our day started at the crack of dawn, around five in the morning, after which we got washed and had a hearty breakfast in the farmer's house. Directly afterward, at about six, we set out for the fields. Except for a few short breaks that lasted long enough to enjoy homemade apple cider, we worked until noon and had our lunch in the fields. After a one-hour lunch break, we worked until dinner.

Those two weeks were a difficult experience and I've had the greatest respect for farmers ever since. Our stint at the farm sounds short, but when we were digging potatoes with our bare hands for ten hours a day, the time felt interminable. Everyone was relieved when it was time to return home.

When I got back to Paris, I discovered that my mother was refusing to leave for Argentina without me. I knew that I had to find a way to convince her to take Clarice and go. One evening, when I was at Aunt Leah's place with my cousins and a number of friends for our regular Saturday night card game, I discussed the matter with my aunt and came to the conclusion that only something drastic and a bit deceptive would work. I felt pretty sordid about the whole thing, especially since I had to involve my aunt in the conspiracy – she was an extremely Orthodox woman who never went against Jewish law. She alleviated my feelings of guilt, however, by reassuring me that the scheme was for a righteous cause and was therefore not a sin. To this day, I am convinced that Aunt Leah and I saved my mother and sister's lives.

HICEM had become aware that my mother was refusing to go to Argentina unless they could persuade the French authorities to let me leave with her. At the same time, they knew very well that they had no power to change that decision. They explained to my mother that they had already obtained passage for two on a French freighter and that if she was not on board, she would miss her last and only chance to get out of France. It was now up to me to do whatever it took to ensure that my mother and sister were on that ship. Time was of the essence; I couldn't allow myself to be swayed by her crying or by her fears of leaving me alone in wartime.

Day after day my mother and I talked in circles, having the same futile discussions while her position remained adamantly unchanged. Finally, I impressed on her that, should the Germans break through the French defenses and, God forbid, occupy France, we would all be trapped and it would be far easier for one person to escape than three. Then I brought out my strongest weapon: I told her in no uncertain terms that if she continued to refuse to leave at once with Clarice, I would leave home and never return. I said that if she doubted my determination to carry out my threat, she could confirm it with her sister Leah. My mother, of course, didn't take me seriously, but she did speak to Aunt Leah the very next morning and Aunt Leah confirmed everything.

When my mother finally realized that I was serious, she was very hurt. That was never my intention, but it had to be done. For the first time, my mother was forced to seriously reconsider her unwillingness to leave the country without me. That very evening, when I got home from work, my mother told me that she had reluctantly decided to take my advice and leave for Argentina with Clarice. I knew that I had won an important victory, but the reality of remaining behind by myself still hit me hard. With the issue finally settled, we began preparing for their departure. During the process, my mother suddenly had a change of heart and burst into tears. Before long, she almost had me crying, too. Nevertheless, she managed to overcome her hesitation when I reminded her of the serious hazards we all faced should she remain in France. The next day, we went to HICEM to pick up their tickets along with all the other necessary documents.

My mother, Aunt Leah and Uncle Joseph had already decided that I would live with my aunt and uncle, which reassured my mother that I would be well looked after. We made the most of the remaining few days that we had together, talking about the new opportunities ahead, building a new life with a better future. All too soon, however, the time came for my mother and Clarice to leave. In October 1939, the whole family and many of our friends gathered at the station to see my mother and sister off and I did my best to hide my apprehension so that I wouldn't give my mother any reason to change her mind at the last minute. I remember standing on the station platform, exchanging hugs and kisses, and whispering into my sister's ear that she had to promise to console our mother whenever she became sad about leaving me behind. With tears in her eyes, my mother placed her hands on my cheeks, kissing me over and over again, repeating, "How can I leave without you, my beloved son?" She was clutching the first present I had ever given her, a beautiful patent-leather handbag that I had given her as a going-away gift.

My mother and Clarice finally boarded the train and watching them as it slowly pulled away made my heart sink. I continued to wave as the train moved out of sight, having no idea when we would see each other again. At that point, I broke down in tears, crying like a baby. Aunt Leah stood beside me and, with tears streaming down her cheeks, tried to comfort me. I had now accomplished what I set out to do – my mother and sister were on their way to safety. I would now have to learn to fend for myself.

Occupation and Escape

I settled into my new life with Aunt Leah and her family. My aunt treated me more like her own child than a nephew, becoming my counsellor and confidante when I needed it the most. I also had the advantage of living with four wonderful cousins and an uncle who was a true gentleman. I shared a sofa bed in the living room with my cousin Pierre, who was three months my junior. His brother, Philippe, was four years older than us and had his own bedroom, while my youngest cousin, Chai Liba, or Luba as we called her, shared a bedroom with our cousin Hélène, who had come to live with them when Aunt Pola passed away. I was not as close to Pierre, but Philippe and I were already very good friends. I had a bit of a crush on my lovely cousin Luba, although I made sure that no one was aware of it since she was only fourteen and I was already eighteen.

My routine while I lived with Aunt Leah was pretty similar to the one I had followed at home. Every morning after breakfast, I caught the métro to work. The train took me to the Champs-Élysées, where the offices of OSE were located, but instead of starting out from the Simplon station near Montmartre, I now took the train from Places des Fêtes in Belleville.

One day I came home from work to find that Aunt Leah had a surprise for me. She did her best to keep me in suspense, teasing me by holding her hands behind her back to conceal what she had been hiding. I guessed that it had to be a letter from my mother and Clarice and sure enough, once Aunt Leah felt that she had kept me in suspense long enough, she jubilantly flashed the letter from my mother, written for her by Clarice, in front of me. I could hardly wait to read it.

Their journey by freighter had taken longer than expected and it had taken them the better part of a month to arrive in Buenos Aires, where my father and several of his friends had met them at the dock. My mother wrote that they had really enjoyed their trip, during which they had stopped at many different ports, including Lisbon, Casablanca, Dakar, Rio de Janeiro and Montevideo. There were two photographs enclosed in the letter, one for my aunt and the other for me. My mother, father and Clarice all looked wonderful in the photos and I was particularly delighted to see my mother holding the handbag I had given her.

Clarice also wrote her own part of the letter, telling me about a Frenchwoman she met on board ship named Mme. Dalière, who had a daughter my sister's age. Mme. Dalière had been visiting relatives in France when the war broke out and had decided to return to Buenos Aires, where she and her family had been living for some time. Mme. Dalière proved to be of invaluable help to my sister – it was through her that Clarice landed her first job as a governess to a wealthy Argentinean family that owned a vast estate in the country. Her sole responsibility was to teach their children French.

My sister also wrote that my mother had found a full-time job as a fur finisher, but that my father's physical and mental health still left much to be desired and he frequently had to go to various doctors. According to my sister, he hadn't bothered to look for any accommodations before they arrived and they had had to spend their first night in a hotel. My father's friend Shloime had helped them find a suitable place to live the next day. The letter ended with my mother expressing concern for me, saying how much she missed me and that she hoped to see me soon. I was so relieved to know that they were out of harm's way. Over the next little while many more letters arrived, all describing that the conditions for my family were continuing to improve.

Life proceeded pretty normally for me for several months after my mother and sister left. As 1939 ended and 1940 began, the political situation was volatile, but most people continued to go about their daily business. I was no different from anyone else, adopting the same nonchalant attitude. No one was willing to believe that this was the calm before the storm. But the country seemed to be swarming with fifth columnists and Nazi sympathizers, and the Germans were spreading rumours that they intended to attack the Maginot Line and smash their way through its defenses. To everyone's surprise, when they unleashed their spring 1940 offensive, they instead invaded Belgium, Holland, Denmark and Norway, penetrating into France through Belgium, initially bypassing the Maginot Line altogether. The French were not at all prepared for this strategy.

The German invasion of Denmark and Norway occurred on April 9, 1940, and despite the gallant resistance of the French and British forces, their war machine broke through into Belgium, Luxembourg and the Netherlands on May 10. For the first time, the general public began to show concern, but their uneasiness soon gave way to a restored optimism when the French government put up enormous posters throughout Paris with the slogan "Nous vaincrons parce que nous sommes les plus forts" (We will be victorious because we are stronger). The poster also showed a map of France and Great Britain with their vast colonial empires, showing the two countries' massive resources. It's strange how easily a whole nation could be lulled into a dangerous deception.

Over the next few weeks quite a different picture emerged. The Germans kept up their momentum and advanced swiftly with the support of their superiority in the air. Everyone around us was overcome with fear, gloom and insecurity. The French government began making plans to leave Paris and relocate to Tours. Even OSE was in the process of moving to Vichy. Since I couldn't go with them to their new quarters, they assigned me to another one of their branches that was still functioning in Paris under the direction of a non-Jewish French director named M. Chevrier.

After I'd been working for M. Chevrier for just over a month, he called me into his office to ask how I was managing on my meagre salary and, during the course of the interview, learned that I had been separated from my family and was living with an aunt. This caring French gentleman then told me that he would raise my salary to 1,000 francs a month from 600 francs. I will never know for sure, but I suspect that a dear friend and colleague of mine at OSE, an Austrian Jewish refugee named M. Brandeis, had influenced M. Chevrier's decision.

There was another Jewish gentleman on our staff, M. Bloch, whose family had been in France for generations. He was our purchasing agent, responsible for the provision of clothing and a variety of other items essential for Jewish refugees interned by French authorities in detention camps in the south of France. I worked quite closely with him and through our many conversations he learned that my uncle was a shoe manufacturer and asked me to inquire whether he would be willing to take on an order for men's boots. He persuaded me to act as a go-between in negotiating a deal with Uncle Joseph for a sub-stantial boot order. This was the first business transaction in which I was personally involved and I received a substantial commission from my uncle for my efforts.

There were two other people working for our organization but I no longer recall their names. One was our accountant, a gentleman who always arrived at the office impeccably dressed, and the other was a young woman, rather good-looking, who worked as a stenographer.

We were shaken out of our routine one morning when we re-ceived the shocking news that the Germans were quickly advancing on Paris. All communications were disrupted; we were no longer able to dispense aid to the Jewish refugees and had to close down our of-fices. I was left without a job, without an income, confronting the most serious crisis of my life. Fortunately, I had managed to save up a fair amount of money.

The grim prospect of a German occupation was finally a reality. Only a few months ago this had seemed a remote possibility, but now the French were simultaneously despondent and confused, searching for someone to blame, accusing the government for their lack of pre-paredness and mismanagement. People now panicked and hundreds of thousands started fleeing the city, by vehicle, by train and on foot. Those who remained feared the worst, resigning themselves to what-ever lay ahead. Among those who stayed behind were my aunt and uncle, their children and me. There was an air of gloom and eeriness throughout Paris, everyone wondering what to expect and how they would be able to provide for themselves and their families.

On the morning of June 14, 1940, we woke to a rumbling noise and ran out into rue de Belleville to see a German cavalry detach-ment slowly making its way up the street. At intervals, they entered courtyards to water their horses. All the normally boisterous French people who were watching stood dumbfounded. This is what I most vividly remember about the first day of the German occupation of Paris.

With the occupation a fait accompli, my life changed drastically. I had to figure out some way to support myself so that I wouldn't have to be dependent on my aunt and uncle. I needed to find some work and some means of joining my parents and sister in Argentina. I was sure that I would never be able to get an exit visa from the Germans, so I had to consider other options, however hazardous.

In their first months of occupation, the Nazis wasted little time in introducing restrictive measures against foreign Jews, including forbidding them to travel to the unoccupied sector of France that was under the control of the Vichy administration. The Germans had only occupied half of France as well as the entire Atlantic coast down to the borders of Spain. The south-central and southeastern parts of France were called the *zone libre* (free zone) and came under the jurisdiction of a collaborationist French government headed by Maréchal Pétain. The administrative centre was in the town of Vichy.

French industry ground to almost a complete halt following the occupation and the ensuing economic crisis affected everyone. I spoke to my friend Avrom Kirsch nearly every day about how we might earn a living and came up with what turned out to be an ill-fated scheme. The plan consisted of purchasing as many chocolate bars as we could from the bakeries in our vicinity because we knew that the Germans were buying up all the chocolates they could lay their hands on and sending them back to Germany. We accumulated several hundred bars each and set off for the German army camp on the outskirts of Paris.

When we got out of the subway, it was still quite a long trek to the camp. At the gates, we were met by several guards who told us that the camp was off limits to civilians. I explained in my best German – I had picked up the language from the German Jewish refugees I met in the *asile* – that we had come to sell them chocolate bars and opened the small case I was carrying to substantiate our story. The sight of all that delectable chocolate was all it took to win them over and before long a crowd of German soldiers had appeared, only too eager to snap up every chocolate bar that we had. We left the camp with lots of cash, buoyed by our success.

About ten minutes later, however, while we were on our way to the subway, we were intercepted by the French police. They asked us to produce our vendor's permits and when we were unable to do so, we were taken to the local police station. When we got there and the police opened our suitcases, they found them empty. To our amazement, the police officers asked us what we had done with the chocolates. We were so taken aback by the fact that they knew about the chocolates that we proceeded to compound our troubles by denying that we'd ever had any. The policemen beat us until we confessed and, as further punishment, confiscated all the money we had. Fortunately, they left us with a few métro tickets to make our way home.

So much for our business venture. All we had achieved for our efforts was to get beaten up; we not only lost our profits but also our original investment. There is no doubt in my mind that the Germans themselves, knowing that we were Jewish, had informed the police after we left. The Germans got their chocolates and the French police got our money. Perhaps I should consider myself fortunate that the Germans and the French were not yet deporting Jews. Several years later, Avrom was murdered in Auschwitz.

When I got home on the evening of my misadventure, my aunt and cousins were horrified to see how bruised I was from the police beating. That same evening, I made up my mind to talk to them about applying to the German Kommandantur for an exit permit. I already had the document from the Argentinean government granting me permission to enter their country and I was hoping the Germans might grant me the exit permit on the basis of it. I found out where to go and was advised to get there at four in the morning because the lineup of people seeking permission to leave the country stretched for blocks. I got up very early the next morning and went to the Kommandantur, but even at that hour there were already hundreds and hundreds of people in line ahead of me. I had a long, exhausting wait of about six hours before I was finally shown into a huge office staffed by hundreds of German female office workers and military men.

I was struck right away by the sight of so many tall, handsome, tanned men, literally glowing with health, and the equally tanned good-looking young women. I was ushered into the office of a German official, a rather pretty young woman who asked me to state my business. She spoke French fluently with only a trace of a German accent. I told her that my parents and sister were already living in Argentina and that I wanted to join them. I then produced the document stating I had been granted entry into Argentina. The official took some notes and then asked me some questions. In particular, she wanted to know if I was Jewish, to which I of course responded in the affirmative. She

left the office to consult with her superiors, returning some five minutes later to inform me that foreign Jews were not permitted to travel
more than twenty kilometres from the city limits and that there was
absolutely nothing more she could do for me. I was very upset – this
was my last chance to leave the country legally.

When I went to the Kommandantur, I had never had any illu-
sions that my chances of success were very good, but I had to try.
When the Nazi official confirmed my suspicions, however, my heart
sank. I didn't know what to do next and began pleading with God
to enlighten me as to how I would ever see my parents and sister
again. My situation was becoming more precarious by the day. Not
having a job was bad enough, but now I felt somewhat demoralized.
Nonetheless, at eighteen I had become quite self-reliant and started
discussing plans with Aunt Leah to escape from France. Despite the
risks, she never once discouraged me; on the contrary, she was very
encouraging, although the prospect of my leaving made her and my
cousins tearful.

Toward the middle of August 1940, I surprised my relatives one
evening by announcing that I had bought a train ticket to Bordeaux.
My plan was to travel southwest from Paris to Bordeaux, nearly 600
kilometres away, then continue on to Bayonne and from there to
Hendaye, the last border town between France and Spain. Across
the Spanish border from Hendaye were the towns of Irun and San
Sebastian, from where I could make my way to neutral Portugal.
Although I took everyone by surprise and they were concerned about
the great risks I was about to undertake, my sudden decision was
not completely unexpected. I had been hoping that at least one of
my close companions would be willing to come with me, but since
none of them were in my situation, with parents in a far-off country,
I would have to go alone.

On the eve of my departure, my friends and relatives gave me a
festive send-off. Everyone was advised not to see me off at the station so they wouldn't attract attention and alert the Gestapo or the

French police. As another precaution, I carried no luggage except for a backpack. My savings, along with accumulated gifts of cash from my relatives, would be more than enough to pay for my passage to Argentina.

When I got to the station the next day, I boarded the train and selected a compartment with a number of other French passengers. Throughout most of the journey everything appeared normal and I assumed that I would reach my first destination of Bordeaux without any problems. But I was proven wrong when a train inspector suddenly appeared and asked for our identity cards. By this time the train was close to Bordeaux and I was stuck. I left the compartment and went out into the hallway, where I peered into the next car to see three or four men checking out each compartment. There wasn't much time to reflect. The train was moving very slowly and my only chance to avoid inspection was to jump off. My heart thumping with fear, I made my way to the next car, away from the inspectors, went to the door and jumped from the steps. Shaken, I managed to get up and started walking toward Bordeaux.

When I got to Bordeaux, finding a hotel for the night presented a problem because the law required me to leave my identification papers with the hotel clerk when I registered. The papers would be inspected by the police and returned to me the next morning. I knew they would figure out that I had left Paris without the approval of the authorities and would arrest me, so I hit upon the idea of telling the clerk that I had forgotten my suitcase with my identity card on the train and that I would personally report to the police first thing in the morning. What really persuaded him to overlook the matter, though, was the large tip I gave him.

The next morning I asked directions to Bayonne and Hendaye and was told that there were regularly scheduled trains to Bayonne, which was about 200 kilometres away. I would have to ask about getting to Hendaye, another thirty-six kilometres further, when I got there. I had been assured by people in Paris that there were no identity card inspections on this route. I bought a ticket to Bayonne and within a matter of hours was heading in that direction.

In Bayonne I stopped for lunch, got directions to get to Hendaye by bus and soon reached the town. I was now only a few kilometres from Spain, so if I succeeded in crossing the border, all that remained was to catch a train to Barcelona and from there get to Lisbon. If and when I reached Barcelona, I had been told that there were people who would help to smuggle me into Portugal, where I could find a ship heading for Argentina.

I made my way from Hendaye to the Spanish border, about one and a half kilometres away, on foot. Before leaving, some friendly residents in Hendaye gave me directions. To avoid detection by Nazi frontier guards, however, whom I had erroneously assumed only guarded the main frontier crossings, I walked many kilometres out of my way to seek out some isolated spots where it might be safe to cross. I walked and walked, looking in vain for an unguarded crossing until I started to get very tired. As I persevered in my search, I suddenly heard gunshots. Although I had no way of knowing if they were aimed at me, I sure as hell wasn't going to wait around to find out. I dropped flat on the ground to take refuge in the tall grasses, not daring to budge an inch. The high grass there gave me some protection.

I'm still not certain whether the bullets were aimed at me, but never have I been so close to death or so overcome with fright. When I recovered from my initial fear, my very next thought was that they would be coming after me. I crawled on my hands and knees as fast as I could through the deep grass to get as far away as possible. When I had travelled what I hoped was a safe distance, I lay flat on my back, not daring to move for the next hour. At that point, I slowly stood up to look around, ducking back down quickly and then peeking out again. To my frustration, I saw nothing but German soldiers as far as the eye could see. My plan to make it across to Spain had clearly been foiled; it seemed futile to even consider trying. Getting out of this dangerous situation alive was now my prime concern.

Much to my chagrin, I had to accept that I had reached the end of the trail. The frontier was too well guarded and it would be suicidal to attempt to cross it. Even standing up and walking away from my present position would be too dangerous. My only options were to either wait for nightfall or crawl away through the grass on my hands and knees. I decided to try both – first to crawl as far as I could and then wait for the cover of darkness to flee. To make sure that I was going in the right direction, I peeked out at various intervals, quickly ducking down so I wouldn't be seen. I continued this process until the sun began to set and I could no longer see any German soldiers.

It may seem odd, but even as I lay in the grass, my pulse racing and terrified of being caught, I couldn't help marvelling at the breathtaking scenery around me – the majestic beauty of the Pyrenees mountains rising against the clear blue sky. The memories of that scenery and the trauma are inextricably linked for me.

When the skies began to darken I decided that I was far enough away from the German guards to make a getaway. It would still take me quite a while to get back to the road and even longer to reach Hendaye. I would have to make a dash for it or it would get too dark to find my way. I hesitated for the longest time, not knowing what course of action I should take. Finally, I decided to take my chances escaping in the semi-darkness rather than waiting for dawn. I just wanted to get out of my present situation. I headed in the direction of the road, slowly trudging along, feeling dejected about my failed mission.

I reached Hendaye a few hours later, caught the first bus back to Bayonne and from there on to Bordeaux, where I learned that the next train back to Paris wasn't due for many hours. While I was passing the time, I met a couple of young fellows who told me, to my great relief, that the Germans didn't carry out any inspections on trains going to Paris.

On my return trip, I mulled over everything that had happened and wondered how I could face my relatives after failing to reach

Spain. I fell asleep thinking about it all. Exhausted by my efforts over the last forty-eight hours, I only woke up when the train jolted to a stop in a Paris suburb. A few minutes later I got off at Gare d'Austerlitz and headed for the métro. Within half an hour, I arrived at the Place des Fêtes, where my unexpected arrival at my aunt's house caused quite a stir. I described what had happened, telling them how difficult it was to cross over into Spain because the frontier was so well guarded. My information soon spread throughout the community, dissuading many other Jews from making the same attempt. I didn't want to discourage them altogether – there might have been places where the border crossing was easier.

For the next two weeks or so, I devoted all my energy to finding a safe way to cross the demarcation line separating German-occupied France from the Vichy-administered unoccupied zone and soon had enough new information to plan another escape. This time, I would have to be much more cautious. I learned that some of the people who helped arrange for foreign Jews to be smuggled across into the free zone had been betrayed by informers. Fortunately, the ones we knew about had been able to outsmart their informers by beating a hasty retreat at the very last moment. I resolved to succeed no matter what the dangers, but, despite my brash self-confidence, the thought of facing those dangers alone was difficult.

By this time, the overseas mail had slowed to a trickle. The last letter I received from Argentina was a source of some comfort because everything seemed to be going well. When my parents sent the letter, however, they knew that the German occupation of France was imminent and they expressed concern for my safety that hadn't been mentioned in their previous correspondence. Little did I realize that that letter would be the very last one my parents were able to send me in Paris.

By the end of August 1940, during the third month of the German occupation, I conceived a new plan to escape into the free zone. It came about as a result of information filtering into Paris from people who, for one reason or another, had found it necessary to travel back and forth across the demarcation line and were reporting back to friends about the safest way to do it. The information was not completely reliable and I considered it more as a tip rather than a guarantee.

Restrictions against travel for Jews were becoming increasingly severe, so I had to make a decision based on the most reliable sources of information available and work out a practical strategy that would, I hoped, lead me across the demarcation line. I was afraid that if I waited much longer it would become impossible to get out of occupied France and felt that I had no choice but to act quickly.

Sadly, so many Jews did not see the necessity of escaping, relying instead on Providence, hoping that the good Lord's mercy would see them safely through this turbulent period. Even when they became aware that there was danger in staying, many chose to ignore it, unwilling to abandon everything they had worked so hard for to flee empty-handed to an unknown fate. My own aunt and uncle with their three children were among them. They lived in a lovely apartment with all the advantages of a secure economic future and chose to remain in Paris. In 1942, the Gestapo came knocking on their door. The three members of my family who were home, my aunt Leah, her son Philippe and her daughter, Luba, were interned in the transit camp in Drancy and from there deported to Auschwitz, where they perished in the gas chambers.

The night before I left Paris for the second time, all my friends again gathered to bid me farewell. We talked long into the night, reminiscing about the many good times we had shared. I will retain these memories of my good and loyal friends forever. I can still hear their last words to me, "Bonne chance, mon vieux. (Good luck, old pal.) We'll see you after the war."

A few of my friends came to the station this time to help me buy my ticket in case the clerk asked for identification. One of them was a native-born Frenchman, so the travel restrictions didn't apply to him. Pretty soon I boarded the train heading for Moulins-sur-Allier, about three hundred kilometres south of Paris. En route, I had time to think about where I should get off the train – an all-important consideration if I was to avoid running into the German inspection that was most likely to occur at the main station there.

When the train got to within thirty kilometres or so of Moulins, I concentrated on looking for a small station or spot in between stations where it might be safe to jump off. All I had with me was a backpack that contained only a few essentials – the best advice I had been given was to travel light. Looking out the window, I saw the train pulling slowly into a small station, probably Saint-Imbert, and when it came to a complete stop, I saw that the station was almost deserted – there was only one station attendant and a couple of other people; there were no German soldiers in sight. I went quickly to the exit and stepped off the train just before it began to pull out of the station. Cautiously, I walked from the station toward Moulins and the border crossing at the demarcation line to assess my chances for crossing over to the free zone. Needless to say, the actual checkpoint was swarming with German guards as far along the banks of the Allier River in either direction as I could see. From where I was standing, my prospects appeared hopeless, but this time I was determined not to turn back.

From my vantage point I could see – with much envy – how easily French people were able to cross over into the free zone. Even if I were remotely inclined to try requesting legal permission to cross over, they would arrest me on the spot for violating the rule that restricted stateless persons from travelling beyond a twenty-kilometre radius from Paris. On top of this, foreign Jews were not permitted into the unoccupied zone without first obtaining a permit from the Kommandantur.

The limited equipment I had brought with me included a pair of binoculars that I had purchased at the Marché aux Puces (flea market) just before leaving Paris. My first escape attempt had made me realize how useful binoculars would be in spotting German soldiers from a distance. Since any attempt to cross the demarcation line at Moulins would clearly be futile, I decide to follow a route south along the river. After trekking along roads and through fields for about four hours, I came across a farmer's field that seemed like a good place to rest for a while.

I made an important discovery while scrutinizing the area around the field with my binoculars: the German observation posts were thinning out as they got farther away from town. These gaps might give me the opportunity I needed to sneak across the river. From my hiding place in the farmer's field, I could observe the Germans' every move and learn their routine. I watched them for hours until my hands were practically numb from holding up the binoculars and my persistence finally paid off. I was able to discern the pattern of their movements that would tell me when exactly to make a break for the river and swim across to freedom.

I noticed that at regular intervals the German guards strolled over to the next post quite a distance away, stopping to chat for up to half an hour at a time. Everything seemed to be in my favour except for the fact that the sun would soon be setting and it would be much too difficult to make my escape in the dark. I didn't look forward to the prospect of spending the night in an open field, but there didn't seem to be any other choice. Fortified by the wonderful sandwiches my aunt had prepared for my journey, I settled down for what felt like the longest night I had ever experienced. As twilight gradually turned into pitch darkness and I could no longer see anything through my binoculars, I tried to use my backpack as a pillow and fall asleep. But try as I might, I couldn't get comfortable and I spent a very cold and restless night. Daylight couldn't come soon enough.

By the time dawn broke, all I wanted was a hot café au lait. My wristwatch told me that it was five o'clock, and it was becoming fairly light out. When I looked through my binoculars, however, I wondered if I was hallucinating. There were no Germans anywhere. By some strange miracle they had all vanished, leaving me free to safely make my escape across the river. I was so nervous that I kept checking to make sure that they weren't just napping or hiding, ready to jump out and grab me. I gathered up my courage, picked up my backpack, slung it across my back and cautiously moved toward the German control post until I was near enough to see that, beyond a doubt, the German sentry was not at his post.

To say I was baffled would be an understatement, but without any further hesitation, I took advantage of the situation and went straight to the river and took off all my clothes except for the bathing suit I wore underneath. I then packed my clothes into the backpack and strapped it tightly across my shoulders. With one final look all around through the binoculars to satisfy myself that I was alone, I plunged into the frigid river. The sudden shock left me gasping for air and my cumbersome backpack made every stroke more laborious than the last.

I wasn't a particularly strong swimmer and could only swim short distances before running out of breath. I also tended to panic unless I stayed close to the shore. Under the circumstances, I had to rely entirely on willpower to keep me going. The freezing water temperature was only a minor concern compared to the far more serious problem of remaining afloat. As my strength waned, my arms felt as heavy as lead, forcing me to stop and rest. I went into a real panic when several times I swallowed mouthfuls of water. When I checked my progress after these incidents, I saw to my dismay that I had only covered about a third of the distance. Using every ounce of energy to increase my pace, I forced myself to labour on mechanically, afraid that my strength would give out at any moment.

The realization that the Germans might spot me and shoot me gave me the impetus to keep going. By the time that I had covered two-thirds of the distance and was within reach of the free zone, however, my strength began to seriously fade and I was consumed with fear. I was so exhausted that I could only occasionally kick my legs. At the very moment when my strength gave out completely and I was no longer able to stay afloat, on the verge of going under, I found within myself a renewed energy that came from pure determination. I managed to fight off my fatigue and before long I found myself grasping the shores of the unoccupied zone of France and my entry into freedom.

Across the Pyrenees

Hidden in a secluded area beyond the banks of the river in the free zone, I rested until I could regain my strength, waiting for the sun to come up and dry my clothes before heading for the town of Vichy to make contact with O S E. When the sun finally rose, I lay there absorbing its warmth, my whole being suffused with a sense of calm – I was at least temporarily out of reach of the Germans.

By the time the sun had dried my clothes, I felt completely revitalized and ready to begin my walk to Vichy, still about forty kilometres away. I was famished, though, and had no idea how far I was from the nearest town. I walked as quickly as I could and within a couple of hours was comfortably seated in a café. After my meal, I asked the waiter for directions to Vichy and set off along the road again, racing against time so that I could arrive before the O S E offices closed. I walked so quickly in the hot sun that I got blisters on my feet and had to rest under a shady tree. I had to continue my travels, though, blisters and all, and before long I reached a sign that told me I was close to Vichy.

My memories of Vichy are of beautiful white buildings, of a clean holiday resort town that was quite out of the ordinary. My first priority was to find a post office to get the address of O S E. When I got to the O S E building, I found that I was somewhat anxious, not out of any sense of fear – far from it – but from an almost staggering disbelief that I had actually made it. At the same time, I was relieved at the prospect of being among friends who would help me take the next step toward freedom. I knocked on the door and standing before me, looking as if she'd seen a ghost, was none other than Mlle. Levine. When she had recovered from the shock of seeing me, she reached out to welcome me enthusiastically and ushered me into the main office. Everyone crowded around me, asking how on earth I had managed to get across the demarcation line without being intercepted by the Germans. I felt like a celebrity.

When all their questions had been answered, an uncomfortable silence came over the room as Mlle. Levine regretfully told me that the extremely rigid antisemitic laws enacted by the Vichy government meant that I couldn't stay there. Among other restrictions, Jews were not allowed to work in Vichy or change their place of residence without reporting to the police within twenty-four hours or risk being arrested. In light of this, the OSE staff decided to send me to one of their newly established branches in Marseille as soon as possible. The staff at OSE had been given a temporary exemption from the above laws because they were a charitable organization that received most of its funding from American Jewish sources.

Even though my main plan was still to get to Lisbon and from there to Argentina, I was outraged and disappointed to learn that there was no way for me to stay in Vichy and resume my former job at least temporarily. Even worse, I learned that the Vichy government would not grant me an exit permit nor issue a Nansen passport for travel to a designated neutral country. I had been convinced that once I was in the so-called free zone, the French would no longer have a reason to stop me from leaving the country. It was now clear that I no longer had recourse to any legal solution – I would have to find some way to escape illegally, just as I had from occupied France.

My stay in Vichy was short-lived and I soon found myself on a night train to Marseille. Before leaving, however, the OSE staff treated me to a great meal in an elegant restaurant, after which they escorted me to the station and gave me a letter of recommendation to be presented to their Marseille branch. I am happy to report that most of them were able to escape to Switzerland at the end of 1942 and spent the rest of the war years there.

Once the train was underway, I drifted off into a light sleep, thinking of the fact that no one is an island – dependence on the goodwill of others had played a significant role in my flight to freedom. It could be said that I had taken all the risks, but the truth is that I had plenty of assistance along the way, especially from people like the OSE staff and many others. Without them, my life would probably have ended in disaster. I cannot stress enough what an important role luck and the human concern of others played in my survival.

As the train pulled into Marseille in the fall of 1940, I was struck by how different this journey was from the many I had taken in the past three months – I felt completely relaxed and free from the fear of encountering any Germans. How good it felt to once again breathe what I thought of as the air of freedom, even though the Vichy government was collaborating with the Nazis. When I got to Marseille, I handed over my letter of recommendation to the OSE branch and was offered a job with them. I was told to report for work the following morning. In addition to providing me with a job, the organization also arranged for me to stay at the Hôtel du Levant, where hundreds of Jewish refugees were being accommodated free of charge.

At the hotel I met a Jewish lad named Wolf who was only sixteen but had recently had an incredible experience. Amazingly, it also turned out that he was from Argentina and had only arrived not long before. What a strange coincidence! Like me, Wolf was born in Poland, but when he was only four years old his family had immigrated to Argentina. Both his parents had worked hard to provide the family with a comfortable life, but other than that remained aloof and strict in their treatment of Wolf. After his father's death and his mother's remarriage, he felt so unloved that he ran away from home. A strong Zionist, his most ardent wish was to go to Palestine. He had attempted to achieve this goal by going to the docks every day and befriending merchant sailors with the intention of stowing away. He wanted to defend the Zionist cause and hoped to join the Haganah, the Jewish Defense Force.

Wolf had left Argentina with the help of one of the sailors at the docks in Buenos Aires, who had told him about a ship that would soon be sailing to somewhere in the Middle East. He had slipped on to the vessel and found a safe hiding place. He fell sound asleep and when he awoke the next morning he found himself on the high seas as a stowaway. There was no turning back. When he got so hungry that he risked coming out of hiding, he was discovered by one of the cooks while raiding the kitchen and promptly reported to one of the officers. During his interrogation, the officer began to feel sorry for him and promised not to turn him in; instead, he agreed to leave him ashore when they docked at Marseille. That is how he came to be there when we met, two Jews from Poland whose parents lived in Argentina, and we developed a wonderful friendship.

It embarrasses me to say that I didn't understand the significance of his noble cause – I didn't even know that a Jewish state was in the making. This was the first time that I had met someone who knew about Zionism and who was prepared to act on his convictions. Wolf had had a traditional Jewish upbringing and was taught Zionist philosophy, but, other than learning from my uncle Morris when I was a child in Winnipeg, I had not been so fortunate. To my everlasting regret, I didn't know enough to take up Wolf's appeal to join our fellow Jews in the defense of our beloved land. Instead of pursuing his brave course, I advised him to return with me to Argentina.

From the first day I started working for OSE in Marseille, I had felt an irresistible urge to flee, to keep up the momentum that first led me to escape from Paris and not give up until I was reunited with my parents. The thought of precious days slipping away without doing something that would bring me closer to my goal was intolerable. Wolf and I discussed the issue at length and decided that we would try to escape to Spain, from where we hoped to first reach neutral Portugal and then make our way to Argentina. Each of us had something to offer the other: Wolf could speak Spanish and I had enough money to meet our expenses. Wolf had arrived in Marseille penniless and at the time of our first encounter was totally dependent on Jewish charitable organizations.

In my fifth or sixth week in Marseille, while eating in a clandestine restaurant operated in an apartment by a Jewish refugee couple, members of the Groupe Special de Securité, the Vichy equivalent of the Gestapo, suddenly burst through the door. Everyone present was caught up in this *rafle*, or raid, hustled down the stairs and put into a paddy wagon. The majority of us didn't have proper identification to show that we were in Marseille legally. Our worst fear was that we would be sent back to occupied France. Among those arrested was the poor couple who ran the illegal restaurant.

When we got to the main police station, we were all interrogated separately and then sent to a camp. I no longer recall the name of it – I was only there for a short time because I managed to sneak out unnoticed, make my way to the nearest town and catch the first available transportation back to Marseille. My status had suddenly become even more precarious – I was now an escaped prisoner from an internment camp. Every day that passed exposed me to greater danger, especially at a time when the Vichy government was introducing even more stringent measures against Jews in general and foreign Jews in particular. It was no longer safe for me to be there.

While all of this was going on, my work for ose continued. They were aware of my difficulties and on occasion I talked to the staff about my idea of escaping to Spain just to get their reaction. They were noncommittal but they didn't try to dissuade me. The more I brought it up, the more they realized that my mind was made up and nothing short of a catastrophe would stop me.

Wolf and I got together every day to plan our escape. When the details were sufficiently fleshed out, we began to make preparations for the long hike over the Pyrenees, the mountains that separated France from Spain. Given Wolf's fluency in Spanish, we decided to try to pass ourselves off as members of the Basque people who lived in that region. We would have to dress accordingly, including wearing the traditional berets. Since I didn't know any Spanish at all, we decided that I would pretend to be a deaf mute. My savings would be more than enough to see us safely across Spain to Portugal and cover both our fares to Buenos Aires. All that remained was to select our departure date.

No sooner had we picked a date than we heard about a much easier and less risky way to get out of France from a Jewish friend at the Hôtel du Levant. He knew a Frenchman who could guarantee Jews safe transportation to Casablanca on a freighter because he was a friend of the captain. The only condition was that he had to find a minimum of fifty passengers who could each pay a deposit of fifty dollars in US currency in advance; the balance would be paid when they boarded the vessel on the night of departure. The proposition was too good to pass up and the number of prospective passengers, Wolf and myself among them, soon exceeded the minimum. The captain agreed to take all fifty-three people and told us to be ready to board his ship at two o'clock the next morning. We all knew that the ship would be making a stopover in Lisbon and began scheming about disembarking there by one means or another.

The arrangements called for us to rendezvous near a warehouse at the docks, where the ship would be berthed. When we arrived at the appointed hour, we waited anxiously for the captain to show up. The vessel was nowhere to be seen and many of us began to get uneasy. Our suspicions were further aroused when the captain didn't show up at the appointed hour. The very patient among us suggested that we wait another hour and then appoint someone to try to find out what was going on. There were a number of theories as to why the captain hadn't shown up, but most people suspected that we'd been tricked.

We finally bowed to the inevitable – we had clearly been the victims of an experienced swindler. That was confirmed when one of the people in our group learned that our vessel had in fact sailed more than twelve hours earlier. Some people panicked, but others just felt terribly disheartened and frustrated. Here we were, fifty-three frightened and desperate people seeking refuge who had found ourselves robbed of our hard-earned money, leaving many with little to fall back on. This was the first of many hard lessons I would have to learn about trust.

Wolf and I now had no choice but to return to our original plan. Since we were starting from Marseille, our route would take us first to Perpignan, the last major city on the French Mediterranean coast, and then across the Pyrenees. I knew that I should tell the wonderful staff of OSE of my impending escape before leaving, but I didn't because I wasn't sure if they would agree with our plan. I decided instead to send a pneumatique, a kind of telegram, bidding them farewell and conveying my deepest gratitude for everything they had done for me, promising to write them when I arrived in Buenos Aires. I still regret that I didn't say a proper goodbye, considering how much they went out of their way to help me and my family.

It had been seven years since I left Winnipeg and there had been a lot of water under the bridge since then. These had been the formative years of my adolescence, the time in which character-building and self-esteem develop, along with learning to express oneself and learn a skill. Last but not least, these were the years to learn about relationships with the opposite sex. I, unfortunately, had never really experienced the latter. At eighteen, I was on the run like a hunted criminal, completely absorbed with basic survival. To have lived in Paris, which I will always think of as the city of romance, through my adolescent years in the 1930s was an education of sorts, but now all this was behind me.

A month or so after my nineteenth birthday, in December 1940, Wolf and I boarded the train to Perpignan. We had a compartment to ourselves, which gave us a chance to go over our plans to get across the Pyrenees and what we would do once we were in Spain. We weren't sure whether to use some form of transportation or proceed on foot. We also needed to figure out how to exchange our French francs – travelling through Spain without any Spanish currency would be very risky and we would need cash to buy food.

We conducted our entire conversation in Yiddish since it was the only language we had in common. Immersed as we were in our intense conversation, we didn't realized how quickly time was passing until the train was pulling into Perpignan. We stepped off the train and went to the waiting room, still tossing around various ideas. We finally decided that the best plan was to find a rabbi in Perpignan and ask him for advice, following in the traditions of our forefathers. We looked up the address of a rabbi in the telephone book and not long afterward, we found ourselves ringing his doorbell.

The man who opened the door was very dignified but clearly bewildered to find two teenaged boys on his doorstep. As soon as we explained that we were Jewish and had come to him for advice, however, he welcomed us into his house. He showed us into his study, where we came straight to the point, explaining that we were planning to escape across the border into Spain. He listened carefully and then told us that while he knew of many successful attempts, he knew of many more in which people had been apprehended. He made it quite clear that our undertaking would be extremely dangerous. Realizing that we were set on proceeding, he advised us to exercise extreme caution. He also recommended that we seek out Basque farmers who lived on both sides of the Spanish border and elicit their help in exchanging our currency. He explained that many of them augmented their income with smuggling and therefore always had Spanish pesetas.

We left, thanking him for his advice and kind concern. I have often wondered what became of the good rabbi of Perpignan. For the life of me, unfortunately, I cannot remember his name, but, as Jews, our discussion with him reminded us of the wisdom and comfort in seeking the advice of the teachers of the Talmud before venturing out into dangerous territory.

Not long after leaving the rabbi's house, we started cautiously walking in the general direction of the border separating France from Spain, looking out for frontier guards. Rising majestically in the distance were the beautiful Pyrenees, their greenery releasing a fresh scent into the air. It was a sunny day, enhanced by a gorgeous view of softly rolling hills covered with sweet-smelling flowers. We were so captivated by our surroundings and our determination to succeed that a strenuous day of walking became almost effortless and pretty soon we found ourselves approaching a Basque farm.

The farmer came to greet us and was so friendly that we felt immediately welcome. We began cautiously engaging him in casual conversation, not wanting to give away the reason we were there. Nonetheless, he astonished us by guessing our intent and offering to help us in any way he could. We clearly weren't the first Jewish fugitives who had come to him nor would we be the last. Once we had gained his confidence, he confessed that he had helped many others like us cross into Spain. Nothing could have given us a greater boost to our morale. Up to this point, we had had to rely only on our own resourcefulness. The farmer's kindness overwhelmed us as much as his offer to help us. He said that he could exchange our French currency into Spanish pesetas and invited us to join him and his family for dinner and then stay overnight with them so that we could start our long trek the next morning. We, of course, paid him for all his generous hospitality and no one was more deserving. As Wolf and I lay contentedly in our beds that night we were in high spirits, talking and laughing about how easy the first leg of our journey was proving to be.

After a peaceful night, we woke to a dazzling blue sky filled with sunshine. After a hearty breakfast, our host exchanged five thousand French francs of my funds into Spanish pesetas, which still left me with a small reserve divided equally into the American dollars and Swiss francs I had acquired in Marseille. This was a considerable sum of money in those days. We bid farewell to all the members of our host's family and set off with the farmer. He took us to a safe area that would lead us across the Spanish border and, in a completely isolated spot, came to a stop, telling us that this was as far as he would go. He gave us some very complicated directions and extended his hand to bid us farewell, wishing us the best of luck. We thanked him sincerely and, to show our appreciation, I gave him an extra fifty francs.

Left to our own devices, I began feeling apprehensive about the reality of venturing into a strange country illegally. When we first set out, we felt as though we could keep walking forever, but our seemingly inexhaustible energy gradually began to wane and we stopped for a rest. According to our watches we had been walking steadily for well over six hours and, apart from being tired, we were famished. So we sat down high up on a mountain top and ate some lunch with wine. Our satisfying meal soon revived us and we were ready to keep going.

For miles in every direction we could see nothing but mountain after mountain and we inevitably began to wonder whether we had lost our sense of direction. We suddenly got a strange feeling, as though we were lost in a forest or thick jungle like the scenes we'd seen in many movies, and we began to feel a little afraid. Fortunately the sensation didn't last very long. Part of the problem was that we had no idea whether we had actually crossed the border or were still in French territory. As if the situation weren't fraught enough, Wolf and I began to disagree over which way to go. We each stubbornly tried to persuade the other as to who was right, almost coming to blows over it. In these situations reason does not necessarily win out over emotion and we foolishly decided to go our separate ways, taking off in opposite directions without saying a word. I'm not sure which one of us was more scared at the prospect of being left alone in the middle of nowhere. I had a sinking feeling in the pit of my stomach and a desire to cry out for help. Never before had I felt such utter desolation.

As the distance between us increased so did my anxiety. I was too obstinate to give in but kept looking over my shoulder so I wouldn't lose sight of Wolf. I was hoping that he would come to his senses and turn around, even if it was only because I had all the money. Unfortunately, my friend instead disappeared from view. I became frantic and just as I started to turn back, to my relief I heard a loud, shrill voice calling my name. I responded in kind, shouting at the top of my lungs until I saw Wolf in the distance and we ran toward each another. We hugged and agreed to figure out some kind of compromise.

After another five-hour trek in a direction chosen by mutual consent, the sun was about to set without any signs of civilization. The compromise that Wolf and I had reached was to walk in one direction for a number of hours, then return to our point of departure and switch to another direction until we reached a village or farm. If we had accurately followed the instructions from our Basque guide, then we should have been in Figueres by now; obviously we were lost. Exhausted and hungry, we stopped to eat. With almost all our food now gone, we absolutely had to find some inhabited area that night or the next day. We took stock of our situation and decided that it would be safer to keep going right through the night rather than lose valuable time bedding down. We headed out along a path that was difficult to see because it was already dark.

Hours passed without us seeing anything. We carried on walking through the night, peering through the darkness, hoping to see some sign of civilization. Plodding along, climbing up one hill and down another, the minutes ticking away into hours, we grew increasingly anxious. Fatigue began to overtake us, slowing our pace and diminishing our spirits. We began to despair that we would ever see civilization again. Huge black clouds were gathering overhead. All around us was nothing but barren hills, devoid of any shelter in the event of a downpour.

The rain finally descended between one and two in the morning, at first lightly and then steadily increasing until we were drenched to the skin. Then, when the rain stopped temporarily, Wolf saw the outline of a house dimly through the dark. We both went from the depths of pessimism to the heights of optimism. Wolf was so elated that he nearly lost his balance and we both raced enthusiastically toward the house that was just over a kilometre away. I found myself hoping that it wasn't just a hallucination. Fortunately it was real and the closer we got, the more oblivious we were to the pouring rain.

We still didn't know whether we were in Spain, but we were too drenched, exhausted and drained to worry about it. When we at last reached the farmhouse, we summoned the courage to hesitantly knock on the door. When no one answered, we knocked a little harder. Still no answer. Frantically, we continued knocking for almost another five minutes. Then, just when we were about to give up, someone shouted from an upstairs window in Spanish, demanding to know what we wanted. Wolf spoke to the farmer in Spanish, asking him if he could offer us shelter for the night, for which we were prepared to pay handsomely. The farmer apologetically responded that he couldn't let strangers into his house at that hour of the night, but offered instead to let us take refuge in a tiny shed until morning. I reminded Wolf to ask him where we were and to our immense relief, the farmer replied that we were one kilometre inside Spain. Months of danger trying to get out of France had finally come to fruition. Everything seemed to be going according to plan.

Capture

Wolf and I ran to the shed and found ourselves in a cramped space that was barely wide enough for us to squeeze into side by side on a narrow board. Even that didn't dampen our spirits – we were so delighted to be on Spanish soil, to be in a country that was not controlled by the Germans. We changed into dry clothes from our backpacks and talked about our plans for the immediate future. We were exhausted but too proud and excited to sleep. We spent the rest of the night talking and laughing.

At about five-thirty in the morning, the farmer came to invite us into his house. Greeting us with a "Buenos dias" (Good morning), he apologized for showing up later than he had intended, explaining that it had taken his wife an extra half hour to prepare our breakfast. Considering how hungry we both were, we couldn't have been more grateful. The farmer's wife served us a very substantial breakfast that included as much coffee as we could drink. Over breakfast, Wolf asked the farmer how to get to Barcelona. Our host gave him very detailed directions to Barcelona by way of Figueres and then offered to take us part of the way in his horse and wagon. We appreciated his generosity and were a little embarrassed when he refused to accept any payment for feeding us and starting us off on our way. We climbed in the back of his wagon and rode through the hilly Spanish countryside.

After we'd travelled for a little while, the farmer told us that he had gone as far as he could and pointed the way toward Figueres. We made one last attempt to offer him money and when he once again declined, we repeated our fervent gratitude and shook his hand. Left on our own, Wolf and I headed down the road to Figueres and Barcelona full of eagerness and burst into song. The beautiful sunny day felt like the height of perfection.

After many hours of walking, we arrived in Figueres. Dressed as Basques, with Wolf speaking fluent Spanish, we never for a moment suspected that we would arouse any suspicion. The long walk to Figueres had left us thirsty and hungry and we decided to look for a bistro or restaurant. Close to the centre of the town we came across several bistros and decided to go into the one that was the most crowded so that we could avoid drawing attention to ourselves. We were disappointed to find that there weren't any empty tables and that we had to sit at the counter. Wolf picked up a menu and very quietly read it to me in Yiddish, then he put in our order with a request for lots of water. We thoroughly enjoyed our meal and after about half an hour, we paid the bill and went on our way.

Just when we felt so happy, when our prospects never looked brighter, everything suddenly fell apart. We had stopped about five or ten minutes outside the town to look over our maps and decide how far we should go that day when out of nowhere, we were confronted by two Spanish *carabineros* (soldiers) with rifles demanding that we put up our hands. I was petrified. They frisked us and took my wallet, which contained all the money I had – the equivalent of more than one thousand dollars. Not a penny was ever returned to me; these so-called protectors of law and order robbed me of all my possessions.

After our arrest, Wolf and I were taken to the police station in Figueres, where we were separated. We never saw each other again. It took many years for me to figure out why the *carabineros* had separated me from my dear friend Wolf. I'm now sure that it was because they didn't want their superiors to know that they had removed the contents of my wallet. Knowing that Wolf spoke Spanish and I didn't, they wanted to make sure that I couldn't accuse the two arresting officers of taking my money.

Serious as the matter of the theft was, however, it did not begin to compare to the sadness I felt at being separated from Wolf and the realization that all my efforts to reach my family in Buenos Aires now seemed to have been an exercise in futility. Locked in a prison cell and left alone for what seemed like an eternity, my hope of seeing my parents or sister again dwindling, I could only think of the worst – that I would be returned to France or turned over to the Germans. Nothing short of a miracle could change what had happened.

I desperately tried to figure out what had gone wrong. Perhaps we should have avoided the stopover in Figueres. Perhaps we should have used local transportation, travelling by bus or train. We had certainly left ourselves exposed among a small local population who would have immediately noticed strangers in their midst. Since we'd been caught just a short distance out of town, I can only assume that some local people or the owner of the restaurant had reported our presence to the police. What we hadn't known is that the Spanish authorities had tightened up their border regulations because so many people were escaping to England through Spain to join the Allied armed forces. A foreigner crossing the border from France into Spain illegally would have had to be exceptionally adept and experienced to avoid being caught by the *carabineros*.

My solitary confinement on the first day of my arrest continued well into the night. Not knowing what was going to happen to me was the most difficult burden to bear. Just as I was falling asleep, exhausted by the day's events, I was aroused by the clanking sound of the prison cell door opening. Several prison guards walked into my cell and motioned me to follow them outside to a police van that contained a dozen or so other prisoners. We drove off into the night until the van came to a stop in front of a massive old, grey prison. When we got out, the police officers lined us up and marched us into a huge hallway leading to a spiral staircase. The climb to the very top seemed endless and when we finally reached it we turned down a dark hallway where, about halfway down, the officers unlocked an ordinary-looking door. When they flung it open, I was shocked to see at least seventy people crowded into one large room crammed to capacity. There was barely enough room to move, let alone stretch out on the tiled floor to get some sleep.

I spent twelve of the most miserable days and nights of my entire life in these appalling conditions. Apart from not getting any sleep, the three meals a day we were given amounted to little more than a starvation diet. Still, I was grateful for the fact that I hadn't been returned to France or turned over to the Germans, so I resigned myself to facing whatever came my way. I had to come to grips with the reality of my new predicament. Each passing day became a test of endurance as I craved food. We all looked forward to our meagre rations so eagerly that we almost became like wild animals.

During my twelve-day confinement in Figueres I made a number of acquaintances, among them a Belgian, two Frenchmen and an Englishman. Each day pretty much resembled the previous one, in which almost all our time was spent in that crowded room. On the twelfth excruciating day, I was selected along with some others to be transferred by freight train to Barcelona. Our destination only became clear when we arrived at Barcelona's main railway station, from where we were marched to a prison. It felt so good in the early dawn to experience the freedom of walking through the streets of Barcelona after twelve days of imprisonment. Breathing the fresh air and looking at the beautiful structures, with their rows upon rows of stores, it became apparent to me just how precious my lost freedom was and to what lengths I would go to recover it.

All too soon we arrived at the prison. We were led through enormous iron gates and toward the entrance. Once inside we were taken to what appeared to be a prison cell but actually turned out to be an enormous room filled with hundreds of prisoners. Our temporary freedom had come to an end. Later that same day I met a Spanish prisoner who spoke French and during our conversation I was amazed to discover that he was a Republican soldier who had fought in the Spanish Civil War against Franco. He was one of the hundreds of thousands of Republican combatants who were still in prison. It was shocking to find that almost two years after the Civil War the Franco regime was holding so many of their own people prisoner. At least the prisoners' families were allowed to bring in food every day. Most of these people were a pathetic sight to behold, bitterly resentful over the fact that they had supported the party duly elected by the Spanish people and yet their government had been forcefully over-thrown with arms and men supplied by Axis collaborators Mussolini and Hitler.

My days and nights in the Barcelona prison began to take their toll on me. Under the stress of not knowing how long I would be there, I began imagining myself in a luxurious French restaurant, ordering gourmet food, or arriving in Buenos Aires to see my mother, father and sister standing at the docks waiting for me. My reality, however, was entirely different – I had become completely subdued, sad and frustrated, and, above all, always so hungry. Hunger reduces a person to the point that he or she will eat anything to satisfy their hunger. I also had to lie on a cement floor with one blanket spread beneath me and another as a cover, using my backpack as a pillow. At some point, unable to withstand my hunger any longer, I offered to sell the only pair of shoes I owned to one of the Spanish inmates in exchange for three loaves of bread and a pair of sandals. I hid the bread in my backpack so it couldn't be stolen.

I was very lonely without Wolf. I had his mother's address, so I thought of writing my mother and asking her to contact her. After thinking it over, though, I decided that I really didn't want my mother to know that I was languishing in some God-forsaken Spanish prison.

Just when I had almost grown accustomed to the rigours of my confinement, learning to live with hunger, solitude and sleeping on a stone floor, an official arrived to remove me from the prison. Having already spent a total of twenty-four days in prison, half of them in Barcelona, the Spanish police now transferred me to a new prison. Once again, I was hustled out of jail and led to a freight car with other prisoners. We didn't know where we were being taken; all we could do was hope that whatever lay in store for us wouldn't turn out to be worse than our last place. There was even speculation that we might be headed to the French frontier and handed over to the Germans or that we were going to be released on condition that we leave the country. It was, of course, ridiculous to even dare hope for the latter, but what else is there when all hope vanishes?

After a long and bumpy train ride, we stood on the station platform, filling our lungs with brisk, cool winter air. Looking beyond the station, we caught a glimpse of countryside. For a brief spell, we again savoured freedom before being marched off to the jail in Saragossa, about three hundred kilometres west of Barcelona. When we got there, I discovered that it had a few improvements over the last prison: we were given cots to sleep on and the food was much better. What I didn't yet know was that I would be confined to a cell in which I could only take five steps in one direction and three in the other, all on my own without seeing or hearing another human soul except, of course, for the prison guard who brought me my food rations. Not having anyone to talk to all day or so much as a book or newspaper to read drove me crazy. Despondency and disillusionment became my constant companions as the days ticked away.

After another twelve days, just as I was beginning to lose all hope of ever being released from the Saragossa prison, my situation changed again. As if in answer to a prayer, I heard the sound of heavy footsteps that came to a stop outside my cell door. Learning that I was being transferred brought a smile to my face for the first time since I arrived in Saragossa. I had by then been incarcerated for thirty-six days in three different jails.

Throughout my confinement in the various Spanish jails, I was constantly exposed to Spanish and as a result picked up some of the language. As a Latin language, Spanish has many similarities to French, so it was not at all difficult for a French-speaking person to learn. I never quite spoke it fluently, but I learned enough to make myself understood.

When I left the prison, some other prisoners – almost all of whom had escaped from France – and I were organized into formation and marched off to the railway station to wait for a train. About an hour later, we boarded a train heading for a new destination. On the journey, the prisoners all speculated about where we were going. Once again, some were afraid that we were being returned to France, while others predicted that we were being relocated to another prison. As it turned out, none of us were right. Our destination remained a mystery and the Spanish guards, of course, never told us anything. I spent most of the time talking to my new companions, refusing to dwell on all the uncertainties. Instead I told them about my own experiences in crossing the Spanish border. We also discussed possible plans to escape but eventually concluded that the risk factors far outweighed the chances of success.

After travelling through the unknown for many anxious hours, the train pulled into a station and our fears were somewhat assuaged. We weren't in France – the sign in the station told us that we were in the town of Miranda de Ebro, in the Spanish province of Burgos.

Miranda de Ebro

It was a cold January day in 1941 when we arrived at Miranda de Ebro, and we were kept waiting on the train for about half an hour before being let out onto the platform. It was sunny but crisp and most of us were not dressed for the cold weather. Hungry and freezing, we were lined up and marched off to the gates of a camp identified by a sign that read "Campo de Concentración de Miranda de Ebro" (Miranda de Ebro Concentration Camp). Through the gates we could see enough army-style barracks in rows to accommodate hundreds of prisoners. As soon as we entered the grounds we saw shabby-looking prisoners dressed in drab grey uniforms with a round cap with the letter P for the word *prisionero* (prisoner) printed in black on the front. I had never heard of a concentration camp, but it was clearly not an inviting place to be.

From the moment we entered the camp we were made to feel the indignity of being prisoners. The first thing that the military camp officials did was shave off all our hair. That felt really humiliating. I tried to tell myself that being bald wasn't the end of the world – it's not as if there were any girls in the camp. After our haircut, we were all taken to another room and issued our own drab grey uniforms, two blankets and a round metal dish and a spoon. It was shortly before noon, so the guards took us to the far end of the grounds where the kitchen was located. We saw some prisoners placing two huge circular vats side by side about three metres apart on the ground. The rest of the prisoners formed two lines in front of the vats and the guards ordered us to join the end of the line. When we got to the front of the line, one Spanish soldier handed out miniature loaves of dark cornbread and another dished out soup from the vat. Each prisoner's ration consisted of only two full ladles of soup and one tiny loaf of bread that had to be shared between two people. If we were dismayed at how small our lunch ration was, we were in for an even bigger shock when we discovered that for supper we would receive the same two ladles of soup but without the bread. Breakfast the following morning was even worse: it consisted of only two ladles of ersatz coffee with absolutely nothing else of substance.

Since the prisoners were not allowed to have knives, the only way we could divide our bread was to use either the handle of the spoon or our hands. Tempers often flared over the inevitable uneven division, so some weeks later I suggested to the person I was regularly paired with that we each take turns keeping the entire loaf on alternate days to avoid conflict. He readily agreed.

After a lunch that left us almost hungrier than before, a distin-guishcd-looking man with grey hair, a moustache and a German accent called out the names of the newly arrived prisoners and asked us to follow him. We stopped in front of one of the barracks and he introduced himself as Señor Pfeffercorn and gave us a brief outline of how the camp was run. He was a kapo, a prisoner-overseer, who was responsible for maintaining order in our barracks. Apparently, whenever there were new arrivals to the camp, Señor Pfeffercorn was in charge of the incoming Jewish prisoners for his own barracks. A German-born Jew who had lived in Spain for twenty-five years, Señor Pfeffercorn told me that there were about 25,000 Jews living in Spain, quite a number of whom were native-born, with the remainder being foreign nationals.

As soon as he arrived in Miranda, the Spanish military authorities recognized Pfeffercorn's intellectual and linguistic abilities – he was highly educated and spoke a number of languages, including Spanish, French, English and German – and wasted little time in making him a kapo. The position afforded him a number of advantages denied to ordinary prisoners, such as a generous space to himself at the entrance of the barracks that was cordoned off from the other prisoners with army blankets, the luxury of a small stove and food rations that were substantially larger than those given to regular prisoners. He was a man of imposing stature and his very presence and his superior intellect commanded respect from everyone in the camp, including the commandant.

Pfeffercorn assigned me a place on a lower platform about three-quarters up the barracks with two Jewish gentlemen. On my left was a German Jew, who had lived in Spain as long as Pfeffercorn, and on my right was a Danish Jew who was the president of the Zionist Federation of Denmark. I'm not sure how he came to be in Miranda. We all had to sleep on bare wooden planks, spreading one of the blankets allotted to us beneath us and using the other as a cover. The winter was cold, the grounds were covered with snow and the barracks were completely unheated.

It didn't take me long to strike up a few friendships. That first day, I talked to my two neighbours as well as others in the barracks. We became so absorbed in each other's accounts that we were temporarily oblivious to the appalling conditions around us. When it got dark, we all had to retreat to our bunks. Before going to bed, the German Jew on my left tried to make us laugh by handing me a metal mirror, pulling off my cap and saying, "How would you like to see what a good-looking monkey looks like?" When I caught sight of myself in the mirror, I had a very rude awakening and did not feel the least bit amused. But I didn't want to spoil everyone's fun, so I played along, pretending I wasn't really affected by my appearance and even joining in the laughter.

I had a difficult time settling down on the hard wooden planks, twisting and turning from side to side in an effort to relieve my discomfort. I eventually fell into a deep sleep and only awoke to the sound of Señor Pfeffercorn loudly ordering us to follow him into the parade grounds by six a.m. sharp for the playing of the Spanish national anthem. Getting to my feet after such an uncomfortable night was difficult – every part of my body ached and felt as rigid as the planks I had slept on. Nevertheless, I joined my fellow prisoners in the parade grounds, where we were assembled in rows facing the commandant and the military band. The commandant stood at attention on an elevated platform and, as the band played the national anthem, the prisoners had to raise their right hands in the Fascist salute and keep them there until the anthem was over. At that point, each of the three times that the commandant shouted the word España (Spain), we had to respond in unison by first calling out "Una!" (One!) followed by "Grande!" (Great!) and finally "Libre!" (Free!) After that we were dismissed.

We returned to the barracks to pick up our metal dishes and join the lineup for breakfast, for our two ladles of ersatz coffee. Next, we had to report for forced labour. At about seven a.m., a detachment of guards led us out of the camp grounds to a quarry where we spent the morning picking up heavy rocks and loading them into woven baskets until the baskets were filled to capacity. Then we had to heave them onto our shoulders and carry the load a considerable distance to be dumped. The extremely arduous work made us sweat profusely, but we weren't allowed to drink any water until we had reached our quota or it was time to quit for the day.

The quarry was quite a distance from the camp, so we were under the watchful eye of heavily armed guards to make sure that no one escaped. If they thought that anyone was shirking their duty or moving too slowly, they didn't hesitate to hit him on his back or legs with the butts of their rifles. This happened to me on my very first day. One of the guards saw me struggling to lift the heavy basket of rocks onto my shoulder and slammed me full force on the back with his rifle butt. I was sore for weeks and before it had time to heal, I received the same treatment during a subsequent work period. At eleven a.m., we stopped work and were escorted back to camp. Thank heavens for the Spanish siesta – we were spared from forced labour for the remainder of the day. Those four hours of hard labour on an empty stomach had sapped most of our energy.

The Miranda de Ebro camp was on an elevated plateau next to the River Ebro. The camp was like a fortress, surrounded by barbed wire fences and guards, beyond which lay the river. Across the river were still more guards. Some prisoners thought that the fences were electrified and that if anyone touched them they would be electrocuted. Any notion of trying to escape seemed suicidal, although one Jewish prisoner did manage to escape and reach Portugal during the time of my incarceration in Miranda.

The prisoners in the camp were of many different nationalities, most of whom had been caught trying to escape from France. Among the roughly nine hundred foreign nationals – including only about ninety Jews – were people from Britain, France, Poland, Belgium, Czechoslovakia and the Netherlands, as well as some other nationalities. At this early stage of the war, in 1941, the British embassy in Madrid became aware that there were British citizens detained in Miranda and Britain had begun the process of obtaining their release in exchange for petrol, which the Spanish needed badly.

The process unfortunately proved to be extremely slow. We had access to Spanish fascist newspapers through the camp canteen, where people could buy basic goods if they had money, and it became clear to us that, as the war progressed and the Germans gained military advantage over the British forces in the North African campaign, Franco favoured the winning side, adversely affecting British negotiations. German Field Marshal Erwin Rommel and his army landed in Africa on February 12, 1941, and by February 14, his Afrika Korps had launched its campaign. By March 24, the German offensive had re-captured El Agheila and the British had been routed all the way to Tobruk. Despite all of this, the acute shortage of petrol in Spain was a powerful incentive for the eventual exchange of prisoners.

Toward the end of my second month in Miranda, a British envoy showed up to interview non-British prisoners who wished to go to Britain to volunteer for their respective armed services. The interviews were conducted in our barracks, where Señor Pfeffercorn's quarters served as an office and he acted as interpreter. Señor Pfeffercorn himself was beyond military age and therefore not eligible for release to Britain. When my turn came, although I didn't need Señor Pfeffercorn's assistance as an interpreter, he nevertheless stayed to give me moral support. He sensed my shyness and discomfort in the presence of the envoy and his support put me at ease. He also said some amusing things that even had the envoy laughing and before long my application for release to Britain was submitted.

During my interview, the envoy was quite puzzled as to how I had come to spend more than half my life in Canada. After he left, I had time to think about whether the whole idea of going to England made any sense. My life had taken a totally different turn – after all, my whole future was supposedly bound up with going to Argentina to join my family. On the other hand, going to England sure beat living in the appalling conditions of the concentration camp. Out of nowhere, I was being offered a great opportunity.

By the time my incarceration was well into its fourth month, having persevered through a severe winter, I was still in the dark as to when I might be released. It had been impossible to stay warm – not only was there no heat in the barracks and only one blanket, but I had to walk in the snow every day with only sandals on my feet. To make matters worse, I had to endure the scourges of lice, fleas and a severe case of dysentery. The longer I stayed in the camp, the weaker I got. Day in and day out we were subjected to the same morning parade and fascist salute, followed by a march to the quarry to put in a four- or five-hour stint of heavy labour. Then, as usual, we lined up for our paltry rations and spent the remainder of the day sleeping away our misery or chatting with friends.

Fortunately for everyone, the advent of spring made everything a little easier as the warm sun and fresh mountain air helped restore some of our energy. By this time I had even more friends, both Jews and gentiles. My closest gentile friend was a Scotsman named Jock. I still have a photograph of him with me and another Jewish friend by the name of Hershorn. Like most of us in the camp, Jock had been apprehended in Spain after escaping from France, where he had been trapped while attached to a fighting unit of the British forces. We were roughly the same age and got along extremely well – so well, in fact, that he spent more time with me than he did with his British mates. In certain respects, his background was similar to mine – he had grown up in poverty, his father barely eking out a living as a rag-and-bone man. Jock was kind and considerate, and showed genuine concern for all I had been through.

My friendship with Jock unfortunately only lasted about three months. Just as we were about to begin our fourth month in the camp, in April 1941, Señor Pfeffercorn was summoned to the commandant's office and came away with a list from the British embassy naming the first British prisoners to be released, and, as a British soldier, among them was my friend Jock. He was absolutely ecstatic when he heard Señor Pfeffercorn call out his name and I heartily congratulated him. He was sorry to learn that I wasn't on the list and tried to cheer me up, reassuring me that my turn would come soon.

Within a matter of days, the British envoy showed up to escort the released prisoners out of the camp. Everyone who remained had suddenly become more optimistic because they now had reason to hope that they too would be released. Even the non-British prisoners celebrated because most of them were eligible for release through their embassies as well, although, as it turned out, subsequent lists did not include the names of any Jewish prisoners. Being stateless, with no embassy to turn to, I had no idea when my turn would come. Before he left, Jock and I told each other that we hoped to meet again soon in Britain. We had taught one another songs – his were about his native Scotland while mine were in French. Whenever he attempted to sing in French his accent made me roar with laughter, but other than that, he picked up my songs fairly quickly. Thinking about him now, I wonder if he still recalls some of the songs I taught him, for I certainly remember several of his. Life being what it is, however, we never met again.

Shortly after the first release of British prisoners, in the early spring 1941, a tragic event occurred concerning my German-born barracks neighbour. The camp was visited by Gestapo officers who had come to Miranda specifically to find out how many Jewish German nationals were interned there. Among the ninety-odd Jewish prisoners in the camp, only two were born in Germany: my Jewish barracks mate and our kapo, Señor Pfeffercorn. For some reason, Señor Pfeffercorn's name was not given to the Gestapo – I believe that the Spanish commandant, who genuinely liked and respected him, did not want to turn him over to the Germans. At any rate, the only German national identified was my barracks mate and the Gestapo officers insisted on interviewing him. When we heard about it, all the Jewish prisoners were terrified for his safety.

My German friend was summoned to the commandant's office for his interview with the Gestapo and several hours later returned to the barracks completely shattered. It was horrifying to see this dignified and intelligent man so overcome that he wept as he flung himself onto the floor. Seeing an adult cry with such abandon left me at a loss; I had no idea how to comfort him. When he finally rose from the floor, he said, "Max, my dear friend, they are coming for me in a few days." He then added, "Please forgive my odd behaviour. I feel like an innocent person who has just been condemned to death. I feel strongly that my upcoming journey to Germany will be my last and nothing but death awaits me there." How does one respond to a person who knew exactly what fate awaited him? I put my hand on his shoulder and did my best to comfort him.

Just before the Germans took him from the camp, this wonderful man (I regret that I don't remember his name) spent quite a bit of time talking to me about Jewish history, about how we Jews were driven from our homeland and forced into exile. What he said made a profound impression on me, especially his strong convictions that we absolutely had to have a state of our own. He made me understand that, to survive as a people, as many of us as possible needed to reach Palestine by whatever means necessary.

The day before he left the camp, my friend asked for my parents' address, saying that he would let me know what was happening to him. To my great sorrow, I never heard from him, leading me to conclude that, as he had predicted, he became a victim of the Holocaust. He left me some of his belongings, including the metal mirror that had made me the object of a joke on my first night in Miranda. As he handed me some of his possessions he ruefully remarked, "I won't be needing any of these where I'm going." When he left, I couldn't resist giving him one final embrace. His last gesture was to hand me twenty-five pesetas, which I tried to decline but he insisted I keep. It was the first money I had received since being robbed by the Spanish civil guards in Figueres and I used it to buy food from the canteen.

As the weeks dragged on, many new lists arrived from the British embassy for the release of prisoners and, although some of them did include a number of non-British prisoners, my name wasn't among them. Nor, I must add, were the names of any of the other Jewish civilian prisoners. In most cases, even for the non-Jewish civilians, the waiting period was no more than a month or two. After six months without any word, I became really anxious. One of the new arrivals in the camp at that time was a Jewish captain in the French army named D'Alsace and I decided to ask for his help. I hoped that since he was an officer, his appeal to the British representative on my behalf might carry more weight. Capitaine D'Alsace and I had struck up a friendship on the day that he arrived and he decided to take me under his wing. He would look for an opportunity to meet with the British envoy to advocate on my behalf.

Capitaine D'Alsace met with the British representative and

brought the matter to his attention, pointing out that many non-British civilian prisoners who had arrived long after me had already been released. Capitaine D'Alsace himself barely spent three weeks in Miranda before being released, although, of course, he was a French national with the military rank of captain. When he emerged from his meeting with the British envoy, he brought me the good news that the envoy had promised to look into my application and try to speed up my release.

Sitting all alone on the ground near the barracks on the afternoon following Capitaine D'Alsace's release, I took off my prisoner's jacket to delouse myself – it was a daily ritual – and was suddenly overwhelmed by my loneliness, frustration and constant hunger and began whimpering uncontrollably. I realized that it was time to let go of my resolution to conceal my whereabouts from my parents. I had to end my silence – that in itself was no doubt torture for my parents – and allow myself to ask for help. My original plan had been well-intentioned, but it had gone on far longer than I envisioned. My parents hadn't heard anything from me in more than eight months.

I had to find a way to get a pen and paper and an airmail stamp, all of which required money that I didn't have. My few possessions were of no value, so my only hope was to figure out something to barter with the prisoners who still had money. What did I have that would be of any value to another prisoner? The only thing I could come up with was my life-sustaining bread ration, the only substantial food we received. Trading it away for money took courage, not to mention an enormous amount of willpower. It would take a week's rations to get enough money to buy what I needed. Going without bread for that length of time would be extremely difficult, but what other choice did I have?

I can't begin to describe what it was like to be without bread for a week. The lack of nutrition affected my morale and the gnawing emptiness in the pit of my stomach gave rise to severe cramps. All I wanted to do was sleep to get some relief from my debilitating hunger. But I accomplished what I set out to do: I managed to get enough money to send a letter to my parents.

During the week that I deprived myself of bread, there were some other stressful events in the camp. The first involved a Jewish man I barely knew – he was the prisoner I mentioned earlier who had somehow managed to escape from the camp. His absence went undetected for a while, but before long all the prisoners were buzzing with the news of his escape. We were all baffled as to how he had pulled it off. To my knowledge, no one else had ever succeeded in breaching the camp's defenses. The Spanish commandant was outraged by the escape, even more so when he received a letter from the escaped prisoner railing against the treatment he had received while incarcerated in Miranda. We heard about the letter from Señor Pfeffercorn who translated it from French to Spanish for the commandant. Little did the escaped man realize the repercussions his letter would have on the prisoners: the commandant took his anger out on us by extending our work hours at the quarry and reducing our food rations for a week.

The second incident also happened because of the escaped prisoner. There was a quiet Jewish gentleman named Mr. Silverman who lived in our barracks. A middle-aged man in his fifties, he was in failing health – mainly because of the terrible conditions in the camp – and had a weak bladder. It was difficult for him to walk to the washroom, so he had to resort to urinating in a can, especially at night. This was a problem for the fellows with whom he shared his space, but they felt sorry for him and overlooked it. Mr. Silverman also considerately concealed the can as best he could.

One of the harsh new measures that the commandant implemented as a result of the escape and the subsequent letter was a daily inspection of the barracks. The inspections started the morning after he received the letter and no one was prepared. Three officers entered the barracks without any warning, exchanged a few words with Señor Pfeffercorn and began inspecting everyone's quarters. Starting from the left side, the side I was on, they went all the way down one side and then back up the other side, meticulously checking every object in view. Somewhere between halfway and two-thirds down the right side, in the space Mr. Silverman occupied, one of the officers found the can that still contained Mr. Silverman's urine.

As a rule, Mr. Silverman got up early to empty the can of urine in the washroom. This time, however, the officers arrived before he could do so. When the officer inspected the can more closely and discovered its contents, he exploded into a thundering rage. Before the officer even had a chance to find the guilty party, Mr. Silverman stepped forward to claim the can as his own. The officer, sneering at him with disgust, ordered him to pick it up and carry it outside. By this time, the poor man was trembling with fear.

Señor Pfeffercorn was reprimanded for allowing the situation to occur. His explanation that Mr. Silverman had a weak bladder only further incensed the officer. All the prisoners were ordered to leave the barracks immediately and form a circle outside. What happened next left me stunned – it is the most disturbing spectacle I have ever witnessed. One of the Spanish officers grabbed Mr. Silverman by his jacket collar and brutally shoved him into the circle of prisoners. The highest-ranking officer among them dug a small hole in the ground, took Mr. Silverman's can of urine, poured some of it into the hole, then ordered the poor man to get down on his hands and knees and lick it up. When he was done, the officer poured more of the urine into the hole and again mockingly ordered Mr. Silverman to lick it up. The process was repeated over and over again, with the officer jeeringly asking how good it tasted. The officers forced Mr. Silverman to drink every last drop from the can. But the man's deep humiliation didn't end there – while all of this was going on, his tormentors hurled antisemitic insults at him. Finally, when Mr. Silverman lay sick on the ground, half-dazed with cramps, they decided to end the torture.

Silverman was quite ill after his terrible experience, but we all did what we could to help him recover. We took turns helping him to the washroom, even in the middle of the night. He was embarrassed by our support, but he never failed to show his appreciation. Thanks to everyone's concern, he was never again subjected to such a horrendous experience.

The days went on, still without any hope of my leaving Miranda. It was hard to watch so many of the prisoners being released without my turn ever coming up. As much as it pleased me to see anyone released from the camp, I couldn't help feeling envious. I was desperate to escape my confinement and experience freedom again. At least there was the occasional relief from hunger – on the Spanish holidays we were treated to traditional Spanish rice in lieu of the customary watery soup. Although the rations were still far from adequate, at least the rice was more filling and much more nourishing. But six months in a concentration camp plus thirty-six previous days of imprisonment had taken their toll on me. It had been six weeks since I'd written to my parents and instead of giving me hope, my frustration increased. For the most part, sleep was the only escape from my misery.

The friendships I developed with my fellow prisoners were my saving grace in Miranda. We talked about our experiences and took great delight in poking fun at one another and at our intolerable situation. Together we found the strength to get through another day. I consider myself fortunate to have had such outstanding people to share my abominable experiences with. Without their companionship, my life there would have been a whole lot bleaker.

For the most part, the routine in the camp never varied. We were occasionally called for potato-peeling duty, performed in the barracks where they were stored – and God help anyone who dared to steal any. Just before bed, people got together to chat while we carried out the thoroughly disgusting but necessary chore of taking off our clothes to get rid of the ever-present lice and fleas. The heat of the summer particularly aggravated the situation because the pests increased so much that it was hard to sleep and almost drove us mad.

Toward the ninth month of my incarceration, in fall 1941, there was a sudden ray of light. Señor Pfeffercorn motioned me over to him and the closer I got, the broader his smile became. "Bornstein," he said, "you are to report to the commandant's office immediately to pick up a cabled money order from your parents in Argentina." I was elated, not just at the prospect of the food I could buy, but also at the thought of my parents knowing that I was alive and well.

I went straight to the commandant's office and exchanged the money order for cash. Leaving with a pocketful of money, my first priority was a visit to the canteen to indulge myself in whatever I wanted. After going hungry for so long, gorging myself with food felt even better when I realized that I could do the same thing the next day. Of course, my stomach wasn't used to so much food, so it's not surprising that I felt quite ill after eating so much. But no matter how sick I became, I couldn't resist the temptation. After a few days of limitless indulgence, however, I did try to regulate what I ate, as well as the quantity. I craved bread more than anything else, which probably contributed to the ill effects I suffered. The bread in the camp was of poor quality and extremely heavy, making it hard to digest. That didn't really matter to me though; I was simply obsessed with assuaging my hunger and couldn't get enough.

Several days after I received the money order, Señor Pfeffercorn told me that there was a registered airmail letter waiting for me at the office. When I picked it up, the first thing I noticed was that the envelope had Argentinean stamps on it – my first letter from my parents! I wanted some privacy so I went straight to my sleeping quarters before opening it. It was so wonderful reading the first news I'd had from my family in more than a year. Over the next two days, I read that letter over and over again countless times, relishing every word, especially the encouraging information it contained. My mother had apparently notified Aunt Sadie by cable as soon as she learned of my circumstances. Aunt Sadie took immediate action, making every effort to remedy the situation. She tried to get permission to bring me over to Canada and when that failed, she went to New York City to find relatives on my father's side, one of whom held an important position in Washington, DC. As a result, an application had been forwarded to the US State Department to have me admitted on compassionate grounds. Although nothing came of those efforts, she also bombarded the British embassy in Madrid with correspondence. Aunt Sadie sent several letters to me in Miranda that outlined all her efforts on my behalf. Although it was late in coming, she was finally showing compassion for me, and each of her letters helped to ease my stress.

As I sat down to write a reply letter to my parents, it dawned on me I could try to find out what had happened to my friend Wolf. I sent my parents his parents' address, hoping to learn whether they had heard from him, and asked my parents to report back to me.

As long as the money from my parents lasted, my diet improved considerably. However as the funds gradually dwindled and I could no longer purchase any extra food, my health took a sharp downturn. This time the hunger pangs were even harder to withstand. Along with them, my loneliness, anxiety and frustration returned once again. I had seen a winter, spring and summer come and go and now the fall of 1941 was coming to an end without any sign of my release. The thought of spending yet another winter in the freezing barracks was almost too much to bear. One of my friends, the middle-aged Danish Jew, dreaded another harsh winter in Miranda even more than I did. He wasn't a well man and his health was steadily deteriorating in Miranda's crude conditions.

By this time, our population in the camp consisted of roughly ninety Jews and about another eight hundred gentiles. The one thing we all had in common, irrespective of nationality and religion, was that we were all the innocent victims of a madman, namely Adolf Hitler, and his Nazi henchmen. We had been thrown together in terrible conditions, caught up in a supposedly neutral country because its Fascist dictator, the Caudillo Francisco Franco, favoured the Axis powers.

I was once again feeling despondent when one day, as I returned from forced labour and headed for the barracks, I saw Señor Pfeffercorn standing at the entrance with a mischievous grin. He kept me in suspense as long as he could, then asked me to follow him to his quarters. When we got there, he picked up a document from his table and announced, "Your name is listed among those to be released to the British embassy within the next two weeks. Take a look for yourself!" I nervously scanned through the list until I saw the name Max Bornstein. No words can describe my joy at that moment. Unable to contain myself, I burst into tears and hugged Señor Pfeffercorn. He told me that it was a time for celebrating, not crying, and added, "You are the first among ninety civilian Jewish refugees to be privileged with this honour." He went on to say that, given my good fortune, it was my duty to help the remaining Jewish prisoners by trying to secure their release through the appropriate organizations in England and telling them about the terrible conditions in Miranda. I solemnly promised him that I wouldn't rest until the Jewish organizations gave me their assurance that they would help.

We didn't know that during the war all our letters were being censored by the Spanish authorities. If anyone dared write anything derogatory about the conditions in the camp, the letter would automatically be destroyed. Many Jewish prisoners had written to various Jewish organizations asking them to come to our aid, but, unbeknownst to us, none of the letters had ever reached their destination. We also didn't know that by 1941 most Jewish organizations in France had evacuated. The only way we could inform Jewish agencies about the situation in Miranda was through word of mouth. I was only too aware that ninety Jewish men were depending on me to give an uncensored account of their terrible circumstances.

The day that I found out that I was going to be released and word spread throughout the camp, I became the envy of all the other Jews.

They all gathered around to wish me good luck and ask me the secret of my success. I wished that I had some magical answers for them, but the reality was that I couldn't really explain my good fortune. I told them that it was more than likely that my Canadian aunt in Winnipeg could take most of the credit for my release, along with Capitaine D'Alsace and my own application. I started thinking about my future plans, but it was hard for me to grasp the reality that my long-sought freedom was now within reach.

Before I left Miranda, I received one more letter from my parents. I couldn't wait to tell them that I was about to be released and made a mental note to cable my mother on the very day of my arrival in England. My parents wrote, however, that they had visited Wolf's parents and learned that they hadn't heard a word from him since the day he stowed away. That was distressing news and I wasn't sure what I could do next to find him. More than ever, I felt guilty about having gotten him into such a terrible situation. Working on the assumption that all foreigners caught in Spain would sooner or later wind up in Miranda, the fact that he hadn't arrived in the camp during the eleven months that I was there led me to assume that he had been returned to France and caught by the Germans. I couldn't think of any other explanation for his long silence.

Finally, only one more day separated me from freedom. I still wouldn't completely believe it until it actually happened, but my friends' confidence in my release was unshakable. They wrote letters to the various Jewish agencies and gave them to me to smuggle out of the camp and deliver when I got to England. Of particular importance was the letter written by my Danish Jewish friend who had been president of the Zionist Federation of Denmark. His chilling account of conditions in Miranda de Ebro – the hard labour, the dysentery, the starvation diet, the lice and fleas, the unheated barracks – included a plea that, given his age, he could not be sure that he would survive another winter and his very life depended on some organization coming to his rescue and to the rescue of all the other Jews in the camp.

I spent my last evening in Miranda bidding farewell to friends and casual acquaintances alike. Many of them wept openly and I cried right along with them. It was hard to break the bonds of friendship nurtured under such difficult conditions, even for so happy a reason. Knowing they would be going hungry while I was well fed, spending their nights sleeping on bare wooden planks while I slept in the comfort of a bed, was very disturbing. I was somewhat reassured by my own experience working for a Jewish agency, knowing that these organizations worked tirelessly to come to the aid of Jews in dire straits.

On that last night, I had trouble sleeping. I was too excited, my mind racing with the anticipation of whatever the future held in store for me. I eventually fell into a deep sleep from sheer exhaustion and the next morning woke up filled with exhilaration. I had just spent my very last night in that God-forsaken place. As humiliating as life in Miranda de Ebro was, however, I cannot ignore the fact that it inadvertently saved us from falling victim to the Nazis.

In the morning, Señor Pfeffercorn announced the arrival of the British embassy representative, who told me to get ready to leave quickly. Unfortunately this took place while my friends were out performing their daily forced labour, which prevented my saying a final goodbye. Only Señor Pfeffercorn, who was exempt from work, remained behind to wish me Godspeed on my journey to England, hugging and kissing me as if I were his own son. I promised that I wouldn't forget my commitment to try to get him and the other Jewish prisoners released. He escorted me to the commandant's office, where thirty or so other prisoners were waiting to be released with me. Less than half an hour later, the British representative announced with a broad smile that we were all now officially released and added, "I'm sure all you fellows are only too anxious to depart, so let's get the hell out of here and not waste another moment."

When we got to the gate, Señor Pfeffercorn waved for the last time and I waved back. It was early December 1941 and this marked the end of my harrowing experience in the concentration camp of Miranda de Ebro.

Freedom!

As soon as we passed through the gates of Miranda de Ebro concentration camp, our group broke out into a loud cheer. I couldn't believe it was really happening. When we arrived in the town of Miranda proper, the British representative surprised us all by taking us to a cozy restaurant with tables covered in red-and-white-checked tablecloths. Just imagine what it felt like to be treated to my first regular meal in almost a year, and in a restaurant. For inmates of a concentration camp, the luxury of a regular meal was like a feast. We savoured each course, hoping the meal would continue indefinitely, eating until we couldn't take another bite.

After our splendid meal we went to the railway station to wait for the train to take us to Madrid. I spent the time talking to the British representative and it turned out that I was the only one of the released prisoners who spoke English. All the others were either French or Polish or various other nationalities; none of them were British. As a result, I was given the task of acting as interpreter.

We sang and laughed and conversed in French on our trip to Madrid; our mood was in marked contrast to how we felt in the camp. Very little, if anything, could diminish our exuberance, so intoxicated had we become with our new freedom. When we arrived in Madrid and got off the train, we followed the British representative to a vehicle waiting outside to take us to a section of the British embassy compound where we would be deloused, have a shower and get new clothes. It's hard to describe how wonderful the soothing spray of a warm shower felt after almost a year.

After we concluded all the formalities in the British embassy, we were driven to a hotel where we were served another wonderful meal and where we would stay the night. All these luxuries were almost too much to take in. The bed looked so inviting, but I was seized with guilt, thinking that surely this bed could not be intended for me. Long-term confinement can play havoc with the mind – after experiencing long incarceration, it doesn't seem that anything good can happen again. It takes time to restore one's self-confidence. In the end, I enjoyed that night in the comfort of the hotel bed and awoke the next morning reassured that what was happening was real.

The British authorities assumed that all the non-British prisoners released from Miranda would join their respective national forces when they got to England. This also applied to me, although my status was complicated by the fact that I was officially stateless. Since I was born in Poland, it should have followed that I would join the free Polish forces based in England, but the Polish officials in Paris had refused to issue me a Polish passport; they had informed me very emphatically that they no longer recognized me as a Polish citizen. My intention, when I got to England, was to assert my allegiance to Canada and join the Canadian forces.

It was still amazing to me that, in addition to being free, I now also had the freedom to achieve whatever goal I set for myself. Being released from incarceration was like recovering from a lengthy illness, like surfacing from darkness into bright sunshine and fresh air. When I woke up the morning after my first night's sleep in freedom and saw light streaming in through the window, the realization that I was no longer a prisoner overwhelmed me. I got out of bed and went straight to the window, revelling in the sight of people freely coming and going. Rarely have I ever been so overcome with joy. That feeling was further enhanced when I went to the washroom and saw an ordinary, clean, white enamel sink with hot and cold running water, sweetly scented soap and soft fresh towels.

After washing up, I joined the others in the hotel dining room for breakfast. We had no idea what to expect next and speculation ran rampant – some of the suggestions were hilarious. In the middle of all this hilarity the British representative announced that we should prepare to leave for the railway station, where we would be boarding a train for Gibraltar. We were all surprised that our trip to Britain, which had already involved a journey from the province of Burgos in the north of Spain to Madrid in the centre of the country, would now also take us right down to the southern border with Gibraltar. Thanks to my training with OSE in Paris, I had a very good grasp of geography and knew where Gibraltar was. Under British sovereignty, the rocky peninsula was considered the gateway to the Mediterranean and was of very strategic importance.

In high spirits, we boarded the train for Gibraltar to complete the last lap of our journey to freedom. As the train sped along the tracks to its destination I couldn't help having some lingering anxiety of being intercepted by the Spanish Civil Guards and returned to Miranda. There was absolutely no chance of that happening, but my experiences had left me feeling insecure. My fears were soon allayed when we safely crossed the border into Gibraltar. Deafening shouts of "Hip, hip, hurrah!" reverberated through the group in various languages when we set foot on the free soil of British Gibraltar.

When we arrived in Gibraltar, we were driven to a military camp, assigned to sleeping quarters and given a meal, the same food rations as the enlisted men. For the rest of our stay, the military authorities didn't impose any restrictions on our movements, so we saw most of the area. One thing that stands out most was our visit with some servicemen to see the famous Barbary macaques, the only wild monkeys in Europe. That was a lot of fun, especially when a few comedians in our group began imitating the monkeys. After barely a week of rest, food and freedom, we had become just another bunch of high-spirited young fellows full of life. I remember Gibraltar as a haven where the sun shone under clear blue skies; our time there was like being at a vacation resort.

We were given little warning when it was time to leave and had some regrets about saying goodbye to Gibraltar. Strict wartime security regulations dictated that no one could know the exact time of departure or the name of the vessel that we would be sailing on and we boarded in absolute secrecy. Only on the following day, when our vessel was far out at sea, did we discover that we were part of an escorted convoy of eleven vessels because of the serious threat from German U-boats.

While we were in Gibraltar I had decided that it was my duty to serve the British in whatever capacity I could to defeat the Nazis, regardless of the danger. For a Jewish person in particular, no sacrifice would have been too great in the battle to defeat them. I volunteered my services wholeheartedly at the army camp, deeming it an honour and a privilege to serve. But I had hardly had a chance to get used to the army routine before we all now had to learn to live as sailors. The transition went fairly smoothly, except for my first experience of sleeping in a hammock. Trying to sleep while suspended in mid-air between two posts is not easy if you've never experienced it. I kept thinking that the hammock would flip over while I was sleeping and I would fall flat on my face on the hard floor. That first night, I spent long sleepless hours before exhaustion finally took over. I woke up to find my fears unfounded – I had managed to stay safely face up in my hammock. The very real threat of German U-boats was far more serious, though. They prowled the Atlantic corridors searching for Allied vessels and posed so much danger that our convoy was forced to travel far out of its way to avoid being intercepted, coming within six hundred kilometres of the Canadian coast. Under normal conditions the trip from Gibraltar to England would take no more than a day or two whereas our journey lasted for eleven days.

Britain was experiencing some victories in the war at this time.

In December 1941 they had taken the upper hand in the North African campaign, driving Rommel's forces clear across Cyrenaica to El Agheila. This news further buoyed our sense of optimism, which reached a high point when some members of our group sighted land and a great cheer rose up. In a flash, most of us raced to the deck to see Liverpool in the distance.

After we had docked and disembarked, we were taken to a military camp and interviewed one at a time by a British officer. I was interrogated very thoroughly and then, in a painful blow to my expectations, assigned to the Polish armed forces. I was appalled. Without even trying to hide my resentment, I told my interviewer, "Sir, you need to understand that the Polish government has refused to recognize me as a Polish citizen, that I do not speak a word of Polish and that, as far as I'm concerned, the Poles are extremely antisemitic." It didn't matter what I said, though. The officer was completely unmoved and insisted that his word was final. Here in Britain, he added, I had to do as I was told.

I felt completely humiliated and tried to explain that my intention wasn't to avoid being inducted into the armed forces. Far from it – joining up had been my sole reason for coming to Britain. But I couldn't join the Polish forces. I pleaded with the officer to understand my position and allow me to join the Canadian or British forces, both of which it would be my honour to serve. The British officer heard me out but didn't change his position. I didn't realize at the time that official government policy barred foreigners from joining the British forces. For the first time since my liberation, I lost some of my exuberance.

As it turned out, this was not the end of the matter and the final verdict I received within the week was a surprise. At a second interview with a different officer, I was told that I would be excluded entirely from the armed forces. He explained that there was simply no regulation that would allow a foreigner to join the British forces, but as an alternative he would find me some kind of employment that was vital to the war effort. He then asked whether I would be interested in working in a sugar beet factory. Caught completely by surprise, I hesitantly replied that I still preferred to serve in the armed forces, but since that was no longer an option, I would do anything that would contribute to the war effort. The fact that a young refugee boy was given a choice of employment at all showed how well the British treated me.

The day after the interview, the British officials had made arrangements to send me to the city of York, in the north of England, to start a job in the lime kiln of a sugar beet factory. They had also arranged accommodation for me, sharing a room with another fellow, a black man. Unfortunately, I can only describe my first meeting with him as weird. First he didn't acknowledge my greeting, and then he rushed toward me as though he was going to hit me. When I tried to calm him down, he glared at me contemptuously. His eyes filled with hatred, scaring the hell out of me, and he said, "You must think you're a better person than I am because you're white and I'm black."

I was shocked by his accusation and retorted, "My dear friend, as a Jew, how can I possibly be prejudiced? I love all people regardless of race or the colour of their skin." But he continued to hurl accusations at me and, terrifying me even more, produced a switchblade. I pretended that I wasn't afraid and told him that I was going to sleep, praying all the time that I would come out of this predicament alive. I guess that calmed him down somehow, and we didn't exchange another word for the rest of that night.

The following morning, I got up early while he was still asleep, dressed quietly and rushed out of the room. Once I was safely out on the street, I heaved a tremendous sigh of relief and went straight to the appointment that the authorities had set up for me with a social worker. She was a very nice woman and I felt comfortable with her. She began by asking me how I had enjoyed my first night in York and when I told her about the horrifying night I had just endured, she was aghast and contacted the police. She immediately started looking for new accommodations for me, assuring me that in the next place I would have a room to myself. When I went back to see her some time later, she told me that a doctor had found my first roommate to be severely mentally disturbed and apologized for my terrible experience. True to her word, she placed me in a boarding house with my own room and all my meals included. All the other boarders were from Ireland, having come to England to work on the construction of new airfields. I settled into my new living quarters and looked forward to a peaceful night's sleep and the start of my first job in England.

Unfortunately, my first job only lasted three weeks. Working in the lime kiln entailed shovelling heavy bricks of lime into a wheelbarrow, wheeling the load to the huge blast furnace, shovelling the contents into the furnace and returning to a different place to fill the same wheelbarrow with coke. This was repeated all day long and it required great physical strength. In a weakened state from my long incarceration in Spain, the job was simply beyond my physical capabilities. The intense heat from the furnace also exhausted me by the end of the day. I might have been able to tackle the job after about six months of recuperation, but even then, given my background of tailoring and office work, I might never have been up to such hard physical labour.

At first I tried to persevere, but I had a change of heart when I had to spend my only day off lying in bed all day, all my joints stiff and aching. I realized that I should change jobs before I got seriously injured. I set up an appointment with my social worker and during the interview I told her about my past so that she could understand why I was so weak. She was shocked to hear what I had endured and said that she would do whatever she could to improve my situation. Through her kind efforts, I got an appointment with a gentleman named Mr. Edwards, who was a social worker with the labour exchange.

Mr. Edwards worked in York but lived in Leeds, about forty kilometres southwest, and we soon developed a friendship. A tall, lean and affable man, his mission in life was to help people in any way he could. He found me a new job as a milkman and, when he got to know me better, invited me to have Sunday dinner with him and his family. I didn't realize until we set out in his car to drive from York to Leeds that his wife was Jewish, which lent a special significance to my invitation to dinner. I had barely been in England for four weeks and the excitement of my liberation was beginning to wear off, replaced by loneliness. Mrs. Edwards was the first Jewish person I met in England.

When Mr. Edwards pulled up in front of his house, his wife and their two grown sons greeted us on the steps. We went into the house, where Mrs. Edwards served a traditional English Sunday dinner of roast beef and Yorkshire pudding. Everyone was very curious about my escape from France and asked me lots of questions. I not only enjoyed the company and the dinner but also got some valuable information from Mrs. Edwards about the various Jewish organizations in Leeds. This gave me the first opportunity to do something to help my friends in Miranda because there were no Jewish organizations in York. Leeds had a sizeable Jewish population, whereas there were almost no Jews living in York.

Before I returned to York with Mr. Edwards, I thanked him and his family for the best day I had spent in England so far. On our drive back I asked Mr. Edwards if he could use his influence to get me permission to take a day off work to return to Leeds to contact one of the Jewish organizations. Later that week, Mr. Edwards told me that he had gotten permission for me to take Friday off. On Thursday night, I carefully put in my wallet the letter that my Danish Jewish friend had asked me to deliver to an appropriate Jewish agency.

I lay awake all Thursday night, rehearsing over and over in my mind what I would say to concisely describe my experiences. I didn't want to let my friends down and ruin their chances for release by failing to convey how terrible the conditions in the camp were. The organization had to understand that leaving the prisoners where they were for much longer would jeopardize their chances for survival. They had to believe that what I was telling them was the absolute truth. Ninety suffering people were depending on me.

On Friday morning I got up early to take the train to Leeds. As soon as I arrived I asked for directions to the Leeds Jewish Refugee Committee (JRC) and requested a meeting with the director, explaining to the woman at reception that the matter was urgent. Within fifteen minutes I was led into the director's office, where two women sat with him. After introductions, the director asked me how I had managed to get into the country under the war restrictions. I responded that before talking about myself, I would like to speak on behalf of ninety desperate Jews who faced sickness and starvation if they didn't get assistance.

I told them about the Jewish prisoners in the Miranda concentration camp who, like me, had all fled their home countries to escape Hitler's tyranny, trying to travel through Spain to reach Portugal. Like myself, many of them had been prisoners for almost a year or more and were living under unsanitary and crowded conditions, infested with lice and fleas, on little more than a starvation diet. Most of the inmates were suffering from dysentery. Throughout my incarceration in Miranda, I continued, my own weight had dropped from sixty-one kilograms to just over thirty-eight kilograms. In addition to being extremely undernourished, the prisoners were forced to perform hard physical labour. I added that I had spent a total of thirty-six days in three different Spanish jails before eventually ending up in the Miranda concentration camp.

I concluded by telling them that my report was by no means a full account of the horrible circumstances faced by the Jewish inmates of Miranda. To supplement and corroborate my statement, I gave them the letter entrusted to me by the former Jewish leader from Denmark. As the director read the letter aloud, his expression showed outrage and revulsion. When it came to the portion of the letter where the writer said that if he were to spend another harsh winter in Miranda he doubted whether he would live through it, that he implored them to come to their assistance, the director could barely speak and the two women were in tears.

As soon as he regained his composure, the director commended

me for safeguarding the letter and bringing such important information to his attention. He assured me that he would do everything in
his power to bring immediate relief to the prisoners in Miranda, that
he would contact the Central Council for Jewish Refugees in London
at once to report on our meeting. Before I left they thanked me and
asked me to leave my name and address so they could keep me posted. I felt as if a heavy burden had been lifted from my shoulders. I
was grateful to have been able to help my friends, so much so that I
wrote to them that very same day about my successful meeting with
the J R C. Within about six months, I learned that the J R C officials had
managed to secure visas for all ninety Jewish prisoners in Miranda to
immigrate to the United States. No news could have given me greater
pleasure and I'm proud to have played some part in it.

On my return home from Leeds that day, I felt both a sense of
accomplishment and good about once again being in the company
of Jews. I began to think about how I could make that a regular part
of my life. As I've mentioned, there were practically no Jews in York,
so the obvious answer was for me to move to the hub of the Jewish
community – the city of London. I looked into how much the travel
to London would cost and realized that it would take at least another
several weeks of work to save enough for the train fare.

Over the next couple of weeks I managed to save enough money
to start making plans for my move to London. I had made every decision so far in consultation with Mr. Edwards and sought his approval
for this one as well. Although he was reluctant to see me leave, he
nevertheless understood why I wanted to go to London. He reminded me that I would have to report my move to the York police and
report to the London police when I arrived. After the York police
gave me permission to go, I reported back to Mr. Edwards. At our
last encounter he wished me the very best, adding he would be very
pleased to hear from me when I got settled. I packed my few belongings into a small suitcase, including my very first purchase in Britain,
a safety razor that I amazingly still have after all these years.

Breakdown

By sometime in February 1942 I was on a train to London, reflecting on my time in England. I felt thwarted by my inability to join the British or Canadian armed forces, my prime reason for coming to the country in the first place. I felt lonely and inadequate, unable to engage in what I considered any useful service, unsure of what direction my life should take. It was quite a contrast to the optimism of my joyous arrival in England only two short months ago.

It was in this state that I arrived in London and was directed by the Jewish Board of Guardians to a Jewish shelter, where I was introduced to a lovely middle-aged Jewish woman. She commented on how terribly undernourished I looked and said, "We'll soon get him back to a healthy weight." From that moment on, she fussed over me like a true Jewish mother, feeding me the most tasty and nourishing meals I'd had in years. I'm so sorry that I was later unable to recall her name so that I could thank her for her kindness during a very vulnerable stage of my life. She eased my loneliness and truly made me feel at home, reminding me of my own mother. It was wonderful to be able to talk to her in Yiddish, my *mameh loshen* (mother tongue).

This kind woman didn't only make sure that I was well fed, she also gave me the opportunity to meet young Jewish girls at the shelter's weekly dances. At one of these dances I met a girl whom I danced with and talked to for the whole evening, and after the dance I es-

corted her home. When we got to her apartment building, to my surprise, she invited me in to meet her parents. I was shocked to see the
poverty in which the family lived – the small two-room flat reminded
me of my own miserable past in Paris. There and then I resolved not
to enter into any long-term relationships with girls for the duration
of the war, to first establish myself in a career so that I could earn
enough to properly support a family. Besides, I was only twenty years
old, too young to tie myself down.

Three weeks after I arrived at the shelter, I had my first interview with the Jewish Board of Guardians. They placed me in a home
owned by a Jewish woman named Miss Jacobs, where I shared a room
with another Jewish refugee approximately my age. Since I had some
skills in the needle trade, they also set up a job interview for me with
a cloak manufacturer the following day. Everything finally seemed
to be moving in the right direction, although I was sorry to leave
the Jewish shelter and my guardian angel. I settled into my first real
Jewish home away from home with Miss Jacobs and at first all went
well. She was a refined, intelligent and accomplished housekeeper
who, despite British food rationing, managed to produce nourishing and tasty meals. Although she did her utmost to make us feel at
home, I have to say that she was not as warm and compassionate as
the Jewish woman from the shelter. I also had difficulty striking up
a friendship with my roommate. He was always courteous, but he
had already established friendships and for the most part he kept his
distance. I never let on to what extent my feelings were hurt by his
aloofness.

The Jewish owner of the ladies' cloak factory hired me without
hesitation when he discovered my proficiency as a sewing-machine
operator. When I was directed to the main factory, which had two
rows of sewing machines, twenty on either side, and was placed at a
sewing machine, I found that sitting directly across from me was the
most beautiful girl I had ever laid eyes on. I was dazzled, but my shyness with girls inhibited me from talking to her. She was my dream

girl, so much so that her presence interfered with my concentration; all I wanted to do was wrap my arms around her. Knowing only too well that this was likely only a fantasy on my part, I tried to keep my composure. A number of other girls sat on either side of her, but none could hold a candle to her startling beauty.

Although she was a brunette and I was generally more attracted to blonds, I couldn't resist her. She was about my height, with a statuesque figure that curved in all the right places, a pair of legs to match and a smooth, creamy complexion. Her high cheek bones added depth to her intelligent looks, as did her piercing black eyes, and she had a perfectly sculpted nose, cherry-tinted lips and long, black, silky hair. Seeing this heavenly creature in the middle of a shmatte (clothing) factory somehow did not seem appropriate, but I learned that she was a Jewish refugee from Poland.

After several weeks, I summoned up the courage to ask her out, offering to take her to dinner and a show. My heart pounded while I waited for her reply. My assumption that she wouldn't even consider going out with me proved correct when she turned me down cold. In addition to feeling humiliated, I had to suffer the torture of facing her every day at work and it began to wear on me. My sense of inadequacy from the rejection gradually became so extreme that I started to behave irrationally. I have no explanation for the fact that for years I had been fully capable of coping with matters of life and death under the most adverse conditions yet could not cope with this personal situation. It doesn't make sense, but the more I tried to accept my lot, the more complicated my reactions became.

Working in the factory turned into an unhappy experience and returning home to spend my nights alone in my room was very depressing. I decided that I had to find a way to change my situation, but rejected most of my ideas as impractical. One day, however, I had a brainwave: I would go back to Liverpool, some three hundred kilometres from London, and apply to join the Merchant Navy. This idea appealed to me for a variety of reasons, not the least of which was the fact that I might be able to get assigned to a freighter going to South America. Now that I was in England I had been corresponding with my parents and sister regularly and was very eager to see them.

I figured out that I would have to work for at least another four weeks to save up enough money for the trip. Unfortunately, it didn't even occur to me to check whether my plan was viable, nor did it occur to me to seek help from any of the Jewish organizations or try to make friends in London through any of the Jewish activities. I was becoming more and more introverted and afraid to try to connect with other people. I think that a number of factors contributed to my condition, especially my extreme loneliness, but I have no doubt that if I had had more education I would have been able to better understand my problems and come up with a possible solution. I knew absolutely nothing about psychological stress at the time.

Since I was spending all my time after work alone, I resorted to poring over the daily newspaper, which served both as a morale booster and kept my mind occupied. The newspapers had been full of encouraging war news since I arrived in England. During December 1941 and January 1942, the Soviets had succeeded in stemming the German advances towards Leningrad, Moscow and Sevastopol. The shocking bombing of Pearl Harbor by the Japanese had brought the good news that the Americans had come into the war on the side of the Allies. Any mention of an Allied success became a source of encouragement and hope. In particular, the reports of Allied air raids on German war plants worked miracles in raising my spirits.

In this favourable atmosphere I continued my preparations to travel to Liverpool. I hadn't accumulated very many possessions during my short stay in England and everything I owned fit neatly into one small suitcase. The money I had saved would barely cover the cost of a week's lodging, so if I needed a return fare to London, I would be broke. I had also foolishly made the mistake of writing to my parents about my intentions without having first checked out my plan. I was so enthusiastic about the prospect of seeing them again that it never dawned on me that anything could go wrong. Even worse, I gave up my lodgings without even giving Miss Jacobs, who depended on the income from her boarders, the courtesy of notice. I was hesitant about revealing my real motives for joining the Merchant Navy and I didn't have the heart to tell her that I considered this to be a permanent move. It was a heartless way to repay someone for their kind treatment. In one irresponsible move I managed to hurt both my wonderful landlady and myself by delving into uncharted waters.

As soon as I arrived in Liverpool, I asked for directions to the Merchant Navy headquarters. To my horror, after a very brief interview, they rejected me outright. I was upset and angry at what I perceived to be a complete injustice. It simply hadn't occurred to me that the same regulations that had prevented me from joining the British or Canadian armed forces also applied to the Merchant Navy. Since I wasn't a British subject, I couldn't serve.

The shock of being turned down affected me deeply. For the first time in my life, my entire nervous system went off kilter and threw me into a panic that caused facial tremors that particularly affected my lips. I was, in fact, having a complete nervous breakdown. I had never before been seized by feelings of such utter helplessness. My condition was clearly very serious, but I could neither accept nor understand it and tried to just carry on without seeking help.

It was late in the afternoon and I was hungry by the time I left the Merchant Navy headquarters, so I first went to a restaurant and then looked for a room for the night. When I found one, I asked the proprietor for a telephone book to find out whether there were any Jewish organizations in Liverpool. Sure enough, several were listed and I resolved to visit them the following morning. I had very little money left, so I needed their help to find a job.

At this point, I didn't really care whether I worked in Liverpool or London, since there was nothing waiting for me in either place. I arrived early for an interview with the Jewish agency and, after the person in charge talked to me at length, I was temporarily placed with a nice elderly Jewish couple. Before the week was up the agency told me that they had decided to transfer me to Manchester, where there was a hostel that catered exclusively to young Jewish refugees. That sounded like exactly what I needed. Unfortunately, time would show that their help had come too late to repair the damage to my mental health.

I travelled to Manchester by train courtesy of the Jewish agency. I had to go to a temporary shelter for Jewish refugee families called Kershaw House until a space opened up in the Jewish refugee youth hostel. There were very few young people there – only one couple had a daughter and son my age. The girl was quite pretty and three or four years younger than me, roughly sixteen or seventeen. Although she was very appealing, our friendship remained platonic. Her mother was overprotective and suspicious of my intentions toward her daughter, so, to my great frustration, any communication with her was limited to the few moments when her parents were not around.

The labour exchange soon provided me with a job in a ladies' garment factory as a sewing-machine operator. It was a relief to start working because it not only gave me the means to earn a living but also distracted me from my anxieties. In the evenings, I wrote letters to my parents and sister, though I never let on that anything was wrong. On the contrary, I was careful to only relay encouraging news. I also wrote to my two aunts in Winnipeg, but to them, I didn't hold anything back about my emotional health. I knew that they wouldn't be as affected by the news as my mother and writing to them gave me a good outlet.

When they replied many months later, my aunts chose to omit any reference to my illness and instead only addressed totally irrelevant matters. I was hoping for a few words of sympathy, but all I got were generalities. They kept to their philosophy of not wanting their serene lives disrupted; it's as if they were saying, "If you don't have any good news to report, don't tell us anything." Only much later would Aunt Sadie realize that there were serious repercussions from her lack of response to my situation.

After little more than a month I was transferred from Kershaw House to the Jewish refugee youth hostel at 25 Northumberland Street in Salford, Manchester. The hostel was in a huge mansion that had been converted to create numerous bedrooms. There were probably about thirty or forty refugees living there, all of them from either Germany or Austria. Their parents had managed to send them out of the country on the Kindertransport, the British-organized rescue of Jewish children from western Europe in 1938–1939. Most of them were close to my age, between sixteen and twenty-one. Their backgrounds varied, although they all came from affluent, well-educated families, which was evident in their behaviour and refined manners, and their appreciation for fine art and classical music. Quite a number of them had had training in playing musical instruments, including the piano. It took no time at all for me to discover that I was living with an elite group of young people with whom I had absolutely nothing in common. Amazingly, though, many were very modest and did their best to put me at ease.

On the main floor of the house was a large dining room that was next to a completely enclosed kitchen, except for a small pass-through with a wide flat ledge in front of which we lined up to get our meals. The dining room led to a hallway and two recreation rooms, one of which contained a piano. Both rooms had fireplaces that were only lit during the winter months and we spent a great deal of our leisure time in those two spacious rooms. Some people read while others listened to classical music. There were also a few people who simply sat in silence, staring into the fireplace. We all felt the same desire to be free to resume our old lives once again; we all sensed that our youth was withering away during a war that had no end in sight. None of my companions were going to pieces as I was, though. If anything, they all displayed patience and an optimistic attitude. They were a tough breed of young people who, although separated from their parents and relatives, were not going to let the war get them down. They tried to make the best of every day.

Our sleeping quarters and the bathroom were upstairs. In addition to the efficient kitchen staff was Mr. Hughes, a gentile Englishman who served as the hostel's social worker and supervisor. He was a truly thoughtful and caring individual who had our welfare at heart. As a young Jewish refugee, the hostel was everything I could have hoped for under wartime conditions. It gave me the opportunity to once again be with companions my own age, many of whom became my friends.

Unfortunately, however, my mental condition continued to deteriorate. I could no longer function without being periodically overcome by severe anxiety, which eroded my self-confidence. As time passed, I developed an uncontrollable twitching of my mouth that caused me great embarrassment. Despite my efforts to control it, I began to avoid people as much as possible. How pathetically ironic that just when, at long last, I had found a home with friends that I so desperately needed, I felt compelled to isolate myself.

The events leading up to my breakdown had started long before I came to England and was rejected by the armed forces and the Merchant Navy. There was, for example, the trauma I experienced as a young boy who could not return home to the country in which he spent the happiest and most secure years of his life – Canada. I had also met my father after a ten-year separation only to find him sickly and destitute, unable to support himself let alone his family. Then there were the four years during which my father had had the ever-present threat of deportation hanging over his head and his erratic behaviour constantly erupted into violent fights with my mother. Then came the occupation of France, my enforced separation from my family, my perilous escape and my eleven months of incarceration in Spain.

Had I been allowed to join the British or Canadian armed forces when I arrived in England or been placed right away in a refugee youth hostel with other young men my age, my condition might never have surfaced. As it was, I lost my ability to withstand all the pent-up pressures of my circumstances. The harder I fought to resist, the more confused and frustrated I became. The ongoing struggle to keep my anxiety in check while trying desperately to maintain a normal, healthy façade and perform my job well was a very demanding task. I was always exhausted by the end of the day.

I didn't understand the nature of my illness at the time, but I had to finally admit that there was something terribly wrong. I thought that my anxiety had to be a symptom of a physical disease – it never occurred to me that it could be mental illness. The symptoms were not only incomprehensible to me, but the very thought of being mentally ill was repugnant. I could never see myself in that light. I had an image of myself as a healthy, robust, daring individual. Now the very foundation of my manhood and self-esteem was being seriously undermined.

When a neurotic condition affects an adolescent male just at the point when he wants the companionship of young women, the experience can be terrifying and demoralizing, especially if it includes a paralyzing fear and a desire to disappear into thin air. It's hard not to think of suicide as an escape, but in a moment of calm you think about the people who will be hurt by your actions. In my case, I thought about my mother. My love for her took precedence over any personal anguish I was feeling and controlled the destructive thoughts I was having.

The most surprising development during this awful period happened one evening at dinner. Directly opposite me sat two lovely girls who shared the same room and were close friends. I summoned the courage to talk to one of them, a girl named Kitty, and she actually seemed to be interested in me. We became good friends and our relationship eventually resulted in a courtship that I wasn't at all prepared for.

Kitty was a pretty, rosy-cheeked girl about my height with a sparkling personality and a fine figure. Our courtship started off gradually by meeting in one of the recreation rooms and, as we got to know each other better, discussing more personal issues. She was from Vienna, Austria, and, like everyone else at the hostel, was from a fairly comfortable background. Her father was a successful merchant and both he and her mother had been active members of the Jewish community. She had a very pleasant disposition and a refreshingly cool temperament. In the evenings, Kitty treated me to biscuits and a hot cup of cocoa that she prepared in her room on a tiny alcohol burner. We enjoyed the cocoa and each other's company, talking until it was time to go to bed. One of her hobbies was knitting and after we'd been friends for a number of months, she surprised me with a beautiful pair of wool socks that she had knitted herself. Everything about her was special and my attraction to her grew stronger.

Our friendship continued to develop and there was no doubt that she had a calming effect on me, but deep down I remained troubled. Sadly, I realized that I wasn't in love with her, so I decided that I shouldn't lead her on. I felt guilty and, not wanting to take advantage of her good nature, I reluctantly decided that I should tell her as soon as possible. It's quite possible that my condition led me to make this hasty decision, but no matter what the reason, the sad outcome was the break-up of our beautiful friendship. Kitty and I had not been intimate beyond caresses and kissing, mainly because of my sexual inexperience, but she was my first serious relationship.

After I broke up with Kitty my mental condition continued to deteriorate until I realized that I could no longer function without help. I turned to Mr. Hughes, who stepped in to play a very significant role in this crisis. When I confided in him about my disturbed state, he set up an appointment for me with a female psychologist. I didn't know what a psychologist was, but it sounded impressive enough to suggest that she was a special kind of doctor who would help me get well. Completely ignorant of any kind of psychological treatment, I was disappointed to learn on my first visit that my treatment would consist exclusively of verbal sessions in which I was supposed to reveal and relive all my worst experiences.

After attending several such sessions with no noticeable improvement in my condition, my patience began to wear thin and I told Mr. Hughes how I felt. He consulted the psychologist on my behalf and they decided to try another approach. I was very disappointed that I wasn't being treated with some kind of medication. I thought that anything would be better than just talking about myself. Although I think that the psychologist was extremely competent, I also believe that her form of treatment wasn't suitable for my severe neurosis. I also believed that I needed someone with a Jewish background who could better understand everything I had gone through.

With my anxiety increasing, the psychologist recommended that I be referred to a psychoanalyst. When I paid my first visit to the new doctor, I was amazed to learn that he was not only Jewish, but also a refugee. He gained my complete confidence from our very first meeting. After doing a thorough analysis of my condition, which took a number of visits to his office, he diagnosed it as a serious nervous breakdown that required immediate and drastic treatment. He recommended that I be admitted to a hospital as soon as possible for electric shock therapy.

Unfortunately, the hospital where he wanted to send me was filled to capacity at the time and there was a considerable waiting period before they could admit me. That did little to relieve my anxieties and my condition further deteriorated to the point where I could no longer face anyone. The muscular spasms at my mouth had now extended to my eyelids and the reaction increased whenever I was with people, making me extremely self-conscious and embarrassed. My attempts at self-control didn't make any difference; I prayed for relief, but none was forthcoming. At my wit's end, I decided once again that suicide was the only solution that would release me from my misery. As soon as I made the decision, a sense of calm came over me.

Mentally drained and morally crushed, I had no more stamina to put up any resistance. I just wanted to vanish; with death would come the peace and tranquility I so longed for. I was barely two months from my twenty-first birthday in November 1942, and I wanted to be like any normal person my age, not a pathetic anxiety-ridden neurotic who couldn't face the world. I desperately missed my mother and the war was dragging on without any sign of an end. The thought of suicide was firmly entrenched – it was no longer a matter of will I or won't I, but when.

I was no longer concerned with how long it would take for me to be admitted to the hospital; instead I became obsessed with how soon I could bring my wretched life to a close. This should tell you how serious my illness was. Fortunately, at this critical juncture, the will of God guided me toward the rational, reminding me that I could never resort to any action that would hurt my mother. Whenever I sank into the depths of depression, it was as if a guardian angel appeared to prevent me from committing an irresponsible act. Somehow or other, I managed to weather the storm without succumbing to my emotional torment.

Finally, Mr. Hughes arranged for me to be admitted to the hospital. My first impression of the place was that it was extremely depressing. The dreary room I was assigned to contained a large number of beds lined up on two facing walls and I was plunked down roughly three-quarters of the way up the aisle. The doctor in charge of my case came to see me every day for nine days and each time he brought with him a huge electrical box. I could see him approaching from a distance as he made his way down the corridor. I remember with great trepidation the first time he appeared with the monstrous-looking contraption. Without a word of exaggeration, the very sight of it scared me to death, especially because I had no idea how it worked. The doctor reassured me, explaining that the machine would just knock me unconscious and I would wake up feeling better. His reassurances did little to diminish my fears and before I knew it, the headgear was placed over my head, snugly fitted against my temples, and a respirator placed over my nose. Within seconds a sudden jolt put me out like a light. I have no idea how long I was unconscious, but when the doctor came down the aisle the next day to administer my second jolt of electric shock therapy, I knew that he was the last person on earth I wanted to see.

Sometime during the course of those nine electric shock treatments, I turned twenty-one. Imagine spending one's most important birthday in the dreary confines of a hospital. I had never felt more abandoned, dejected and alone. One visitor did come to wish me happy birthday, though, and thoughtfully brought a special twenty-first birthday card in the shape of a key: it was none other than Mr. Hughes. I will always remember his considerate gesture with gratitude.

At the conclusion of the series of shock treatments, I was released from the hospital. Frankly, I don't remember much of what happened when I left – my thoughts felt very fuzzy. The traumatic effects of the electric shock therapy had severely impaired my thought processes, although this was fortunately only a temporary condition. It gradually improved with time.

I was taken back to the hostel and returned to the same room I had occupied previously. After a brief period of recuperation, I wanted to return to work at my old job, but I'm not sure that my health had really improved. In the short term, before the effects of the shock treatments wore off, my anxieties may have been temporarily dispelled. But before too many months elapsed, my condition began to gradually deteriorate again, prompting my psychoanalyst to conclude that I had not responded to the therapy and that my condition was getting much worse. Due to the very serious nature of my illness, he said that he would have to find an alternative treatment. The following week, he recommended that I be sent away for treatment to the Crichton Royal Hospital in Dumfries, Scotland, an institution for severe mental disorders that was the only one of its kind in all of Great Britain.

I was accepted to the Crichton, but getting there wasn't a smooth process. There wasn't a space for me right away so I was put on a waiting list. The institution apparently badly needed funding, so there was only one way to avoid a lengthy wait: the hospital was willing to shorten the waiting period for those who could pay the full fees without needing any government assistance. In those cases, the waiting period would be reduced to three or four months instead of anywhere from one to two years.

When I realized how impossible it would be for me to avoid the much longer wait for admission, I became distraught. I knew how seriously ill I had become and I had to do something. Maybe there was someone I could ask for a loan. But who? The obvious first choice was my parents, but I immediately dismissed the idea because they hardly earned enough to support themselves, let alone pay for expensive treatment and hospitalization, and I still didn't want to let my mother know how ill I was. That left only one other possibility – Aunt Sadie in Winnipeg. Although I was hesitant at first to approach her because of foolish pride, I ultimately accepted the fact that my health had to take precedence. I sent her an urgent telegram, pleading with her to help me.

After what felt like an eternity – in reality it was no more than three days – I received my aunt's reply. When I read her telegram, I could scarcely believe my eyes – she had actually agreed to pay for all my treatment! I was so surprised and relieved that the news made me laugh and cry at the same time. Whatever possessed her to help me this time, I will always be grateful to her.

At my next appointment with the psychoanalyst, I showed him my aunt's telegram. He was delighted and told me that he had confidence that I would soon be cured of my condition. He contacted the Crichton Royal Hospital and arranged for my admission in about four to five months. In the meantime I continued my regular routine as best I could. I started work at eight in the morning and returned to the hostel at six in the evening. After dinner, depending on how I was feeling, I either went to one of the recreation rooms to be with my friends or else avoided them altogether by spending the evening alone in my room. Most evenings I ended up doing the latter because being around people was an enormous strain. The constant mouth and eye tremors were still very present and humiliating. It felt easier to avoid people, but the more I alienated myself from them the more difficult it became to renew contact.

In this five-month limbo while I was awaiting admission to the Crichton, I became attracted to one of the most beautiful girls in our hostel, a girl named Helen. To my surprise, she seemed to feel a similar attraction to me because she often went out of her way to strike up a conversation with me. She personified everything I could possibly want in a girl, so, paradoxically, her very presence brought out all my anxieties. Whenever she tried to make conversation, I froze up and made some polite excuse to avoid her. She wasn't just beautiful – I also admired her intelligence, her grace and her charm. I longed for her companionship, so my inability to be with her was very painful.

Despite my discomfort with girls, I did manage to make a few good friends among the boys. Two of them were named Werner and Wolfgang, and there were a few others whose names I no longer recall. They were all sensitive and intelligent young men with quite a profound insight into psychological problems. I talked to them a little bit about my illness, but we mostly discussed the problem we had in common: our separation from family and friends. Unlike them, however, I would have parents to return to after the war; most of the young refugees in the shelter would learn with grief-stricken horror that theirs had been murdered in Nazi camps.

The months preceding my entry to the Crichton were for the most part bleak and dreary. My condition had destabilized to the point that my psychoanalyst had written to Aunt Sadie that my life was in danger. He assured her, though, that everything humanly possible would be done to pull me out of the crisis. I considered doing away with myself almost every day; life felt unbearable.

Looking for a Way Back

I arrived in Dumfries with mixed emotions. My illness had forced me to become acquainted with a relatively new field of medicine – the treatment of mental illness – that I had never heard of. Only a generation or two before, people with any kind of mental disorders were often locked away for life. The advances in medical science had come along just at the right time for me. At the same time, I was concerned about the stigma of being in a mental institution.

The Crichton Royal Hospital was situated in a beautiful park-like setting, nestled in a wooded area with green lawns and gardens, and cool, pure fresh air. There were a variety of facilities, including ones for sports such as tennis and cricket. From the outside, it looked almost like a holiday resort instead of a mental institution, but the inside and my first glimpse of the other patients unnerved me. Although some of them appeared to be quite normal, others were clearly disturbed beyond any reasonable hope for recovery. My first impulse was to flee. I couldn't stand the thought of being surrounded by deranged people and I was even less happy about being one of them. I continued to struggle with this throughout my confinement in Dumfries. I felt that the place was an affront to my dignity and might delay my recovery. Still, this was where people in my condition were treated.

Even though I had concerns about being in the Crichton, I had the good fortune to be treated by two outstanding psychoanalysts named Dr. Mayer-Gross and Dr. Berliner, both Jewish refugees from Germany who had fled the Nazis and been given asylum in the United Kingdom where they could practise their profession. No words can express my gratitude to them. They were so concerned for my well-being that for many years after I left Dumfries, they carried on a correspondence with Aunt Sadie to ask after my state of health.

I was taken to meet Dr. Mayer-Gross and Dr. Berliner the morning after I arrived in Dumfries. They conducted a lengthy interview and then gave me a complete physical examination. The next few days were devoted to various tests to determine my general mental condition. For example, they tested my recall capabilities by reading me short stories and then asking me questions about them. They made a point of choosing basic stories, about cowboys for example, that would match my limited education. After the tests, the doctors asked me for a detailed account of my past.

Dr. Berliner's professional approach soon won me over and I felt completely at ease in his presence. He had a gentle and persuasive manner that soon had me pouring my heart out to him, describing in great detail every aspect of my turbulent past and my present disturbing symptoms. Both doctors were present at my daily psychiatric sessions but Dr. Berliner took the lead. Based on their findings, the doctors decided that I should be treated with a series of insulin shock treatments, given by injection over sixty sessions. The treatment would begin the very next day, overseen by Dr. Mayer-Gross. Of course, I had no idea what insulin shock was. Nowadays, when some people are appalled at the mention of insulin shock therapy, my response to them is that it saved my life. I'm convinced that doctors Mayer-Gross and Berliner used the best methods available at the time and were genuinely trying to help me.

In my opinion, someone who has suffered a severe mental breakdown will never fully recover from its effects nor be entirely free of occasional anxieties. This doesn't mean that the person cannot be restored to a level of mental stability, function as normally as any other individual and succeed in all endeavours consistent with his ability and intelligence. In order to prevent a relapse, however, it is extremely important to take precautions, to engage in recreational and physical activities and, above all, to engage socially with friends and avoid being alone. These activities are mentally stimulating and help to contribute to a sense of fulfillment and self-esteem.

During my treatment in Dumfries, I was woken up every morning at the crack of dawn and taken to a room in the hospital with several beds where the insulin shock treatment was administered. Hours after the treatment I would come out of an unconscious state with an intense thirst, craving something sweet. Within minutes a nurse would appear, carrying a tray of what I later learned was a lemon-flavoured glucose drink. I had never heard of or tasted glucose, but I must confess that nothing ever tasted so good. As a matter of fact I craved it so badly that I asked for a second and even third glass and even then I didn't feel that my thirst was quenched. Every time I had a treatment I looked forward to that lemon-flavoured glucose.

Over time, I became accustomed to the institutional environment and gradually got to know some of the other patients. A number of them were air force pilots and there was a gentle and considerate parson who taught me to play chess. I was also introduced to and thoroughly enjoyed tennis and cricket. One of the male nurses taught me to play tennis and I took to it like a duck to water. I played as often as I could. All the recreational activities helped the patients recuperate. My overall attitude toward the institution itself varied with my mood. Sometimes I saw the place as a sanctuary where I could recover my health; at other times, it was nothing but an asylum for the mentally disturbed and hopelessly insane. The simplest of events on any given day could affect my mood. The line between feeling at peace or feeling hopelessly frustrated was extremely narrow and it didn't take much to upset my equilibrium. The daily see-saw was just one more symptom of my illness. Sometimes I could see a glimmer of hope, yet on other days I felt that I would never get better.

When my course of insulin shock treatments concluded, some-time between the third and the fourth month of my confinement, in August or September 1943, I saw a marked improvement in my con-dition. I was experiencing fewer depressive episodes, my twitching was easing off and I was starting to put on weight. Feeling much bet-ter and buoyed with a little confidence, my therapy sessions with the doctor began to centre around the possibility of my being released. I was restless and assumed that I was well enough to face the outside world. The doctors, however, didn't share my optimism; they made it very clear that they thought it would take much more time before they felt confident in declaring me fit enough to leave.

This disagreement turned into quite a bone of contention between us. I became so focused on leaving the institution that I found it hard to listen to the doctors' reasons for disagreeing with me. Oblivious to their logic and unable to believe that they were acting in my best in-terest, we reached an impasse and I decided to go on a hunger strike if they did not release me at once. It goes without saying that my decision was irresponsible, naïve and self-defeating, for it had a det-rimental effect on my recovery. My hunger strike lasted for ten days, at which point the medical staff locked me up in the area set aside for the incurably insane. Eventually, when I was threatened with forced feeding, my resistance broke down and I reverted to being a model patient. I spent every day in a variety of activities that left little time for anything else and I accepted whatever was happening to me in good faith.

This attitude paid off handsomely because one day past my six months there, the doctors summoned me to their office and inter-viewed me at length about how I was feeling. Without the slightest hesitation, I told them that I felt well and this time I really meant it. At the end of their interview, Dr. Mayer-Gross and Dr. Berliner pro-nounced me well enough to leave the institution, but cautioned me that they still thought I should stay for at least another six months. I was gratified that they had decided that I was well enough to leave, but torn and confused about their advice to stay. The doctors advised me to think it over for a few days and report back to them.

My initial reaction was that of course I would leave. The thought of being able to resume a normal life was irresistible, far outweighing any other consideration. Even though I had some lingering doubts about not taking their advice, being in a place like the Crichton Royal Hospital wasn't something I wanted to prolong or remember. I wanted to bury that part of my past and everything associated with it. What was important was forging ahead with my life. That night I lay down to sleep with a renewed optimism, thinking of how close I was to spending my last days in Dumfries. It had been gratifying to hear that I made such a good recovery. I would now have to figure out how to maintain some stability in my life.

The day finally arrived for me to leave the Crichton Royal Hospital. Although my determination to go had not waned, the thought of facing the outside world filled me with fear and insecurity. I wasn't sure that I could go back to being with people. Still, I have to confess that one reason that I was eager to leave Dumfries is that I was thinking about the possibility of making up with Kitty. I had no idea whether she could ever forgive me for hurting her, but I couldn't stop thinking about falling into her embrace. That gave me something to look forward to and knowing that I dared hope again showed how far I'd come.

I returned to the hostel in late fall 1943, at a time of day when everyone was still at work. My old room had been held for me and some of my things were still there. I had my first chance to see everybody when we gathered in the dining room for the evening meal. Everyone made an effort to put me at ease and make me feel welcome. They avoided asking me any questions about my stay in Dumfries and focused instead on my plans for the future. A number of them told me how well I looked. It was very encouraging, if a little strained, but they really helped me overcome my first hurdle, my re-introduction to the real world.

Mr. Hughes had picked me up at the railway station and we had
had a chance to talk on the drive to the hostel. He asked how I was
doing and what kind of work I wanted to do. I hadn't considered
giving up the needle trade, but Mr. Hughes had apparently received
advice from my doctors that I should work in a quieter environment,
free from the unremitting noise of the sewing machines. I agreed that
a new trade was a good idea, but wasn't sure what I could do with my
limited education. I couldn't really afford to do another extended apprenticeship for little or no income because I would have to earn my
keep. I asked Mr. Hughes to help me choose what to do. He suggested
that I try working as an assistant window dresser and several days
later found me a job with the renowned firm of Marks & Spencer on
Market Street.

The job started smoothly, then ended rather abruptly three weeks
later because of the abusive way I was treated by the store manager.
I reported my grievances to Mr. Hughes and told him that I would
much rather return to my trade in the ladies' garment industry than
work under those conditions. Before long Mr. Hughes was able to get
me my old job as a sewing-machine operator. I stayed there until I
left Manchester.

After a six-month silence while I was in Dumfries, I resumed my
correspondence with my parents. I didn't have the heart to tell my
mother anything about my nervous breakdown and treatment, so I
made up a variety of excuses for not having written to her. I also suggested that some of the mail might have gotten lost.

My life went back to its normal routine again. I went to work every morning and returned to the hostel in time for dinner. In the
evening I got together with my friends in the recreation room, where
we talked and listened to classical music until it was time for bed.
After several weeks I worked up enough confidence to apologize to
Kitty and try to make up with her. I was very nervous, but decided to
plunge in. As soon as I got close to her, my heart pounding, I immediately sensed her resentment. When I started telling her how sorry I

was for my past behaviour, for hurting her feelings, I broke out into a cold sweat because she completely ignored me. Her only reaction was to give me a defiant stare and dash away from me. Later that night, while I was lying in bed, I reviewed the whole incident. Although I was hurt and deeply humiliated, I accepted Kitty's reaction with regret. Kitty had managed to simultaneously hold on to her dignity and give me a taste of my own medicine.

After Kitty rejected me I really began to experience for the first time the stigma associated with being recently released from a mental institution. I also became aware that my illness had changed my appearance – I had developed premature balding and had deep shadows under my eyes. Once again my self-esteem and morale began to sink and I suffered acute embarrassment every time I tried to talk to a young woman. When I left the Crichton, my self-confidence was still fragile. It could have been completely undermined by the incident with Kitty, but although I felt hurt and embarrassed by the encounter, I still maintained a flicker of hope, remembering what we used to say in France: "Eh bien, tant pis mon vieux. Tu a raté ta chance." (Oh well, too bad, old man. You missed your chance.) I was bruised and humbled but not defeated. Nonetheless, I wasn't sure if I could weather the storm and, even though I craved companionship, I was unable to socialize with girls without being overwhelmed by fear.

~

For the rest of the war years – from the late fall of 1943 to the spring of 1945 – my mental and emotional stability continued to go up and down, depending on what was going on in my life. For one thing, I continued to struggle with relationships with various young women and was frustrated by my inability to experience a satisfying sexual relationship. But there certainly were many days when things went well. After work I could always look forward to socializing with my friends at the hostel. We enjoyed taking long walks, listening to classical music, playing darts, having friendly discussions and, at least once a week, seeing a movie. Often, we wound up going to the huge Manchester public library. I had never read much other than newspapers and magazines before this, and found reading books extremely difficult.

It wasn't until I was in my mid-fifties, after I retired, that I began to read books, and then it was only out of a desire to learn about the history of my own people. Even at that late date, it was hard for me to learn to concentrate on what I was reading. My fascination with Jewish history gave me the motivation to work on my reading skills; I wanted to discover everything there was to know. More than five years of continuous reading, even at a comparatively slow pace, also gave me the incentive to write my memoirs. Once the idea took hold there was no holding me back – I wanted to complete the project while I was still relatively young and my memories were still fresh.

In early spring 1944, I received the startling news from my parents that my sister, Clarice, had left the safety of Argentina and was now on a ship heading for war-ravaged England. I couldn't understand why she would embark on such a dangerous venture. If she had known about the hardships I had experienced during my flight from the Nazis, she might have had second thoughts about coming to a war zone. I was also concerned that her seeing me so changed might lead her to ask why I had never told them about the severity of my mental breakdown. Nonetheless, I had been separated from my family for almost five years and although I disagreed with Clarice putting herself in danger, I was excited about her imminent arrival.

After five years of war, people in Britain were war-weary and it showed on their faces. They were faced with every conceivable restriction, from rationing of food and clothing to blackouts and censored mail. Though food was available in sufficient quantities, we weren't able to get the necessary proteins, fats and, in particular, fresh fruits. Single civilians in wartime Britain were not able to obtain any of these nutrients, including fresh milk.

It was also a time when families were separated, with most of the men serving in the armed forces all over the world and longing to be reunited with their families. Nevertheless the British were a hardy people, bearing their lot in silence, outwardly resilient and proud. And we were inspired by the encouraging speeches by British prime minister Winston Churchill, whose voice thundered across the airwaves with hope and certainty. He was a truly remarkable and courageous leader who fulfilled his task with distinction during the most trying months and years of war.

I must add a tribute to the American president Franklin Delano Roosevelt, a superb war leader who led his nation to defeat the Nazis, and to the Soviets, without whose tremendous sacrifices in fending off the German army, the Allied victory might not have succeeded. We must forever honour the memory of the valiant Allied forces, who gave their lives so that we might live in freedom.

Despite the difficult conditions in England, there was now a ray of hope on the horizon with the favourable reports of the Soviet advances. This gave us something positive to hold on to while we waited on tenterhooks for the invasion on the second front to commence. The suspense kept us all on edge. During all this uncertainty in April 1944, Clarice finally arrived in England. Unable to contain my emotions, I burst into tears when I got the news.

When I met Clarice at the railway station in Manchester, we fell into each other's arms, both of us crying. I then took her to the hostel, where I had made arrangements for her to stay with me. She would only be staying for about three weeks until she was inducted into the services of the Women's Auxiliary Air Force (WAAF), which I learned was the reason she had come to England. She was able to enlist because, being Canadian-born, she was a British citizen. It was wonderful to have her all to myself for that length of time and fill in the years we had been apart. I wanted her to tell me everything about Argentina, about where they were living and about everything that had happened since they arrived in Buenos Aires. The most important thing I wanted to know was how my mother was, as well as my father.

When Clarice was comfortably settled in her room at the hostel, we talked nonstop about everything. While we were talking, I couldn't help but notice a sad expression on her face, as though she was saying to herself, Can this really be my brother? Her eyes moistened and she looked as though she was on the verge of tears at the sight of me. She quickly recovered, however, as if she was suppressing her emotions so she wouldn't hurt my feelings.

Turning away, she reached into her handbag and then handed me an envelope, which, to my surprise, contained one hundred American dollars. She told me that the money was from my mother, to buy whatever I wanted. At this point, Clarice could no longer contain her emotions; she burst into tears and reached out to hug me, wanting to soothe away my years of misery and loneliness. Her affection touched me and just knowing that I was no longer alone lifted my spirits – I now had someone caring close at hand.

Clarice told me that she had been working at the Canadian legation in Buenos Aires and had become friends with a number of girls who had told her about British subjects overseas being recruited as volunteers for the British armed services. She had been intrigued with the idea and decided to join up for two reasons. The first and most important was that she wanted to contribute to the war effort and help defeat the Nazis. Her second reason for joining the WAAFS was that she learned that when she was discharged after the war, she would have the option to return to the country of her birth, Canada.

Now twenty, Clarice had gone through the entire WAAF recruitment process without consulting our parents, despite knowing how upset they would be when they found out. She knew that she would never have gotten our mother's consent, so she didn't ask for it, and only told her after she had been accepted. Our mother eventually gave in, partly because she realized the atmosphere in their home was very unhealthy and my sister's life would be much happier if she was far removed from the constant fights that still characterized my parents' relationship. It was hard for my mother to lose her only child still at home, but she took comfort in knowing that her two children would be reunited after a long separation.

Clarice had not been able to inform me in advance about coming to England because of the stringent wartime restrictions that required all British sailing schedules to be kept secret. As a result, she was only given very short notice before sailing. In fact, when my mother wrote that my sister had left, she still couldn't tell me the name of the vessel or when it would arrive in England.

During this meaningful time together, Clarice and I told each other many things that we had not shared before. I was sad to learn that my father was still in poor health and therefore couldn't hold down a steady job. The situation was very difficult for my mother, who had to be the breadwinner as well as attending to all the household chores. This was the same predicament that had always been such a source of friction between my parents in Paris, the one that had led to all the arguments and physical abuse. The unwelcome news disturbed me very much, as it so often had in the past. When I went to bed that night, the trauma lingered and I knew I wouldn't be able to sleep until I wrote a letter to my parents and told them what a joyous reunion Clarice and I had had. Being without her children made my mother sad and lonely and I wanted to fill that void.

The next morning I went down to meet my sister in the dining room for breakfast. I was very pleased with the letter I had written my parents and asked Clarice to read it. Shortly after breakfast I had to go to work, leaving Clarice to make plans with one of the girls in the hostel. My sister made quite a few friends there, which made her stay even more enjoyable. Unfortunately, the time was going by too quickly and we were fast approaching the day when she would have to join her unit. We had to make the most of every day that was left.

My sister's visit really helped restore my confidence and when we had to wish each other "Au revoir" and "À bientôt" on the day of her departure, we hoped that our next meeting would not be too long in coming. At the railway station she boarded a train for Nottingham and was soon on her way to the WAAFS. We wouldn't see each other again until she got a leave of absence several months later. My morale remained high for many weeks after Clarice's visit and then gradually began to decline and I was faced with the same issues as before. I did my best to stick to a regular routine and live as normal a life as I could, but I wasn't always successful in keeping my insecurities under control.

I occasionally met Helen, the only young woman from the hostel I still had a crush on, on her way to work. The factory where she worked was next to mine and we would stop to chat for awhile. But as usual, my anxiety made me freeze in her presence and cut our encounters short. Helen's many gracious attempts to put me at ease somehow never alleviated my emotional state. I was heartbroken and infuriated about my behaviour but felt helpless to reverse it. The inhibiting mouth tremors returned and I became unable to look anyone straight in the eye. Rather than be constantly humiliated, I opted instead to avoid Helen altogether and withdrew into seclusion.

The Tide Turns

In the late spring of 1944, the war situation was steadily improving and in the evenings my friends Werner and Wolfgang and I met to discuss the positive news. People everywhere began to feel a change and former tensions and fears were beginning to subside. Everyone started confidently looking ahead to a decisive Allied victory and our community of young refugees finally felt able to start thinking about our futures.

The Italian Fascist government of Mussolini had already fallen in July 1943 and the Italians had surrendered that September; the Allies entered Rome in June 1944. On the Eastern front, the Soviets were continuing to batter the German forces relentlessly, advancing steadily against the retreating army. That was by no means the end of the good news. On the morning of June 6, 1944, while I was working at the factory, totally absorbed in what I was doing, there was a sudden interruption in the regular radio programming. Coming across the airwaves was an announcement in French, so I strained my ears to hear what was being said. The broadcast was the extremely important message for the people of France, delivered by none other than General Charles de Gaulle himself, that the Allied invasion of France had begun.

When the reality of the news sank in, I could barely contain my excitement. Everyone around me must have thought that I had taken leave of my senses because I started shouting at the top of my lungs, telling them the startling news. All eyes were on me as I repeated with conviction that the Allied invasion was taking place on the shores of France – it was the beginning of the long-awaited opening of the second front. It was D–Day.

Among the hundreds of workers in the factory, I was the only one who understood French and was therefore the first to hear the information about the Allied invasion. Immediately following the address of Charles de Gaulle, a similar announcement came over the air in English, confirming what I had said. The English broadcast began with a special news bulletin and by the end of the program, everyone was cheering and clapping. When they heard the English confirmation, even the people who had been skeptical acknowledged me for letting everyone know about the Allied invasion and my image among my fellow workers was greatly enhanced. One person even made the joking remark, "From now on, if anyone wants to know what Charlie is mumbling about in French (meaning Charles de Gaulle), all he has to do is consult Maxie." I couldn't keep myself from laughing out loud.

Victory was close at hand. For me personally, the invasion represented the change of fortune that I longed for. For the first time in many years I felt good about myself and I wanted to hold onto that feeling for as long as possible.

On June 13, 1944, the Germans launched their new secret weapon over London, the V-1 rockets. They were like missiles, flying at high speed on a pre-determined course and containing large amounts of explosives that detonated on contact with a massive blast. They caused enormous damage and a great loss of life. A few months later, these missiles were followed by the improved V-2 rockets that could not be easily detected; the only warning was often the explosion. The V-1 actually proved to be much more deadly, with its thunderous roar and sudden engine shut-off that gave little hint as to where it would land or whom it would target.

The Allies met with stiff German resistance on all fronts following the Normandy landings, resulting in very heavy casualties. The battles that followed were fierce and lasted many weeks without any clear signs of progress. The Allied forces eventually succeeded in breaking the deadlock, smashing through the enemy defenses and surrounding their positions, capturing thousands of soldiers. From that time on, the momentum of the war swung to the Allies and the enemy was forced onto the defensive. By mid-August the Allies had also succeeded in landing in the south of France and were steadily advancing to link up with the Allied forces converging from the north. Within a short time, on August 25, 1944, the Allies liberated Paris.

I wept for joy at the prospect of my family and friends being freed from Nazi occupation. None of us knew yet about the horrendous Nazi atrocities, and I didn't yet know the fate of my own family and friends. There was nothing at the time to dampen our euphoria over the liberation. I hadn't experienced such a surge of hope for a very long time.

During this optimistic time, Clarice arrived to pay me another visit. She was a very good-looking girl and seeing her in her WAAF uniform for the first time made me proud. We spent her entire leave together, along with one of her friends from the hostel. In light of the Allied invasion and the prospects of an end to the war, this time we spoke with much more confidence about our future. Too soon, however, Clarice had to return to Nottingham. She was later transferred to Newcastle and from there to the Isle of Man, where she spent the next nine months. On July 16, 1945, while she was still stationed on the Isle of Man, King George VI visited the base and her platoon was selected for review by him. If that wasn't exciting enough, she had the honour of the king shaking her hand and addressing her. It was a moment that she cherished for the rest of her life.

Although Clarice was no longer at home to write my mother's letters for her, one of her many acquaintances, a fine gentleman named Carlos, offered his services. Because of our frequent correspondence we got to know each other very well. His letters were not only thoughtful and intelligent, but also contained so many humorous remarks that I ended up responding in kind and our correspondence turned into a battle to see who could be the funniest. I never got a chance to meet him in person but will always remember him with great affection.

In the fall of 1944 I decided that it was time for me to return to London. I didn't arrive at the decision lightly because I still wasn't sure whether I was ready to leave the security of the hostel, but I knew that in London a Jewish immigration aid organization could help me get permission to join my sister once she returned to Canada. London also offered more access to transatlantic transportation. Despite my decision to go, I was deeply sorry to leave behind all the remarkable young Jewish men and women in the hostel. They had introduced me to a way of life I had come to love and through their influence I had become almost fluent in German and learned to appreciate classical music, the importance of reading, the art of stimulating conversation and, above all, the virtue of patience.

A week before I left for London I received letters from my aunts Jennie and Sadie and in my reply I told them about my upcoming move. I had already written to my parents about it. Then it was time to go. I said goodbye to all my friends and the staff at the hostel. When I arrived in London, I went straight to the Jewish Board of Guardians, where I unfortunately discovered that I was no longer eligible for their services – they were only mandated to help young people up to the age of twenty-one and I had just turned twenty-three. After a long wait, I was finally ushered in to see the same man I had dealt with before. As soon as he saw me, he called my former landlady, Miss Jacobs, and asked her to come to the office. He was the person who had placed me at Miss Jacobs' house and after my inexcusable behaviour in leaving without any notice, he wanted to teach me a lesson. My thoughtlessness had both hurt Miss Jacobs' feelings and her livelihood. When Miss Jacobs arrived, she glared at me. I greeted her politely but she rebuffed me and kept on scowling at me angrily, making me feel anxious and embarrassed. She went into the inner office to talk to the man from the Board of Guardians, but I could still see her staring at me and gesturing in my direction.

Until that moment I had not realized how much my leaving Miss Jacobs' had affected her and I naturally felt terrible to learn about it. Miss Jacobs had done everything she could to make me feel at home. She hadn't deserved the disrespect I had shown her. It was an important lesson for me.

Once the confrontation with Miss Jacobs was over, the man directed me to Bloomsbury House, where the Jewish Refugee Committee was located. My reception there was friendlier and after a brief interview they gave me the address of a middle-aged German Jewish refugee couple who would give me room and board. The next morning I got up early to go to the labour exchange and apply for a job. I was prepared to accept any job they considered essential, but I was surprised when they sent me to work in a sausage factory. My job consisted of chopping up the animal guts that went into the sausage production – it was pretty disgusting work. It was little wonder that I wasted no time in reporting back to the labour exchange. This time I took no chances and asked them for a job in my own trade. In due course they found me a new job as a machinist in a ladies' coat factory and I stayed there for almost a year.

After the first couple of weeks I also became disaffected with my new lodgings because there wasn't anybody there my age. The people at Bloomsbury House soon found me new accommodations with a family by the name of Kneip on Finchley Road near the Hampstead Heath Underground station. Mr. and Mrs. Kneip were a young Jewish couple with two children – a son, Anthony, who was barely two, and a daughter, Yvonne, who was an infant of no more than three or four months. Mr. Kneip, whom I later called Ernie, was a German refugee and his wife, Queenie, was British, London born and bred.

Queenie was a warm, good-natured and friendly woman, despite an unhappy marriage. She had the ability to read my mood and react accordingly. If I was really depressed she knew how to distract me and bring me out of it. She was also adept at getting me to talk about whatever was troubling me. She freely confided in me and we established a wonderful rapport, full of mutual trust and confidence. She came from a large family of five sisters and two brothers. One of her sisters, Sylvia, was married to a young Jewish man serving in the Canadian armed forces.

There was one other boarder at the Kneips, a quiet young Jewish German refugee named Goldschmidt who had just turned twenty-one. Unfortunately, his severe asthma made him look ten years older. He regularly suffered acute attacks and on occasion we had to call in a doctor to administer a morphine injection to relieve his distress. He was very intelligent and, in the tradition of the Jewish German scholars, a voracious reader. I looked up to Goldschmidt and he was someone I would have liked to emulate, if I'd been fortunate enough to have had his educational background. In our many discussions, he taught me about a variety of subjects and we became fast friends.

Ernie eked out a living running a small belt factory from his home with the assistance of Queenie and a female employee named Betty. I later had a brief affair with Betty, who turned out to be a very frustrating enigma. She was extraordinarily beautiful and I fell madly in love with her; regrettably, however, even dream girls have their failings and Betty was no exception. She turned out to be fickle, completely unreliable and unconcerned with other people's feelings, not to mention the world's biggest flirt.

Living with the Kneips was as close as I could come to feeling that I had a home, mainly because of Queenie. Ernie was unfaithful to her and at times treated her without dignity or respect. It's no wonder that the marriage eventually ended up in divorce. In a very real sense Queenie could identify with my own unhappiness and understand my depression, and we gave each other support.

By and large, though, things continued to look up. The Allies were still steadily advancing on all fronts and victory was within sight. In this atmosphere, my trips to work every day became less of a grind. People looked more relaxed and smiled more often. God had intervened on behalf of our righteous cause and justice was at last prevailing over tyranny. We could almost hear distant chimes ringing out the sweet sound of victory.

In these mainly hopeful circumstances I was still concerned with my difficulty meeting girls. I would create imaginary scenarios but they always shattered when I had to face reality. I tried to think of a way to solve my problem and decided to contact Margot, a young woman I had been introduced to in Manchester some months before I left. She didn't live in the hostel, but her background was similar to that of many of the young refugees there. Her parents had fled Poland and settled in Germany, and in 1939 had managed to send Margot out with one of the last children's transports sailing for England. Like me, she was lonely and our relationship grew close but purely platonic. One day, however, I realized that her attachment to me was growing when she took my hand as we strolled through the park. We promised to stay in touch when I moved to London and Margot even hinted that she might join me there.

I wasn't in love with Margot and I knew that it was selfish to ask her to join me but I convinced myself that her companionship would give me a sense of security. Loneliness won out over my concern that I might be taking advantage of her and I sent her a letter asking her to join me in London as soon as possible. After exchanging letters for a few weeks, Margot wrote that she had decided to come. She had a very close friend living in London who offered to put her up in a spare room.

Over the next few months our relationship thrived and having her there really helped me. One evening I invited Margot over to meet Queenie and they became instant friends; from then on, Margot visited often. As the two women got closer, they started talking about the issue of marriage. Margot was very keen on the idea and Queenie wholeheartedly agreed – she thought that being married would be good for my mental health.

During one of Margot and Queenie's conversations, they came up with a plan to entice me into a marriage I did not seek or want. Queenie would arrange for Margot to spend the night with me, hoping that intimacy with the woman she assumed I loved would make me want to marry her. On a holiday weekend, Queenie invited Margot to spend the evening with us. As the evening stretched on into the night, Queenie drew attention to how late it was and suggested that Margot spend the night with us. To my utter amazement, Margot didn't object.

What Queenie had failed to take into account was whether I was in fact in love with Margot. I felt caught in a trap. Queenie's suggestion caught me completely off guard, but I reluctantly agreed and escorted Margot up to my room, feeling guilty about taking advantage of her. Fortunately, although Margot and I spent the night together, we didn't have sex and in the end, the scheme backfired. Not only did I not propose to Margot but our relationship was irrevocably ruined. Since I knew I wasn't in love with her, I concluded that breaking up with her would be the gentlemanly thing to do.

We met in a secluded area in the park to discuss it. I told her that I felt badly about pursuing a relationship that she took seriously when I had no intention of marrying her, that under the circumstances we shouldn't continue seeing each other. Margot was obviously shocked by my announcement. She did her best to hide her disappointment, telling me that there was no rush to get married, but I told her that my decision was final. I felt terrible about the way I had treated Margot and was genuinely pleased when I heard many months later that Margot had married a fine young Jewish man.

After my breakup with Margot, my landlord, Ernie, proposed that I come to work for him in his belt-manufacturing business. His offer sounded attractive and the fact that the factory was on the premises was very appealing. I accepted and that is how I met Betty. She was barely sixteen years old, but she was far more mature than most girls her age. At first we just exchanged casual conversation and then gradually we formed a friendship. As I mentioned earlier, she was incredibly beautiful and I had trouble concentrating on my work. After about a month or so, I returned from my lunch break one afternoon while Ernie was away on a business errand to find Betty standing in the doorway to the workroom, smiling at me. I approached her cautiously but when we touched I lost all self-consciousness, threw my arms around her and started kissing her. All of a sudden, she slipped backward onto the floor, throwing me off balance. Something wasn't right about what was happening. She pulled me on top of her and I had no choice but to hold on to her for dear life – I was afraid that she would slip from my grasp and get hurt. But I was also disgusted by her behaviour. I had longed to kiss her, but I was shocked by her aggressive advances and total disregard for any sense of respectability.

She had me baffled. Did she really think I would have sex with her on our first romantic encounter, right on the bare floor of the workroom during working hours? Apparently that is precisely what she had in mind and it was impossible for me not to respond to the excitement of her body. Afterward, I rushed to the washroom to clean up and returned to work. Betty hardly spoke to me for the rest of that day, making me feel guilty and confused. The next morning, to my relief, she acted as if nothing had happened. I was mystified by her behaviour and the next day, when I decided to ask her out on a date, she let me know in no uncertain terms that she would never consider going out with me, insinuating that I wasn't good enough for her. The more she distanced herself from me, the more I flattered and complimented her. Eventually she became argumentative and critical, making derogatory remarks about me.

~

Not long after my misadventure with Betty, my sister arrived for a visit from the Isle of Man, her first visit to London since she had transferred to the base there. Queenie once again decided to play matchmaker but her efforts were much more successful this time. During Clarice's visit, Queenie talked to her about her sister Sylvia, who was married to a Royal Canadian Army serviceman named Max Stein. Max had met Sylvia on one of his leaves and they had gotten married shortly after. Queenie asked Clarice if she would be interested in meeting a young Jewish Canadian serviceman and my sister replied that she would be delighted. That evening Queenie introduced Clarice to Max's brother, private first-class George Stein from the Royal Regiment of Canadian Artillery. George and Clarice liked each other right away and they eventually got married later in Canada.

After Clarice returned to her base, I found that I couldn't stand working across from Betty every day and resolved that the only way to free myself from the effect she had on me was to move out of the Kneips' house. I had some trepidation about talking to Queenie, but when I explained what had been going on, she wholeheartedly agreed that I had no other option, even though it was a terrible loss for both of us. Queenie was not only a good friend; she actually made me feel like one of the family.

During this period I distracted myself by taking the Underground to London's West End and walking around the crowded streets. Several nights a week I went to a milk bar, a kind of snack bar, where I treated myself to milkshakes and cookies. On the weekends, specifically on Saturdays, I went to a movie and spent my Sundays, weather permitting, in Hyde Park, where I discovered Speakers' Corner, the place where opinionated people get up on a box to speak their minds on a variety of topics. Some would talk about politics, others about religion; some people were simply there to amuse themselves and their audiences. The latter deliberately expressed ludicrous opinions to incite the public to respond to remarks that were intentionally silly, stupid, and, above all, funny. Most of the listeners couldn't help being amused – we knew that it was all in fun and, best of all, it was free entertainment.

I particularly remember a very talented black man who was affectionately called Prince Monolulu, a hilarious character who never failed to entertain the crowd. He was so popular at the time that he could almost be considered a British institution. Just the sight of him in his elaborate costume of white satin, colourfully embroidered robes with a matching hat was enough to make people laugh. When he got up on the box, looking very imposing in his regal attire and his dark piercing eyes, he put forward such unbelievable theories that people couldn't help bursting out laughing. He became funnier and funnier as he went on, keeping his audience spellbound and in stitches.

~

Several months before moving out of Queenie's I met a young fellow named Rudi Netzer who would become a lifelong friend. As I write this, it has only been a year since I learned that he passed away at the early age of sixty. His loss affected me deeply – he was the truest friend I had in the whole world.

After my failed relationships with Margot and Betty, I sank into another depression and realized that I needed the help of a psycho-analyst. I went to Bloomsbury House and asked them to help me find a suitable doctor. Once again they came to my rescue and within a relatively short time I was paying regular visits to a very capable psy-chiatrist. Once he had taken my history, he recommended a series of hormone shots for my depression. During one of our hourly sessions – for which I paid a good portion of my weekly earnings – I confided in him about my loneliness and my difficulty making friends. To my surprise, at my next visit he handed me a note with the address and phone number of a fellow named Rudi Netzer, no doubt a former patient of his. As soon as I met Rudi, we took an instant liking to one another and we became almost inseparable. Rudi understood my problems, could accept me for who I was and treated me with cour-tesy and respect.

Even though we had so much in common, we came from very different backgrounds. His parents had had the foresight to send

Rudi and his sister, Irma, out of Germany before the war started in September 1939. Like many other German Jewish children, they were given refuge in England, although they had tragically left behind a brother who had refused to go without his parents. Since no correspondence was possible from Germany and its occupied territories during the war, Rudi hadn't had any contact with his parents and brother since 1940. We only learned after the war that they had perished in the Holocaust.

Unlike me, Rudi had memories of a very happy and comfortable childhood. His father was a successful businessman in Munich and his mother looked after their home life. Rudi was full of rage over his current situation, which he had no power to change or control. I did my best to console him and give him a ray of hope by convincing him that an Allied victory – and a reunion with his parents and brother – was imminent. Rudi did the same for me, patiently doing what he could to pull me through my bouts of depression. We acted as each other's safety net. Although Rudi suffered from a number of mental and emotional problems, fear of people was never one of them and he had a number of other friends as well.

I mentioned to Rudi that I wanted to move out of Queenie's place and he told me that there was a vacancy where he lived. Needless to say, he not only solved my problem but also gave me the comforting security of not having to live on my own – we would live in the same building and be able to see each other even more often. We would both live on the upper floor of a two-storey house at 61 Fellows Road in Swiss Cottage, where Rudi, his sister, Irma, her husband, Eddy, and their baby shared a flat at one end and I would have a very small room at the other.

Throughout this time, my sessions with the analyst continued on a weekly basis. I experienced some marked improvement and after several months he considered me well enough to reduce my weekly visits to once a month. It wasn't long before he told me that I was well enough to manage without his assistance. My spirits were higher than they had been in years. I continued to get regular mail from Buenos Aires courtesy of my mother's friend Carlos and, on a less frequent basis, letters from my aunts in Canada. I saw my sister on every leave and I always looked forward to her visits.

After I moved into Rudi's building, we were together almost every day after work and on weekends. On our days off we did a number of different things, including a trip to London's West End where we had dinner at Lyons Corner House and saw a movie. On other occasions, we met Rudi's friends at a club that offered various activities. Once we even participated in an overnight outing arranged by the club for both girls and boys. When another pretty girl turned me down at the dance and I took the rejection badly, Rudi suggested that we find other ways to amuse ourselves. The next weekend we went on an excursion to the beautiful English countryside.

We were in high spirits as we strolled in the warm sunshine of that beautiful early spring day in 1945. Many different species of birds chirped overhead, flying over the green grass that stretched as far as the eye could see. We burst into song, getting louder and louder, pretending to be opera singers. After a while we switched to the more mellow sounds of the popular music of the Big Band Era. As we were singing away, a woman approached in the distance and we lapsed into silence. She strode briskly toward us and when we came face to face, she told us how much she had enjoyed our singing and invited us to have lunch with her. She told us that she had a keen interest in music and offered to give us some instruction. Rudi and I were both taken aback and a little embarrassed to have been overheard but we accepted the woman's invitation.

Our hostess was an upper-middle-class woman in her late fifties, well-educated and very knowledgeable about music, who lived in a lovely country home about ten minutes away from where we had met. Inside, her living room contained a variety of musical instruments, including a grand piano. She invited us to sit down and said with some amusement, "Well, it isn't every day we come across two young lads from foreign lands with such cheerful dispositions. Please do tell me something about yourselves, where you're from and how long you have been in Britain. You both strike me as having had interesting backgrounds and I would love to hear about it."

Rudi and I began telling her some of our experiences before coming to England. About halfway through, the kind woman served us lunch and then sat down to listen intently to our stories. She was clearly shaken by what she heard, full of compassion for everything we had been through and begged us to tell her more. She told us that she could have listened all day, but didn't want to spoil our beautiful day in the countryside. For the next half hour or so we talked about music and then she generously offered to give us occasional free music lessons. When we were ready to leave, she offered each of us a wooden flute as a memento. Who would have imagined a stroll in the country would have resulted in such an encounter? We returned home that evening in high spirits, inspired and content.

Victory in Europe

Not long after I moved into 61 Fellows Road, Rudi introduced me to his friend Mrs. Robinson, who lived across the road. We developed an instant rapport and I visited her often. Trained as a social worker, I found her to be refined and intelligent, with a deep compassion for human suffering. She gave me a great deal of support and came to represent something of a mother figure for me. Mrs. Robinson was a Jewish woman who had married a German gentile in the early 1920s and had two children, her daughter, Brigitte, and a son serving in the British army. For some reason I never met her son. Mrs. Robinson and her daughter lived alone in a fair-sized home and when Rudi and I were invited over for tea, Brigitte often joined us.

Brigitte and I discovered that we had a lot in common – Mrs. Robinson and her two children had lived in Paris and had escaped to England just before the war. As a result, Brigitte was fluent in French and it was a tremendous pleasure to be able to talk to her in French about all the familiar people and places we both knew in Paris. We were also much more attuned to French customs rather than English ones. She was much more like vivacious French girls than English girls, who were generally rather shy and reserved.

Brigitte was twenty years old, blond with blue eyes, with a slightly deformed upper lip from a childhood accident that gave her a rather severe expression but took nothing away from her outgoing personality and cheerful disposition. With that special *joie de vivre et manière facile* (love of life and easygoing manner) of French girls, she was fun to be with. It wasn't long before we were dating regularly, although there was no serious attachment on either side. Brigitte also got along so well with Rudi that going anywhere without him was unthinkable. Sometimes, if Rudi had a date, we went out as a foursome.

Several months after I met Brigitte, she asked me if I would like to spend a weekend with her – her mother had to go out of town and would be away for the long weekend. As you would expect, I jumped at the chance to make love to a girl for the first time. All that week I felt light hearted just thinking of the weekend ahead. The evening that Mrs. Robinson left, Brigitte and I went to see a hilarious movie starring the comedian Danny Kaye. After the movie, we returned to Brigitte's house and she made us tea and served it with a cake she had baked herself. Over the tea and cake we talked about making love – like me, Brigitte was an inexperienced virgin – and what we would do to make sure that she didn't get pregnant. On our way home from the cinema we had gone to a drug store and bought a condom.

The time finally arrived for us to go up to Brigitte's room for our long-awaited sexual interlude. I felt calmer than I had for a long time. Unfortunately, though, the event didn't live up to our expectations – simply put, because I was so inexperienced, our attempts at intercourse weren't at all successful. We ended up spending a romantic night together cuddling in each other's arms. The next morning, Brigitte prepared breakfast and we talked about the people and places we knew in Paris, overcome with nostalgia, feeling transported back to the nights filled with music, the café terraces bustling with people and musicians full of song, laughter and romance.

With our easy communication, shared memories of Paris and affection for each other, Brigitte might have succeeded in persuading me to marry her despite my decision not to tie myself down for the duration of the war. She was well aware of how I felt, but she tried her best to get me to change my mind, serenading me with the popular French song "Jeunesse," a song about missed opportunities. The words "Jeunesse, jeunesse, on a pas toujours vingt ans" (Youth, youth, we won't always be twenty) describe how our youthful years can slip away without experiencing romance. Brigitte even resorted to trying to make me jealous by dating other men, a ploy that had unexpected repercussions that brought our relationship to an end when she became seriously involved with another man who wanted to marry her. I had taken her too much for granted.

Losing Brigitte sent me into another depression, but this time I had my friend Rudi to help pull me out of it. Together we filled our spare time visiting museums, going to lectures and movies or just walking in Hyde Park.

Letters were still flowing back and forth between me, my parents and my aunts, all filled with the encouraging news of an end to the war. The Soviets had breached the German front in January 1945 and Allied forces at long last broke through into German territory in late March. Both the Americans and Soviets were pushing ahead to Berlin. The last gasps of the war could now be counted in months or even weeks and my impatience for its conclusion grew with each passing day. Never were a people more optimistic than the throngs of British men and women making their way to work through the streets of London. One could see the national pride on their faces and I shared their optimism. Everyone started concentrating on their post-war plans.

I was still working at the belt factory, where I got to know a Polish Jewish man about ten years my senior. He worked directly opposite me and, since he was also single, we often discussed personal matters. When the topic of sex and relationships with women came up, and I told him about my frustrations, he told me that he didn't have that problem because he went to a prostitute every weekend. He suggested that I go with him to his next appointment and make a similar arrangement. My immediate reaction was to say no, but on second thought I said to myself, What could I lose by trying? So I tagged along with him on his next appointment, feeling a certain amount of apprehension and not at all sure I wanted to go through with it.

We met at an Underground station and travelled to where the prostitute lived on the upper level of a private house. She took us upstairs and into her living room and I sat down to read a magazine while my friend went into another room with the woman. He emerged about half an hour later and told me to set up an appointment. The whole time that my friend had been in the other room, I had been trying to decide whether I actually wanted to go through with this, whether I really wanted to have sex with a prostitute. I was repulsed by the very thought of it and I decided to opt out, but didn't want to lose face in front of my friend or offend the woman, so I pretended to make an appointment, knowing that I had no intention of keeping it.

～

That same spring of 1945 Rudi and I attended a mass rally in support of a Jewish homeland in Palestine. This event was a revelation to me – it was the first time that I had attended any public event connected to the concerns of my own people. I felt a surge of pride in being Jewish; in all my time in England, nothing touched me as profoundly as the subject of a Jewish homeland. It seemed like an almost impossible dream for a young stateless Jew who had been cast from pillar to post. The idea took hold of my imagination and I wanted to be part of the miracle of creating a new Jewish state. Unfortunately, a variety of circumstances, not the least of which was my mental instability, made it difficult for me to act on this new passion. It remains one of my most profound regrets.

While hope battled with impatience with regard to the end of the war, my daily life remained unchanged. I went to work every day and went home in the evening. After supper, Rudi and I usually got together for whatever we had planned for the evening. Some days were more interesting than others, but none were ever boring. In the middle of this regular routine, however, we woke up one morning to glorious news: a radio broadcast announcing the unconditional surrender of the German Wehrmacht, in effect marking the end of the war. It was May 8, 1945. Never had so few sentences meant so much – the words were like music to my ears. In jubilation, I threw my arms open wide and rushed over to see Rudi, Irma and Eddy. We all hugged each other and it was some time before we regained our composure. We just looked at each other in stunned disbelief, afraid that it might be just an illusion. When a second radio announcement officially declared the day a holiday to celebrate our victory, we knew it was real.

And celebrate we did that day, heading downtown to join in the joyous outpouring that lasted through the night and into the early hours of the morning. Rudi and I were literally transported from Trafalgar Square to the banks of the Thames by the exuberant throngs of people dancing, singing, cracking jokes and literally shouting themselves hoarse. Seldom has an event inspired people to the ecstatic joy we witnessed in London on VE Day. Patriotic songs such as "Rule Britannia" resounded through the enthusiastic crowds. I was completely consumed by the infectious spirit of celebration. After years of stress, the contagious clamour of the jubilant crowds removed all my inhibitions.

～

When the dust settled after all the celebrations and I realized that there would be no immediate change to my current circumstances, my great exultation waned. The war was over but I still couldn't join either my parents in Argentina or my aunts in Canada. I learned that it might even be another couple of years before I would be able to leave Britain. It was impossible for civilians to book a place on any overseas transportation, either by boat or by air. Top priority was, of course, given to the returning service men and women. For me, another two years might as well have been ten. Having already wasted close to six years of my youth, the thought of waiting another two years to rebuild my life was a bitter pill to swallow.

In this state of limbo, as days evolved into weeks and the weeks into months, my sister arrived one day in late fall 1945 to give me some wonderful news: she was about to be discharged from the British forces and had been granted permission to be repatriated to Canada, which offered me incredible new prospects. I immediately changed my focus from joining my parents in Argentina to preparing for the new – and infinitely more desirable – possibility of going home to Canada because Clarice could now sponsor me. Canada remained the only country I truly associated with both security and happiness.

Clarice received her embarkation notice in January 1946 and her future husband preceded her to Canada by only two weeks. We spent a full week together before she left and she was exhilarated about fulfilling her life's two most important goals: returning home to Canada and getting married. It was like a fairytale come true and I was so happy for her. On the actual day of her departure, she promised to ask my aunts to intervene on my behalf with the Canadian immigration authorities, and to leave no stone unturned in her efforts to secure an entry permit for me. She did everything she could to make me feel positive about the future and, after one last embrace, left to board her ship. When she turned around to wave for the last time, her face flushed with happiness, I could feel my fortunes about to change.

I stayed on the docks for a long time, waving in the hope that I would see Clarice among the thousands of service men and women. Even after I completely lost sight of her, I couldn't bring myself to leave, caught up in the excitement of the happy people returning home and the loved ones who were there to see them off. I felt good about the world, about myself and about my prospects in general. I couldn't wait to get home and write a letter to my parents describing Clarice's departure for Canada.

After a stormy four-day crossing, during which Clarice spent the better part of the journey seasick in her cabin, she reached Canada.

She was home at last. In early 1946, Clarice stepped off the train in Toronto, welcomed by Aunt Jennie and even more eagerly greeted by George, her husband-to-be.

Clarice had chosen Toronto over her native Winnipeg because Aunt Jennie had moved there and George was from there. Within two weeks of her arrival, Clarice and George got married. Aunt Sadie wasn't at the wedding because Aunt Jennie never told her about it. Aunt Sadie was furious at her sister for keeping her from her niece's wedding and, many months later when she'd calmed down, Aunt Sadie invited my sister and her husband to visit her in Winnipeg. Clarice was only too happy to take her up on her invitation. The trip meant much more to Clarice than merely paying her aunt and uncle a visit. It meant returning to the place where she had grown up.

With my sister now actually living in Canada, my chances of joining her there were even greater, although waiting was stressful. Around this same time I also had to say goodbye to Rudi, the one person who always managed to keep up my morale. He had volunteered to be a German interpreter for the British army for the war crime tribunals. With his flawless German and fair command of English, he was accepted right away. What prompted him to go was learning the terrible truth that his parents and brother had been brutally murdered in Auschwitz. He wanted to confront his enemies, to have some authority over them, expose them for the ruthless savages they were and humiliate them for their defeat. The thought of losing the only friend I had in Britain was upsetting, but this was trivial compared with his tragic loss and I of course encouraged him to go. I grieved with him, only too aware how very close I came to experiencing the same fate had I not urged my mother and sister to leave France when they did. Coming to grips with Rudi's tragedy changed my perception of my own petty problems; they stood in stark contrast to the ones Rudi would have to live with for the rest of his life. Whatever I was struggling with, I was alive and would see my parents and sister again.

Rudi thoughtfully asked Irma and Eddy to keep an eye on me and invite me to drop in on them every evening after work and on weekends. Despite his best efforts, though, after Rudi's departure things were never quite the same. Nonetheless, I was lucky to have friends like Irma and Eddy. Eddy, who was from Vienna, often took me to a Viennese club where we spent hours talking to people, playing games, eating home-baked Viennese pastries and drinking coffee brewed in the continental style.

By the time that Rudi had been gone for just over six months, I still hadn't heard anything from Canadian immigration. Wavering between hope and despair, I set off with Irma and Eddy on my first vacation ever in Britain, to a famous seaside resort in Wales for a week. It had been far too long since I'd last had a vacation and the prospect of spending a week on a sandy beach was irresistible – lying on the sand, soaking up the sun, watching beautiful young women and dreaming life's impossible dreams. We spent a peaceful week there, roaming the beautiful Welsh countryside and enjoying the balmy weather.

When I returned to London, my uncertain future continued to be a mounting pressure and I felt unmoored, totally without direction. We were already well into 1946 – it had been a year since the war ended and there was still no hint of progress on my application to enter Canada. Despondent, I arranged to meet with my psychiatrist. After a few sessions, he contacted the Jewish Refugee Committee at Bloomsbury House and advised them to send me to their convalescent home in Epsom, about twenty-five kilometres southwest of London, as soon as possible. The air there was supposedly good for people suffering from nervous disorders and the tranquility of the surrounding woods would help restore me to health. The necessary arrangements were made, although a space wouldn't become available for about a month.

The time finally came for me to go to the convalescent home in Epsom. During my six weeks' stay, the only people I had any significant contact with were the resident doctor and a Jewish girl several years my senior who worked there. There was also a non-resident doctor I had to visit on several occasions who lived and worked some distance from the convalescent home. He was my official doctor, as our resident doctor was a refugee who did not have a British medical licence. Even though he was not permitted to practise in an official capacity, he had permission to supervise the care of patients in the convalescent home. He was a Jewish refugee from Germany, an intelligent, charming and dignified man who was well advanced in years. He had lost all his worldly possessions and a successful medical practice to the Nazis.

I had many lengthy conversations with him about my problems. His approach in treating me was not only professional, but also warm and concerned, almost like a father-son relationship. As a victim of brutal circumstances, he thoroughly understood what I was going through and went beyond the call of duty in treating my symptoms, taking the trouble to explain how I could overcome them and learn techniques of self-control. Rather than just treating my acute mental anxiety, he explained its cause, helping me to better understand it and avoid future pitfalls. In particular, he emphasized the danger of taking myself too seriously, regardless of how anxiety-ridden I became, because this perpetuated a distorted view of myself and a cycle of negative thinking that in turn led to a loss of self-confidence, inhibitions and fears. In the final analysis, it was not the condition alone that was at the root of my emotional conflicts but my approach to the condition and ability to deal with it. What he was able to explain to me about my condition gave me a more positive attitude and renewed confidence. I will forever feel indebted to him.

The resident doctor at Epsom also prescribed lots of fresh air and long walks in the woods, combined with plenty of good food and rest. This, however, still left me a good portion of the day with little to do except read the newspaper or listen to music on the radio. After several days of this, I became quite bored. On my third day, the Jewish refugee girl on the staff came over to talk to me. It was her day off and we spent a good part of it getting to know one another. She told me about her foolish affair with a married man that had resulted in pregnancy. She didn't have any means to support herself and her newborn child, so she had reluctantly given up the baby for adoption. She was very flirtatious with me and I was in a very vulnerable state. All I could think of was that she was attractive and available and I desperately wanted female companionship. Without considering the hazards of such a relationship, we embarked on a short-lived romance. It soon ended when our resident doctor learned of our involvement. He called the young woman into his office, took her to task for taking advantage of me and insisted that she stay away from me.

At an appointment with me that afternoon, the doctor told me that my condition made me particularly vulnerable in any relationship and he cautioned me to think through the implications of my actions. He also explained the difference between someone making a decision under the stress of an anxiety neurosis and someone who is capable of making a rational decision. I was upset about having to break up with the young woman, but I was grateful for the doctor's concern.

By the time my six weeks at Epsom were up, I felt recovered enough to face the world. When I left the convalescent home to return to London, I only had one regret: losing contact with the doctor who wasn't just my physician but a friend. We did keep up a brief correspondence after I left.

The weekend that I got home, I had a surprise visit from Rudi, who was on a short leave of absence. It was so good to spend time with him, sharing our experiences over the months we had been separated and talking about our hopes for the future. The next week I returned to my old job and soon fell into my usual routine. Now, however, I felt confident enough to face whatever difficulties came my way.

The Wait Continues

After I'd been back at work for some time, I was pleasantly surprised to return home one evening to find a telegram from Aunt Jennie, announcing that she would soon be arriving in London. I have no idea how she managed it given how restricted private travel still was in 1946. I allowed myself some small hope that her visit might have something to do with my return to Canada. After all, she had come to Warsaw some twenty-six years earlier for the express purpose of taking my family to Canada with her. When Aunt Jennie did arrive, however, I shouldn't have been surprised to learn that, as usual, her trip was entirely related to her own business ventures. All she could tell me about my entry permit was that Clarice was continuing her efforts on my behalf. With her unpredictable generosity, though, she did buy me a custom-made suit as a gift.

During Aunt Jennie's visit, I managed to restrain myself from reproaching her and Aunt Sadie for refusing to help get us back to Canada in 1934, leaving us to go through many difficult years. I know that my aunts were only partially responsible – even if they had been willing to guarantee us financially, it might not have been enough to convince the Canadian authorities to allow us to return. Despite the fact that one member of our family – my sister, Clarice – was born in Canada, Canadian government policy in 1934 was not in our favour. Nonetheless, I did hold Aunt Jennie responsible for deliberately separating my mother and father and both aunts for the fact that my sister and I had to be placed in an orphanage for almost six years.

Aunt Jennie only stayed in London for forty-eight hours before setting out on the second phase of her trip, which would combine business with pleasure in Paris. She returned to London two weeks later and brought a most unexpected visitor with her: my cousin Pierre's wife, Simone. The travel restrictions within Europe had been lifted and she was able to come to England with Aunt Jennie as an ordinary tourist. She stayed for a long weekend and I took her around to the various museums and historical sights in London. Aunt Jennie finished her business in less than forty-eight hours and got ready to leave for home. As she left, she assured me that she would do whatever she could to speed up the process for my entry permit. Simone left for Paris that same evening, graciously extending an invitation for me to visit the family there.

Since there was no immediate answer from Canada, I realized that I needed some way to alleviate the stress of waiting. A few weeks later, I came up with a plan that I thought was a stroke of genius, but in hindsight was pretty farfetched. Influenced at least in part by the exploits of my friend Wolf, I decided to stow away on a freighter bound for Argentina. I started preparing to go back to Liverpool without telling anyone except Irma and Eddy about my plan. They did their best to dissuade me. I didn't tell my employer or landlady anything whatsoever, although I did take the precaution of paying two week's rent in advance just in case my plan backfired. With only enough money to last a week after buying my fare, I set out for Liverpool, taking nothing but the clothes on my back. I arrived there in the late morning and headed straight for the docks.

At the harbour, I carefully surveyed the area before attempting to make inquiries without arousing any suspicion. I approached a man who seemed friendly and asked him if he worked at the docks and how I could get a job on a vessel bound for Argentina. I told him why I wanted to go there and he was very sympathetic, explaining how to get a job on a ship. Even though I knew that I could never qualify because I was a foreigner, the conversation allowed me to find out which pier the ships to Argentina sailed from. I told him that I wanted to know so I could speak to a member of the crew to find out what the job entailed.

The man told me to come to his home a few hours later to get the information I needed. When I arrived at his dilapidated residence, the door was opened by his wife, a woman several heads taller than me. With true British hospitality, the man asked me to sit down and his wife served tea and biscuits. While we were having our tea, the man gave me some of the information I had asked for. To my astonishment, he also told me quite openly that he wasn't actually employed at the docks; like many others, he made his living by stealing from foreign vessels.

I was disconcerted by his admission since I had never had dealings with criminals before, but tried to hide my feelings. For some reason, though, I did let my guard down and told him the real reason I had come to Liverpool. My host didn't seem bothered by the fact that I was willing to resort to illegally stowing away to rejoin my parents. He even suggested that we go back to the docks as soon as possible so that he could show me the pier from which vessels sailed to Argentina. I was relieved by this turn of events and even offered to pay him for his services, which he declined.

While we were heading to the docks, he suddenly stopped and said that he had forgotten to get the date of the ship's departure and asked me to wait while he made the necessary inquiries. It took a little longer than I expected, but he finally returned with a gleeful smile on his face and told me exactly when the freighter would be leaving and the number of the pier where the vessel was berthed. He then surprised me by inviting me to come back to his house and, since there was still plenty of time, have dinner with him and his wife before I returned to the docks. I left after dinner, thanking them both for their help and hospitality and offering to send them goods from Argentina that were in short supply in Britain. The man escorted me part of the way and then gave me directions to the correct pier.

After we parted, I strolled along contentedly, feeling extremely pleased with myself that everything had gone so smoothly. Suddenly, out of nowhere, two uniformed police officers appeared in the pitch darkness and startled me out of my wits. They demanded that I produce my identification and explain what I was doing at the docks at that hour. It turned out that my supposed benefactor was actually a police informant who had reported a suspicious young alien who was asking for information about vessels sailing to Argentina. I realized that the game was up, that I had wasted my energy concocting an impossible scheme that had no chance of succeeding. I was taken to the police station and subjected to a gruelling interrogation.

In order to understand what happened at the police station, I have to explain a little about the political situation in Palestine at the time because when I was arrested, I was wrongly accused of being a Jewish terrorist. During this crucial period of our history, the Jewish people were rising up against the British Mandatory government as part of their struggle to establish a homeland. In opposition to these actions, the British authorities were restricting the immigration of Jewish Holocaust survivors. The Jewish armed forces and the Haganah, as well as groups like the Irgun and the Stern Gang, resorted to military action to force the British to abandon their mandate in Palestine. The British, however, had no intention of surrendering Palestine to the Jews, which raised tensions to a feverish pitch. After the Holocaust, neither European survivors nor Jews in Palestine and the Diaspora were willing to be intimidated by a military power.

British Mandate authorities had begun taking strong action against the freedom fighters who were openly defying British rule and chartering ships to bring Jews to their ancestral home. The British considered these freedom fighters to be terrorists and meted out harsh punishment in Palestine, including the death penalty. The daily headlines in the press in Britain highlighted the deteriorating situation there, so it was little wonder that a young Jewish refugee such as myself would be suspect, especially one who was found lurking at the Liverpool docks in the dark.

While not exactly unused to antisemitic slurs, I had experienced very few serious ones in Britain and was outraged when I was subjected to offensive remarks by the arresting officer. Knowing now what Jews had suffered at the hands of the Nazis, I could no longer allow anybody to insult me as a Jew without retaliating. In this instance, when the senior interrogating officer hurled a barrage of abusive antisemitic remarks at me in particular and the Jewish people in general, I got to the point that I couldn't stand it any more and finally exploded, countering his every insult without any regard for what might happen to me. I shot back with all the pride and courage I could muster to defend my Jewish heritage. When the officer concluded his remarks by saying, "We British will never concede Palestine to you Jews, so you don't have a hope in hell of ever getting there," I defiantly responded, "Not only will we get Palestine returned as a Jewish state, but even though you are at least twice my age, you will still have the great displeasure of living to see it happen."

Moments later, I was led to a prison cell where I spent the next seven days. Compared to my prison experiences in Spain, it was luxurious. The conditions were much more humane and I was given enough food to eat. Alone in my cell, I thought about the absurdity of my situation and reproached myself for having made such a stupid move in the first place. What would happen to me now? Where would I go from here?

After the week was up, I was brought out to appear before a judge. To my relief, the judge was compassionate and understanding. When he heard about my desire to see my parents after such a long separation, he sympathized with me and approved my release to return to London on condition that I promised never to try stowing away again. I took the first available train back to London and returned to Fellows Road.

As soon as I got back I went across the hall to see Irma and Eddy, who were surprised but pleased to see me back. I told them the whole story, about my disastrous attempt to stow away, my arrest and my incarceration. They tried to cheer me up by reassuring me that my entry permit would come through soon. My immediate priority, however, was to find a new job because my previous employer had already hired someone to replace me.

At the labour exchange, once the administrator found out that I had applied for an entry permit to Canada, he realized that any job I took would only be temporary. He asked what kind of business my Canadian sponsors were in and when he heard that my uncle ran a fur factory, he suggested that I learn the fur trade so that my uncle could hire me when I got there. The thought had never entered my mind, but I thought that it was an excellent suggestion and agreed to pursue it. He asked me to report back to him the following morning and, sure enough, he had already found me a position in a small fur factory. The owner, a Jewish man, put me to work right away. I was taught to soak fur skins and nail them to a patterned board by stretching them with a pair of pliers. It took me several hours to learn how to do it properly.

Working alongside me was a very friendly gentile man who was quite an amusing character. We got along extremely well even though he was a dedicated spiritualist, that is, he believed that the spirits of the dead communicate with the living through a medium. At the far end of the factory was a young, attractive gentile girl with whom I later became involved, thanks to the persistent and hilarious comments of our friendly spiritualist, who was set on getting us together. Whenever the room was quiet while we were all completely absorbed in our work, for example, he would catch us both unaware by pointing his finger in the girl's direction and loudly exclaiming, "Max, right across the room is your target for tonight." The girl would turn around, smiling with some embarrassment, and look straight at me. Fortunately, the good-natured young woman showed no signs of being offended. If anything, she laughed at my acute embarrassment.

Seeing both the spiritualist and the girl laugh was infectious and I joined in.

As the weeks went by, my co-worker's persistent campaign to get us together succeeded when I at last worked up the courage to ask the girl out and she accepted. I was hesitant to get involved with a gentile girl, particularly if it might lead to any serious attachment, but when it came to girls, I acted more from an emotional than practical perspective. I also didn't have many opportunities to meet prospective dates. Our romance developed over the next few weeks and I still have a photograph of the young woman.

On one occasion, my friend the spiritualist persuaded me to come with him to one of his séances. I reluctantly accepted, but declined a second invitation because it made me uncomfortable. My unwillingness to go to his séances never marred our friendship, though. Some of his comments could be quite crude, even though they still amused me, and working with him was an enjoyable experience.

One day, while I was out on a date with my gentile girlfriend, she confessed that she was involved with a Canadian serviceman who was serving overseas and had every intention of marrying her. In the same breath, however, she confessed that she was now in love with me. She waited for my reaction, hoping to hear that I also wanted to marry her. But I disappointed her by offering the same excuses I had given other girlfriends when the subject of marriage came up – that my unsettled state and uncertain future made it unwise. This didn't deter her from continuing to go out with me. She was a sweet, good-natured, sensitive and extremely thoughtful young woman and we got along very well. She was the only gentile girl I ever dated and the time we spent together was both happy and meaningful. I hope that she married successfully, for no one was more deserving.

~

I knew that I couldn't stay in England much longer – I was desperate to go anywhere to be with friends or family and realized that since I couldn't go to Canada or Argentina in the near future, another option was to return to France. It wasn't an easy decision – in April 1945 I had received the first letter from my cousin Pierre since my 1940 flight from the Nazis, and its contents had filled my heart with grief:

Paris
20 April 1945

My very dear cousins,

It is with great pleasure that I received your letter and was most surprised to learn that Clarice is actually in England. I was profoundly touched by your letter and wish to convey my everlasting thanks. It is good to know that we are thought about after enduring so much suffering.

Oh! My dear Max, you were extremely fortunate to have fled France in 1940. If only we could have foreseen what was coming, the whole family would have happily followed you.

When you wrote to me asking me to send your luggage to Marseille, I made the necessary arrangements, but the cases were returned to us because you were no longer there. Unfortunately, they are gone because the Germans took all your possessions. I think about the wonderful outfit that you were so fond of. Not only did they remove everything you owned, they took everything in our apartment, including all the furniture, and then rented it out. This is the reason that we now find ourselves living in a hotel. Following a judgement of the Paris tribunal, we will be given back our old apartment on July 15, 1945, after the present tenants are expelled.

I can tell you that we have recovered our factory and resumed our work. We are really lucky to have this much. You must understand that in 1942 the Jews were no longer permitted to be self-employed and all their enterprises had to be liquidated by an agent named by the Germans. I took the precaution of assigning our business to one of our French clients on condition it be returned to us after the war. When we returned to Paris our client returned our factory and although all the merchandise was missing, the machines were intact and we had a place to work. This is what allowed us to get production back in full swing.

Hélène Jacobson [our cousin] is working with us in the manufacturing of shoes. The poor girl never had a chance; her husband was deported in 1943. She got married in our home in June 1942, barely six months before the deportation of my mother, my brother and my sister.

We still don't have any news of them and it is most discouraging. Most of the Jewish prisoners of war are returning, but we haven't seen any of the deportees. Only a trickle have returned and according to what they tell us, there isn't too much hope. Nevertheless, although almost all of Germany is occupied and we haven't yet received any word, we will not be discouraged and will hold onto our hopes to the end. My father is so unhappy. Imagine being married, the father of a family of three children, and to find himself alone at his age. It is so sad. We are applying to all the various organizations for information and as soon as we have any news we will send you a telegram. I hope that it will be very soon. This is our greatest hope and would be the happiest day for my father and myself and the end of our heavy burden. I have never been a believer but don't know to whom I should address myself – I plead to God to have mercy on us and return what is most precious to us in the world.

What are you doing, my dear Max? Are you working and in what profession? Why did you leave Manchester for London? And you, Clarice, are you all right in England? I am so proud to have a cousin serving in the British forces. Send us some news of your parents. How are they and what are they actually doing? Give us all the details. My father is very exacting and when we receive a letter, he makes me translate it very slowly. You must have grown into a pretty young girl. Can you send us some photographs?

Things are pretty awful in France, particularly with regard to the food supply and it is impossible to get clothing. If one can even find a cut of cloth, it fetches an astronomical price. We receive regular cor-

respondence from Aunt Sadie and Aunt Jennie and have for some time been receiving food parcels from them. For the present I will close in the hope of sending you a telegram very soon. I leave you both, embracing you with all my heart, as well as your parents. Please accept my best wishes. My father joins me, as does Hélène and her cute little daughter.

Your cousin,
Pierre

In a letter I received from Pierre a year or so later, I learned that his mother, my beloved aunt Leah, his brother Philippe, and his sister Chai Liba had all perished in Auschwitz. He also named ten of our closest friends who had suffered the same fate. The news left me numb with sorrow and pain.

It was this terrible information that made it so difficult for me to make a decision to go back to France; I didn't know if I was emotionally strong enough to deal with the unimaginable tragedy that had happened to my family and friends. I continued to agonize about it and finally decided that I had to see Paris for myself and comfort my cousins, my uncle and what was left of my friends. I wanted to weep along with them and share their terrible pain.

I decided to go back to France within the next three months, so there were a number of things to take care of before then. I had to save enough money to pay for my fare and have enough left over to see me through at least several weeks. I was hoping to be able to get a job in the garment trade in Paris, provided that I could get a work permit – by no means a certainty given France's restrictions before the war. But before I could even begin to think about going to France, I would have to apply to the British Foreign Office for a Nansen passport and to the French embassy in London for an entry permit.

While I was waiting for all these pieces to fall in place, I devoted most of my energies to working and on weekends, I usually went to movies or walked in Hyde Park. Life had assumed an exciting new dimension, in which visions of all my old associations surfaced. I was for the most part free of my unnerving mental disturbances and just thinking about the move made me feel more exhilarated than I had for a long time.

During my walks through Hyde Park, I often stopped to listen to the various speakers and on one particular Sunday I was mesmerized by one I'd never seen before. What first attracted my attention was the unusually large crowd around him, but when I realized that he was talking about the rebirth of a Jewish nation, I moved closer. I saw a Jewish gentleman in an army uniform showing the rank of major, an obviously cultured person with a dynamic personality and brilliant mind, whose eloquence stirred his audience. People were entranced not only by his speaking style, but by the fact that he was making a direct challenge to the British authorities over their rule in Palestine. The crowd's reaction to his blunt statements seemed to be, "The nerve of this bloody Jew, how dare he challenge the authority and might of the British Empire." His subject matter dealt with controversial issues relating to the inalienable rights of Jews to their ancestral homeland. Some people heckled him, but his outstanding speaking ability obviously impressed his listeners and earned him their respect. Not one person left before he was finished; no one wanted to miss a word.

It was the first time I'd seen a Jewish gentleman publically defend a Jewish cause – particularly one as inflammatory as the proclamation of a Jewish state – in front of a belligerent British audience and it was exciting. He stood all alone, defiantly expressing his views. His emphatic message was that the Jews, as all other nations, were entitled to a place under the sun, with or without anyone's agreement. I was completely captivated and listened to him with tears in my eyes. For the first time in my life, I stood in front of a heroic fellow Jew who had the guts to assert our firm intention to establish an independent state so that we would no longer have to be seen as unwanted strangers or, even worse, as intruders.

Just as I thought I couldn't be more inspired, he made an announcement that took everyone by complete surprise. Gazing across his audience with a solemn but dignified expression, he pointed to his uniform and said that he had served with loyalty and distinction, fighting alongside his British comrades for the right of all people to be free, but the same principle had not applied to his fellow Jews. The final straw was that Jewish survivors of the Holocaust were being denied entry into Palestine, blocked by the closed-door policy of the British government. His answer to that outrage was to renounce his British citizenship, to give his allegiance and loyalty to the Jewish people in their struggle to liberate their ancestral homeland and join the Jewish defense forces of the Haganah.

I cannot remember ever being so deeply moved. The more I listened to him, the more I wanted to hear. Until I left for France, I attended the major's session every Sunday in Hyde Park. Each presentation added a little more to my knowledge of Zionist aspirations and taught me the importance of it to our very survival as a people.

Return to Paris

While I was waiting for my entry visa to France to come through I had an unexpected visit from one of my cousins from France, Solomon, the second oldest son of Aunt Pola's three children. He had had the good fortune to get an entry permit to Canada many months before I did and was stopping over in London on his way to Canada. My cousin had survived the Holocaust by escaping from France to North Africa and volunteering for the French Foreign Legion. He was quite a bit older than me and married, so when I lived in Paris our paths had seldom crossed and we hardly knew one another. Nevertheless, we felt a close kinship as survivors after the war. We also shared something else – we were both eagerly anticipating our immigration to Canada – and spent the few hours we had before he boarded his plane discussing our future. He seemed to make a point of not talking about any of the tragedies that had befallen our relatives; it was obviously too painful a subject for him.

Solomon had been sponsored by Aunt Sadie and his older brother, Jack, whom Aunt Sadie had brought to Canada in 1927. I felt as happy and excited about his leaving for Canada as I would be for myself, but it was hard to see my cousin leave while I still hadn't heard anything about my own entry permit in almost two years. Apparently I didn't have the necessary leverage to get my application approved. After my cousin left, I couldn't resist firing off a letter to Clarice, telling her how disappointed I was about his permit coming through before mine even though my application had been filed well ahead of his.

I was so discouraged about this that I told Clarice in my letter I was seriously considering immigrating to Argentina instead. My sister's reaction was to swing into action the moment she received my letter. She wrote to let me know about all the appeals she had made on my behalf, especially the meeting she had arranged with a member of Parliament, the Honourable David Croll, who promised to ask the Canadian authorities to speed up my permit. She begged me to bear with her just a little longer.

My frustration with the Canadian authorities aside, I was still looking forward to going to Paris and seeing my family and friends. Although I could never forget the abject poverty and degrading home life that Paris represented for me, I also remembered the city's vitality and its joie de vivre. I had so many wonderful memories of the years I lived there – the places, the events, the people and, most of all, the friends with whom I shared so many happy times.

As soon as I received the necessary travel documents from the British Foreign Office and my visa from the French consulate, I began making my final preparations for leaving England. I had never flown before and the prospect filled me with both excitement and apprehension. I pictured myself in the airplane as it slowly took off and then soared high above the ground, seeing the panoramic splendour below. Whoever thought that I would have the thrill of flying in an airplane one day? But as I pictured myself returning to Paris, I began to feel conflicted about seeing my family and friends, worrying about whether I would be able to control the still-present – although reduced – symptoms of my anxiety disorder. How would I explain a condition that might make me practically unrecognizable? I was no longer the Max they remembered, the effervescent and confident fellow with a ready smile, full of joy and laughter.

~

The war years began to fade into the background, along with my years of mental torment, as I boarded my flight to Paris in early 1947. The airplane soared into the clear blue sky, blazing a trail into what I hoped would be a bright new future. In this positive frame of mind, I landed at Le Bourget airport in Paris. I could hardly believe it – was I really and truly back in Paris?

I was soon assured that it was real when I saw Pierre and Uncle Joseph in the waiting room for arriving passengers, waving energetically and calling my name. As soon as our eyes met, I was swept up in a heart-warming reunion. For a moment the years of distress vanished, only to resurface when I saw beneath their smiling faces and welcoming arms their grief, pain and sorrow. They both looked pale and quite unlike their former selves. And there were only two family members where there should have been five; I felt keenly the absence of Aunt Leah, Philippe and Chai Liba but fought back my tears, knowing that I didn't want to add to their trauma by breaking down. From the moment we first greeted one another to the time we arrived at my cousin's place, neither Pierre nor Uncle Joseph made any reference to their loss. I only learned much later the shocking details of my aunt and cousins' murder from a survivor who had known them.

Pierre and Simone had been married for more than a year and lived in a rather unusual apartment by Parisian standards: it is rare to see one that only has two levels, including the front court. The entire structure had barely three rooms – a dining room and kitchen downstairs and one bedroom on the upper level – but they made me feel comfortable in their sparse quarters. My uncle lived in his old apartment, where I had lived before escaping from Paris, and had my aunt survived, this is likely where I would have stayed.

When I paid my first visit to my uncle's apartment, I was surprised to find three strangers living there and learned only then that my uncle had remarried. His new wife, Esther, was a pious Jewish woman with two lovely girls about eight and ten years old; the woman's husband had also died in the gas chambers of Auschwitz. I had great difficulty coming to terms with this – not only were my aunt and cousins gone, but three others had seemingly taken their place. It was hard not to resent the poor woman and her children. Over time, however, I came to realize how grief-stricken and lonely she must have been when she lost her husband. It began to make sense that two people who were suffering the same kind of pain had found in each other's company the love, solace and comfort they both so desperately needed.

As I got to know my uncle's wife better, I began to understand about the pressing need for the surviving members of Paris's Jewish community to come together and do what they could to rebuild their shattered lives. They needed to be able to share their traumatic experiences with others who had also lost their loved ones. The Jewish community of Paris was wasting no time in picking up the pieces of their devastated lives. The once-dynamic and thriving community set out to mend its deep wounds by organizing events in community centres and helping survivors get acquainted, which in turn promoted marriages and helped people cope with their loneliness and difficult memories. This also applied to the younger generation and the approach seemed to be working well. In the space of a few short years, survivors who had found themselves alone after losing their husbands, wives, children – entire families – found new hope and a purpose in life, a future for themselves and their children. As a community, we were saying with pride to the Nazis and all other enemies of the Jewish people, "Despite your efforts to destroy us, we are here to stay for all eternity."

The impressions I gathered during my first week in Paris were nonetheless sad and disheartening. I found a great change in the French people. Their sense of humour and carefree attitude had been replaced by a hardened and serious demeanour. Apparently the German occupation had taken its toll as it had in all nations under its yoke. Even though there were few physical changes to the city, Paris and the Parisians that I remembered no longer existed. Paris of the 1930s, with all its exuberance and wonders, its bustling boulevards and cafés, was part of a past that I would never be able to recapture.

I began to look for friends who had survived, even though Pierre had forewarned me that I would not find many of them alive. I naturally started with my best and closest friend, Henri Bruckner, and, thank the Lord, I found him alive, along with his father and one sister. Tragically, however, I learned that his mother, his other sisters and his brother had died in Auschwitz. I was equally heartbroken to learn that most of my friends had perished. The extent of the disaster shocked me and I grieved for the innocent lives lost, for young people whose contribution to humanity would never be known.

The full brunt of the shocking news hit me and it was hard not to fall apart. Along with the pain and grief, I was also overcome with anger and disgust, with a powerful desire to avenge my family and friends. Even more than before, the Nazis became my sworn enemies and, in my emotional state at that moment, I would not have hesitated to seek revenge if any of them were in front of me, whatever the risks to my personal safety. These passions cooled, however, when I reminded myself that the Germans had been defeated and that the Nuremberg trials were meting out the punishment they deserved.

Out of a total of fifteen of my most closest friends, only Henri and Albert had survived. Many others I'd known only casually had also died. What particularly pained me was to learn that, as I mentioned earlier, my mother's best friends, the Silbersteins – Sarah, Favel and their beloved daughter, Esther – had all perished in Auschwitz; only their son, Yosele, had survived and was now living in Switzerland. In my own family, as Pierre had told me in his letter, my cousin Hélène had lost her husband only six months after they got married. The Nazis had taken him away and sent him to his death in Auschwitz. It was hard to celebrate my own escape from the Nazis when I thought about my family and friends who didn't make it.

~

In the first weeks of my stay in Paris, Uncle Joseph and Pierre continued to work in their shoe manufacturing business and had very little time to devote to me other than on weekends. On one of those weekends, Pierre, Simone and a group of their friends arranged an outing to the country and invited me to come along. I still have some mementoes of that excursion – several photographs Pierre took while we were rowing in a boat and some others with all of us posing on the sandy shore with our feet criss-crossed together so that it was difficult to tell whose legs were whose. It was a wonderful day.

On other weekends, we went to the Château de Versailles, Le Trianon, Jardin des Tuileries, Musée du Louvre and many other places of interest. We also went to night clubs in Montmartre as well as to restaurants that served much-celebrated French cuisine. On another occasion, my cousin Hélène and her girlfriend Jeannette took me to a dance hall. Even though I hadn't really mastered the art of dancing, I somehow managed to get around the floor.

Being back in France with my family and friends had already begun to improve my overall mental state, which helped change my whole outlook. I started to feel more hopeful and confident, to feel that zest for life that had lain dormant in me for far too long. It felt wonderful to leave behind my obsessive reactions and revel in the delights of the real world. Just as I was revelling in this positive new outlook, a letter arrived from the Canadian embassy in London and lo and behold it contained the long-awaited news that my application to immigrate to Canada had finally been approved! Surprisingly, though, I didn't feel as elated as I thought I would. After two years of waiting, I had reconciled myself to living either in France or Argentina. I took some time to adjust to the news and concluded that, beyond a shadow of doubt, I should return to Canada. It was the country that I had first loved and longed to return to.

For the first time in my life, I actually had real choices: I could return to Canada, remain in France, immigrate to Argentina or live in England. Having four countries to choose from seemed nothing short of miraculous. On one level, though, these new choices brought up some old resentments. Why had Canada and France suddenly changed their policies when the damage to me and my family had already been done? In the case of France, the years in which my family had been denied the right to work and I was forbidden to leave the country could never be erased. When I look back on my visit to Paris after the war, I am still astounded by the drastic transformation of French government policy toward Jewish immigrants. In 1947, unlike the 1930s, they were willing to offer me the privilege of permanent residency, which finally gave me the right to work.

It seems strange now, but it never actually occurred to me that we could go to Palestine, as did tens of thousands of other Jewish refugees, although it was still illegal at the time. Like so many Jews of past generations, we saw our fate as inextricably linked to the Diaspora. We had the same *galut* (exile) mentality as our parents and naturally wanted to go to a country that offered us freedom and opportunity. Canada was the country that we knew and loved.

After wrestling with all these conflicting feelings and knowing that I would always choose Canada, I left Paris with a heavy heart and returned to London as planned. When I got to Fellows Road, I rushed across the hall to tell Irma and Eddy my good news. They both congratulated me but the mood sobered when I told them the grim news from Paris, not only about the fate of my family and friends, but also that close to 80,000 Jews living in France had been massacred by the Nazis. Our hearts were so filled with grief that when it was time for me to return to my room for the night, we held each other and wept.

The next morning I set out for my appointment at the Canadian embassy. The first thing I had to do was have a medical examination and when that was completed I saw an embassy official who, after a short interview, stamped my Nansen passport with the official authorization to immigrate to Canada. The long, lonely, perilous years were over. It turned out, however, that I would have to clear one last major hurdle – I was shocked to learn that my aunts were not prepared to pay my transportation costs. They were putting the entire financial burden on my sister. I knew that Clarice would provide the funds if she had them, but she barely had a hundred dollars to her name. The total fare to Canada was $350.00 and if we couldn't come up with the money, I wouldn't be able to get there.

I refused to stoop to being a beggar to obtain my fare. If neither of my aunts had it in their hearts to lend me the money then so be it, I would close the door on the whole issue of immigrating to Canada. I would either join my parents in Argentina or go back to France. The second problem that arose, however, was that when I began making inquiries about booking my passage to Canada, I learned that all ships and airplanes were booked to capacity for many months into the future. Another irony – I was finally granted permission to enter Canada only to be prevented from doing so by a lack of transportation. Faced with this reality, I decided to wait out the time for available transportation to Canada in Paris rather than London. There at least I would be in the company of my cousins and two remaining friends instead of being almost alone in London.

It was difficult to break the news to Irma and Eddy, although they knew I would be leaving sooner or later. They understood my reasons for wanting to be with my cousins and friends in Paris while I waited for passage to Canada. The day before I left for France, as a gesture of my appreciation for their friendship, I gave them some of the valuables I had accumulated over five and a half year's residence in England, items that for one reason or another I didn't need to take with me. Irma and Eddy were terribly sad to see me go, but pleased to have some things to remember me by. After all the years I'd spent in England, they were the only ones to say goodbye to.

This drew to a close one of the saddest periods of my life, the time I had spent as a refugee in Britain. It is by no means a reflection on Britain or the British people – without their hospitality I might never have survived the war. My years in England also gave me benefits that served me well throughout my life – the practice of self-education and keeping abreast of international developments, patience, self-restraint and, above all, respect for other people's opinions. In fact, the combined experiences of being Jewish in the various countries where

I spent my adolescent years helped to influence my future judgment and better understand people and the world I live in. My lifelong commitment to self-education that began in England has been immensely rewarding and satisfying.

I was filled with mixed emotions as the plane took off, leaving behind the place I had called home for the past five and a half years. It had represented so much freedom and security as well as so much sadness, illness and loneliness. I left Britain with a fond farewell and optimism for the future.

When I arrived in Paris, I was met by Pierre, Simone and Hélène and whisked off by taxi to Pierre's apartment, where I stayed until I left for Canada. As the days in Paris grew into weeks, the small amount of money that I had brought from Britain was now almost depleted. With no immediate prospects for transportation to Canada and not wanting to take charity from my family, I began to look into getting a job. Simone helped me through the process of getting a work permit from the Prefecture of Police.

Before leaving London I had gone on a small shopping spree to buy things for my cousins that were in short supply or not available in Paris. I wasn't able to buy everything I wanted but I created quite an impression with the train set I brought for Hélène's five-year-old daughter, Paulette. When I got to Paris I was pleased to hear that my aunts intended to bring Hélène and her daughter to Canada. Their application had been filed some time ago and a permit would be coming through soon.

While I waited for some form of transportation to Canada to become available, both my cousins did everything they could to make my stay in Paris as pleasant as possible. Hélène and her best friend took me out dancing on the weekends and Pierre and his friend arranged outings to the country and other entertaining places. I was grateful for all their attention.

My application for a work permit had to go through a review, although I was assured that it wouldn't affect the outcome – it was simply a procedure that applied to all former Jewish alien residents in France. When it was approved, I would have a well-paying job as a ladies' garment operator waiting for me. About a week or so after I had applied for my work permit, however, I received a telegram from my sister with the incredible news that Air France had had a cancellation and she had managed to get me on a flight from Paris to New York on June 20, 1947. I could hardly believe that it was real.

The one issue that remained unresolved was how to pay for my fare. I still couldn't understand how Aunt Sadie could refuse to help me. She was well aware of the tragedies that had befallen the Jews in Europe, in particular what had happened to her sister Leah and her nephew and niece, among other relatives. That alone makes it difficult for me to imagine how she could not follow the Jewish tradition of *tzedakah* and come to my rescue.

I sent a letter to Clarice, asking her to tell my aunt how disappointed I was in her unwillingness to help me at this crucial juncture and that I had decided to take up permanent residence in France. I wrote that I was expecting my work permit to come through within the next few weeks and that I already had a job waiting for me. I also conveyed to Aunt Sadie – through Clarice – that she clearly had no compassion for my situation, comparing it to her refusal to bring us back to Canada in 1934. Aunt Sadie was not usually susceptible to criticism but she was very sensitive about her reputation. She would never want it known that she had withheld a few hundred dollars to help her own sister's son, a survivor of the war, come to Canada. My remarks clearly had an impact because Aunt Sadie called my sister right away to tell her she was wiring enough money to cover the fare and asked Clarice to make sure that Air France didn't cancel my reservation.

As the news of my imminent departure spread from my family to my friends, everyone congratulated me on my good fortune. It was hard to leave them – they represented stability and affection, and most of all continuity with a life I had known. And Paris just has a way of keeping you spellbound. Nonetheless, I had a reunion with my sister and, I hoped, soon with my parents, to look forward to.

Given the short amount of time before I left, there didn't seem to be any point in picking up my work permit or starting up a job that would last less than two weeks. By this time I had no money and I had to rely on my cousin for food and shelter before I left. I promised to repay Pierre as soon as I got my first job in Canada, but he wouldn't accept it. Hélène also generously offered me a ten-dollar loan because she didn't think that I should travel penniless. That ten dollars was the only money I had when I arrived in Canada.

There was one last incident in post-war France that I would like to mention here, although it happened after I left for Canada. Uncle Joseph was honoured by the French government and awarded the medal of La Légion d'honneur and granted French citizenship. The once-struggling Polish Jewish alien who had had to plead with and bribe the pre-war French authorities for permission to stay in the country and carry on his business was now an honoured French citizen. Who would ever have suspected that this would come to pass?

~

June 20, 1947, finally arrived, the day on which I would enter a new phase of my life, one that I hoped would be happier, more productive and peaceful than the previous fourteen years. In high spirits, I exchanged a last affectionate embrace with my relatives and friends at the airport, then headed for the departure room. Soon after, I boarded the plane to New York. In no time at all the plane started to roll and before long we were airborne.

Beside me sat a passenger who tried to engage me in conversation, but I was a little scared about my first transatlantic flight and didn't respond right away. Nevertheless, the kind gentleman soon put me at ease. I learned that he was Jewish, an American from Indiana, married to a gentile woman, and that they had three children. He had just returned from Czechoslovakia, where he was visiting his brother, whom he hadn't seen for a number of years. He had gone prepared to help his brother in any way he could but when he got there he found that his brother didn't need his help; in fact, his brother had given him a substantial gift of money. The gentleman asked me how I had survived the war and was intrigued by my account. We talked throughout the flight and the gentleman even made me promise to visit him in Indiana, discreetly assuring me that it wouldn't cost me anything. I told him that I would reciprocate one day and invite him to Canada as soon as I was in a position to do so.

On the way to New York we stopped briefly at Shannon airport in Ireland and continued on from there to Reykjavik, Iceland. As we approached Reykjavik, I was fascinated by the landscape, which was completely flat and appeared to be barren of any trees or vegetation and limitless, extending as far as the eye could see. I could almost imagine that I could see the curvature of the earth. It was a truly spectacular sight. Our next stop was in Gander, Newfoundland, where we got off the plane for a fairly long time. We were directed to a cafeteria where my companion ordered breakfast for both of us. This was my first taste of Canadian food in fourteen years. Soon it was time to board the plane again for the last leg of the journey to New York; from there I would go on to Toronto.

I had so far thoroughly enjoyed the flight, but during the last few hours of the journey, the going got rough. The airplane began to hit air pockets and as it dropped it vibrated, giving me a sinking feeling in the pit of my stomach and making me nauseous. My travelling companion summoned the stewardess, who gave me an air sickness tablet. It didn't take long for me to regain my equilibrium and the nausea to disappear, and I felt fine for the rest of the trip. My companion was a seasoned traveller who was totally unaffected by the plane's sudden drops in altitude. He kept me in good spirits throughout the flight, for which I was very grateful. Thanks mainly to him, I have very fond memories of my flight back to Canada. Though our paths never did cross again, our brief encounter left a lasting impression.

Finally the captain asked us to prepare for the descent into New York's LaGuardia airport. When I got off the airplane and made my way to the arrivals lounge, there stood Aunt Jennie, waiting on the other side of the customs area. During the process of clearing customs I was given my first official welcome to the North American continent by an American Jewish customs official who spoke a few words in Yiddish – they were music to my ears. He had obviously sized me up right away as a fellow Jew and war refugee. He didn't ask me to open my one small suitcase, just ushered me through and wished me good luck. It was my first taste of American freedom and it felt wonderful. I bid farewell to my travelling companion and went to meet Aunt Jennie. She hugged me and said that we would be staying with her cousin Mrs. Moskowitz in Brooklyn.

Aunt Jennie and Mrs. Moskowitz were more than just cousins – they were best friends, so my aunt felt quite at home with her. With only a few short days to spend in New York, my greatest wish was to meet my paternal grandmother and the next morning we took the subway to visit her in the Bronx. The great anticipation I had built up over my first visit to a grandparent – sadly the only one I would ever experience – faded as I approached the place where she lived. It was an old dilapidated tenement building and I was shocked to see the poverty in which she lived. There were no elevators in the old building and we climbed up many flights of stairs before we reached her floor. When the door opened, I saw a very old well-kept woman with a pleasant smile. She recognized my aunt right away and invited her in, not yet aware who I was.

Aunt Jennie hadn't given my grandmother any prior warning that I was coming because she wanted it to be a surprise. When Aunt Jennie made the announcement my grandmother looked me over carefully and then burst into tears, flinging her arms around me. I was so deeply moved by her show of affection that she soon had me in tears as well. Aunt Jennie looked on with approval, gleeful over the success of her surprise. She sensitively suggested that my grandmother and I spend a few hours alone together and went off to do some errands, giving us an opportunity to get to know each other.

My grandmother lived in a tiny room with a bed, a table and chairs, a stove and an ice box. The view from her one window was a brick wall. After Aunt Jennie left, she put what little food she had out on the table, telling me to sit down and eat. When we began to talk, I learned that she was so poor that she was living on welfare. My heart went out to her and I wished that I was in a position to help her. My poor grandmother was destitute and, to make matters worse, had to endure the terrible late June heat in her tiny unventilated room. It was awful to see how my grandmother was living, but it was also wonderful to finally meet her and spend time with her. When Aunt Jennie returned and it was time to leave, my grandmother gave me one last hug. I promised her that I would write her regularly and visit as soon as I could do so. I had no way of knowing then that she only had a short time to live and we sadly never saw each other again.

My second day in New York was completely different from the first. Aunt Jennie took me out for lunch at an automat, a kind of self-serve restaurant in which food was dispensed from little windows. From there, we walked over to the famous Radio City Music Hall, where we spent an entertaining afternoon. We returned to Mrs. Moskowitz's place for supper and later that evening paid a visit to our hostess's son and his family. When we were returning home, I could hardly contain my excitement about leaving for Canada the following day.

I was almost too excited to sleep that night. I was calmer the next morning but somewhat dismayed to learn that Aunt Jennie wouldn't be travelling with me. Being her usual enterprising self, she told me that she had a prior business commitment that would keep her in New York. She reassured me that she had arranged for Clarice and George to meet me at Toronto's Union Station. I hadn't expected to be travelling alone but it didn't really matter how or with whom I got back to Canada – the only important thing was getting there.

After breakfast on the morning of my departure, I packed my few belongings and thanked my hostess for her generous hospitality. Then, Aunt Jennie and I were off to Grand Central Station in a cab. When we arrived at the station, she bought my train ticket to Toronto and saw me to my seat on the train, giving me last-minute instructions about the customs and immigration procedures. I was finally on the last lap of my journey to Canada, the sweet realization of my dreams. Even as the train pulled away, I still found it hard to believe that I was actually returning. It had been so long since I felt this happy. I was lost in reverie and in what seemed like no time, I could see that we were approaching the Canadian border. I closed my eyes in a prayer to the Almighty for his blessings in guiding me to my destination. In this moment of contemplation, we crossed over the border. I had returned to the country that I had long dreamt about, but thought I might never see again.

Once we had crossed the border into Canada, as Aunt Jennie had warned me, the Canadian customs and immigration officers inspected my documents and looked through my luggage. When the inspection was over, I officially became a landed immigrant with the full privileges of living in Canada.

Home Again

After what seemed like an eternity, on June 25, 1947, I was back home in Canada. I had left as a child of twelve and was returning as a twenty-five-year-old young man. My excitement grew as the train rolled through the scenic stretches of the countryside until we were only minutes from Union Station. By the time the train came to a full stop, I was already waiting at the steps, suitcase in hand, eager to be the first one to descend. As promised, Clarice and George were both there to greet me, their faces beaming. My brother-in-law mischievously asked whether I was ready to get on another flight with him to Holland, to which I happily replied, "No, thank you, this is as far as I would like to go." This set the mood for our happy reunion and we drove off to their home.

About fifteen minutes after leaving Union Station, Clarice, George and I arrived on Palmerston Avenue, where my sister and brother-in-law were renting a two-room flat on the upper floor of a house. When we entered her kitchen, the table was laden with a variety of foods, the likes of which I hadn't seen in years. But even before we sat down to enjoy the feast, my sister and I started talking about a variety of things, the most important of which was bringing our parents to Canada from Argentina. Clarice had rented a room for me on Henry Street, about fifteen minutes away, and also provided all my meals until I found work. I spent my first morning in Toronto exploring the streets of the neighbourhood. Clarice had suggested that I go to the unemployment office or the International Ladies' Garment Workers Union office to look for a job.

On the Sunday following my arrival, my sister arranged a small party in my honour and among the friends she invited was a young Jewish girl she worked with named Minnie. Who could have imagined that this quiet, good-natured young woman would, within a year, become my wife? When Clarice introduced us, I felt instantly at ease with her. She had striking blue eyes, a smooth complexion and was several inches taller than me. She apparently found me attractive because our first encounter was a success. Being with Minnie felt as easy as being with my former friends, but although I was attracted to her, I was still looking for someone who could sweep me off my feet, like a scene from the romantic movies of the 1930s.

While I was trying to resolve my feelings, I continued to date Minnie. We frequently went out on double dates with a girlfriend of hers, Florence, and her boyfriend, who had been discharged from the army a year earlier. Sometimes we went dancing, sometimes to the movies, or to Sunnyside Beach or Toronto Island. Since I had found work as a ladies' coat and suit operator in my very first week in Toronto, I earned enough to pay for our outings. Still, I put myself on a tight budget to save enough money for my mother's fare to Canada. My parents had saved enough for one ticket, so I promised myself that I would pay for the other one. Clarice and I had filed applications to bring our parents to Canada the week I began working. Three months or so later, we received a letter notifying us that they were permitted to enter the country, but processing the various documents, including their official entry permits, took many more months. At least the delay gave me enough time to save up the money I needed.

Somewhere between my second and third month in Canada, I began to have second thoughts about my involvement with Minnie. The whole matter upset me so much that it was literally tearing me apart. I told myself that I had to fight my obsessive tendencies if I was ever going to find love, but the fear of losing my opportunity to experience my ideal of true love led me to gradually break up with my beloved Minnie.

Around the time of my arrival in Canada, a slow trickle of new refugees entered the country. As their numbers grew, the younger ones organized a club for recreation and social activities. When I heard about it, I was extremely interested, hoping that I would meet other refugees, especially ones coming from France. My first visit to the club was during a dance with a small number of girls and boys. The girls outnumbered the boys and I soon spotted a blond girl who was quite good-looking and I approached her shyly and asked her to dance. I still danced fairly clumsily and the girl pretended not to mind. She tried to put me at ease by asking me whether I spoke Yiddish, apologizing that she didn't speak English yet. I replied, "Avade red ich Yidish" (Of course I speak Yiddish). I discovered that she had emigrated from Poland, where she had survived the Holocaust in hiding.

As the evening came to a close, I asked her if she would like to meet again and she agreed. On our first rendezvous she brought along her best girlfriend and from the moment we were introduced I experienced a *coup de foudre* (love at first sight). She was an attractive brunette with a pretty face and radiant smile. Her circumstances were similar to those of her friend – she was from Poland and had also survived the Holocaust in hiding. When it was time to go home my date suggested that I come to her place to meet her aunt and uncle, the relatives she lived with who were responsible for bringing her to Canada.

I was very impressed to learn that my date's uncle was a lawyer. I had never met one socially before. I was very ill at ease in his presence at first – meeting educated people always affected me that way. To my surprise, however, I found him to be a very humble and genial person who went out of his way to treat me as his equal. At the end of our visit, my date asked if I would mind escorting her girlfriend home. I jumped at the chance to see her alone and I left without committing myself to another date. I took the attractive brunette home and just before saying good night, I got up the courage to ask her out on a date. She was caught by surprise and clearly wasn't sure how to respond. I admitted that I knew that it wasn't appropriate because I was dating her friend, but I found her irresistible. I had to wait for what seemed like an eternity before she responded, but in the end, she said that she would accept my invitation. She gave me her phone number and told me to call her to arrange a date for the weekend. I felt elated and walked home whistling and singing all the way.

When I called her up to arrange our date, we decided to meet for lunch at a restaurant. I picked her up at her residence on Elizabeth Street and we walked over to a restaurant on Yonge Street. At first everything seemed to go well, but about halfway through lunch, she suddenly burst into song. I looked at her in astonishment, while she looked me straight in the eye and continued singing as if it were the most natural and rational thing in the world. From then on, whenever I spoke to her, she responded by singing instead of talking. Needless to say, I decided not to see her again and suspect that her behaviour was designed to avenge her friend for my callous behaviour.

At this point, I decided to leave Toronto to move on to Winnipeg, where I had spent some of the happiest years of my childhood. I still hadn't seen Aunt Sadie and it seemed to be the right time to go. I wrote her a letter telling her that I wanted to see her and asked permission to visit her and my uncle. I did this somewhat reluctantly because she hadn't shown any interest in seeing me during the two months I'd been in Toronto. Aunt Sadie responded to my letter quickly and invited me to stay with them. I still had mixed feelings about her but I really wanted to rediscover the place that held so many fond childhood memories. In a spirit of hopeful optimism, I set off on a nostalgic journey to the city of my boyhood. The long train ride to Winnipeg took several days across the vast and beautiful landscapes of Ontario and Manitoba. I had a sleeping berth, which reawakened old memories of my last Canadian train ride in a similar berth in 1933, going in the opposite direction toward Montreal.

Aunt Sadie and Uncle Morris met me at the Winnipeg train station and were clearly happy to see me. Driving to my aunt's house
through the streets of Winnipeg I could see that little had changed
and I recognized many familiar buildings. On Portage Avenue, for
instance, was the old Eaton's building and further north the Hudson's
Bay store. It was fascinating to see my aunt's house again after a four-
teen-year absence. When the car pulled up in front of the house, it
didn't look as grand as I remembered it. Apparently, there hadn't been
any exterior improvements to the house since it was built in 1929,
and its once-shimmering emerald-green stucco surface was dull and
faded. The sprinkling of tiny stones that had once covered the entire
surface of the house had all fallen off. Inside the house itself, the dé-
cor and furniture was exactly as I remembered it. But the formerly
happy and lively home had become sombre, bleak and uninviting. My
cousin Max's death had taken all the vitality out of the house.

It had been roughly ten years since Max passed away and Aunt
Sadie and Uncle Morris continued to mourn him. Uncle Morris, in
particular, mentioned his beloved son, the apple of his father's eye,
in almost every conversation by his Yiddish name, Motele. It is little
wonder that Uncle Morris, still heartbroken, passed away barely a
year after my visit at the early age of fifty-seven. In the years that followed his son's death, Uncle Morris had found the strength to keep
his fur business running but his ambition had waned and the business shrank. Success no longer meant the same thing to him because
the whole reason for his efforts had been his son's future. My aunt,
once the outstanding socialite of her day, no longer entertained in the
grand fashion she was renowned for. She now led a quiet subdued life
with a few intimate friends.

I spent my days in Winnipeg looking for the places I once lived,
including the Jewish orphanage that no longer existed, as well as play-
grounds and parks and movie theatres. Deliberately excluded from
my search were my old friends, who I was sure would not remember
me; my aunt told me that one of them was a law student who had just

passed the bar exam and another was in his last year of medicine. I wondered what I could possibly still have in common with them.

After several weeks staying with Aunt Sadie and Uncle Morris, I started to want some privacy and independence. At the same time, the more restless I got the more I found myself thinking of Minnie. I kept picturing her lovely blue eyes and sweet disposition. Being with her had felt so right, so comforting and easy; looking for my ideal one and only true love now seemed so futile. With this new enlightenment, I finally came to my senses and my indecision, loneliness and boredom vanished. I knew exactly what I wanted and sent a letter to Minnie, hoping that she would respond. In the letter, I told her just how much I missed her and that I intended to return to Toronto very shortly.

When Minnie's reply to my letter arrived, it made me want to see her as soon as possible, so I let my aunt and uncle know that I would be returning to Toronto. I told them the truth about why I was going and although they were surprised, they were very understanding. I arranged for a train ticket the following day and left that same week. During my stay in Winnipeg I had been able to work at my uncle's factory, where one of his employees taught me how to cut up and sew fur coat linings. I became quite proficient within a couple of days and my uncle paid me a reasonable salary for meeting my daily production quota. Uncle Morris also very generously refused to take any payment for my room and board. As a result, I returned to Toronto with considerable savings.

When I arrived in Toronto Clarice was at the station to meet me. She had found me another room but invited me to spend the day with her at her place, where we had lunch and talked. In the evening my brother-in-law returned from work and Aunt Jennie came to take us all out for dinner. The following morning I went to the ladies' garment workers union and they immediately sent me out to a factory, where I was asked to report for work the very next day.

The day that I arrived back in Toronto I had also called Minnie and we arranged to meet the following evening. I was so relieved – ecstatic would be more like it – that Minnie still cared about me and was glad that I was back from Winnipeg. To prove to her that my intentions were sincere, this time I planned to ask her to marry me. If she said yes, I wanted to wait until my parents arrived from Argentina so they could attend their only son's wedding. That night I slept very soundly, without any inner turmoil or uncertainty. My decision to re-turn to Minnie felt very right and it set me free. This peace could only come with a sincere and loving relationship with a girl like Minnie, who had the capacity to give me a feeling of calm and a zest for life.

The next evening, Min and I met at her home on Oxford Street. We didn't talk about our previous breakup, but stayed in the present, where nothing mattered except our love and affection. We both felt that we were destined to be together and the feeling of belonging to each other added a new dimension to our lives. I was transformed into a happier, more confident person. Even my future in-laws whole-heartedly approved and invited me to stay for supper.

Faithful to my intentions, I proposed to Min and she happily agreed to marry me. I first broke the news of our engagement to Clarice, who then told Aunt Jennie. My aunt knew that I was putting aside every penny I could for my mother's fare and that I couldn't possibly afford to buy Min an engagement ring. She surprised me one day by giving me a beautiful miniature diamond engagement ring for my fiancée. Min knew that I didn't have any money to spare for an engagement ring and wasn't expecting one, so when I did present her with the ring, she was overjoyed. We immediately started talking about wedding plans, making sure that the date would coincide with my parents' arrival.

I was very excited about my parents' imminent arrival. They now had all the required documents for their entry to Canada as well as the fare money I had saved. The long years of waiting were finally coming to a close.

Min and I continued to see each other on a regular basis. My daily visits, which I so looked forward to, were made easier because her parents invited me for dinner every evening. Her father, Isaac Grodzinski, was a fine Orthodox Jew who prayed every day and never worked on Saturdays. Her mother, Annie, was engaging, full of mirth, song and laughter. They were extremely poor but contented with their lot, without ambition for monetary gain. If I had to choose between being rich with stress and worry or being poor and contented like my in-laws, I would undoubtedly opt for the latter, for no amount of wealth can buy inner peace. As we had when we first met, we spent our evenings going to the movies or going dancing at the Palace Pier and sometimes we still went to Sunnyside Beach or Toronto Island. We frequently double-dated with Min's best friend Florence and her beau.

While immersed in my daily routine of working, seeing Min and generally feeling good about myself, I received a telegram from my parents in June 1948 telling me that they had boarded a ship in Buenos Aires that very day and were en route to New York City. When I got the amazing news, I thought about how much my fortunes had changed. I felt truly happy and fulfilled. With only weeks before my parents' arrival and our impending wedding, Min and her father were busy preparing for the occasion. We were to be married on July 4, 1948, in a small synagogue with only the immediate family and a few of Min's best friends. After the ceremony, we planned to celebrate the occasion with a strictly kosher dinner at Goldberg's Restaurant on Spadina Avenue.

When my parents finally arrived in Toronto on July 3, it was one of the happiest days of my life. Aunt Sadie had already told me that she would be attending my wedding, so her visit would serve a double purpose. She planned to drive from Winnipeg to New York City to surprise my parents when their ship docked, spend a few days with them there visiting relatives and then head straight for Toronto to arrive the day before my wedding. Aunt Jennie, never one to be outdone by any member of the family on such an important occasion, was also planning to travel from Toronto to New York City to surprise my parents.

Following the surprise reception and a few brief entertaining days in New York City, my parents travelled to Toronto with my aunts. On the day of their arrival, we all stood anxiously waiting for them on my sister's front porch, our tension and excitement growing by the minute. At long last, we all saw a car pull up to the curb and out stepped my mother followed by my father and two aunts. I ran to the curb as fast as I could, straight into my mother's arms. We kissed and hugged, tears of joy streaming down our faces. Then I warmly embraced my dad, basking in his pride at seeing his only son again. And finally both my aunts reached out to embrace me. It was the most joyous of reunions.

The day after my parents' arrival, they participated in my wedding and within a few years became the proud grandparents of four grandchildren. Clarice had two boys, Allen and Morris, and Min and I had a daughter named Linda and a son named Jeffrey. Many years later, Linda gave my mother her first great-grandchild, a boy named Jordan, followed by another, a great-granddaughter named Danielle. The years that my mother spent with her grandchildren and great-grandchildren were among the happiest of her life. Although my father did not live with us, my mother stayed with me and my family until she passed away at eighty-two. Besides being a pillar of strength, she was always a source of encouragement. A true Yiddishe Mama in every sense of the word. Sadly, she passed away during the process of writing this book, in 1983. Even after three and a half years, I'm still just as heartbroken at losing her and I miss her terribly.

For my part, my decision to marry my beloved wife, Min, proved to be the right one. Not only was she a devoted wife and a good mother to our children, but also an easygoing and understanding person with a sweet loving disposition. I still experienced some of my neuroses and her lot in living with me was definitely no bed of roses. Min deserves to be commended for her outstanding devotion, love, consideration and, above all else, her patience, which helped bring me back to mental health. In the face of countless hardships, she weathered all the storms. She displayed courage, decency and above all, trust, knowing and believing in me.

Epilogue

My beloved wife and children encouraged me to write this book in many ways – my daughter, Linda, gave me an Oxford dictionary and my son, Jeffrey, gave me a gold pen. To my amazement, even my grandson Jordan encouraged me by telling me that he couldn't wait to read it. I'm certain that my granddaughter Danielle would have shown just as much curiosity had she been a little older. However, it is Min who deserves most of the credit for her enthusiasm throughout the many years it took to write it. Besides her moral support, she took on the difficult task of typing the entire manuscript, which was made all the more complicated by having to do it from oral dictation instead of copying a handwritten manuscript.

Even though I have had little formal education and could never be considered a professional writer, writing this book is something that I was intent on accomplishing to the best of my ability. I consider it my duty to describe the tragic events of my youth, bound up as it was with the greater tragedies of the Holocaust, and tell future generations about the dangers and hardships encountered by a Jew without a country.

Glossary

Allies The coalition of countries that fought against Germany, Italy and Japan (the Axis nations). At the beginning of World War II in September 1939, the coalition included France, Poland and Britain. Once Germany invaded the USSR in June 1941 and the United States entered the war following the bombing of Pearl Harbor by Japan on December 7, 1941, the main leaders of the Allied powers became Britain, the USSR and the United States. Other Allies included Canada, Australia, Czechoslovakia, Greece, Mexico, Brazil, South Africa and China. *See also* Axis.

antisemitism Prejudice, discrimination, persecution and/or hatred against Jewish people, institutions, culture and symbols.

Auschwitz (German; in Polish, Oświęcim) A town in southern Poland approximately forty kilometres from Krakow, it is also the name of the largest complex of Nazi concentration camps that were built nearby. The Auschwitz complex contained three main camps: Auschwitz I, a slave labour camp built in May 1940; Auschwitz II-Birkenau, a death camp built in early 1942; and Auschwitz-Monowitz, a slave labour camp built in October 1942. Between 1942 and 1944, transports arrived at Auschwitz-Birkenau from almost every country in Europe – hundreds of thousands from both Poland and Hungary, and thousands from France, the Netherlands, Greece, Slovakia, Bohemia and Moravia, Yugoslavia,

Belgium, Italy and Norway. As well, more than thirty thousand people were deported there from other concentration camps. It is estimated that 1.1 million people were murdered in Auschwitz; approximately 950,000 were Jewish; 74,000 Polish; 21,000 Roma; 15,000 Soviet prisoners of war; and 10-15,000 comprised of other nationalities. The Auschwitz complex was liberated by the Soviet army in January 1945. *See also* Nazi camps.

Axis The coalition of countries that included Germany, Italy and Japan that fought against the Allies during World War II. The Axis powers formally signed an agreement of cooperation, the Tripartite Pact, in September 1940. Other countries that joined the Axis included Hungary, Romania, Slovakia, Bulgaria, Yugoslavia and the Independent State of Croatia. *See also* Allies.

bar mitzvah (Hebrew; literally, one to whom commandments apply) The age of thirteen when, according to Jewish tradition, boys become religiously and morally responsible for their actions and are considered adults for the purpose of synagogue ritual. A bar mitzvah is also the synagogue ceremony and family celebration that mark the attainment of this status, during which the boy is called upon to read a portion of the Torah and recite the prescribed prayers in a public prayer forum. In the latter half of the twentieth century, liberal Jews instituted an equivalent ceremony and celebration for girls – called a bat mitzvah.

Bastille Day The annual national day of celebration in France also known as the La Fête Nationale (The National Celebration) that commemorates the storming of the Bastille prison on July 14, 1789. The fall of the prison, a symbol of the monarchy of Louis XVI, was a catalyst for the French Revolution.

Basques An ethnic group that lives in the western region of the Pyrenees mountain range, which is part of north-central Spain and south-western France.

Beneš, Edvard (1884–1948) Second and fourth president of Czechoslovakia (1935–38 and 1945–48). After Germany took control of part of Czechoslovakia in 1938, Beneš went into exile in Britain, where he formed the Czechoslovak government-in-exile. After the war, Beneš was reinstated as president until the Communist coup in February 1948; he resigned in June of that year and was succeeded by Communist leader Klement Gottwald.

Blum, André Léon (1872–1950) Prime minister of France from June 4, 1936 to June 22, 1937, and March 13, 1938, to April 10, 1938; and president of the provisional government of the French Republic from December 16, 1946, to January 22, 1947. Blum, the first Jew and Socialist to serve as prime minister of France, led the Popular Front (in French, Front Populaire) government, an alliance of left-wing parties. After the German occupation of France in June 1940, Blum was arrested for treason and in 1943 he was deported to the Buchenwald concentration camp. He was sent to Dachau concentration camp in April 1945 and then transferred to German-occupied South Tyrol in Italy, where he was liberated in May 1945. *See also* Front Populaire.

British Mandate Palestine The area of the Middle East under British rule from 1923 to 1948, as established by the League of Nations after World War I. During that time, the United Kingdom restricted Jewish immigration. The area currently encompasses present-day Israel, Jordan, the West Bank and the Gaza Strip.

carabineros (Spanish; cavalry soldier) A paramilitary force founded in the nineteenth century whose duty was to guard the Spanish border, especially at the Pyrenees. General Francisco Franco disbanded the armed force in 1939 because thousands had been loyal to the Republican government, and replaced them with members of the police force, the *Guardia Civil* (Civil Guard). Frontier guards continued their border duties, arresting refugees like Max Bornstein, under the title of the *Real Cuerpo de Carabineros de Costas y Fronteras* (Royal Corps of Coast and Frontier Carabiniers).

Churchill, Winston (1874–1965) British statesman who was prime minister of the United Kingdom from 1940 to 1945, and again from 1951 to 1955. A fierce opponent of Nazism from its inception, Churchill led his country in the fight against Nazi Germany and became a key member of the Allied leadership of both the war effort and the post-war peace settlement.

Croll, David (1900–1991) Canadian politician who served as mayor of Windsor from 1931 to 1934 and Liberal Member of Parliament for the electoral riding of Spadina from 1945 to 1955. Croll was appointed to the Senate in 1955, becoming Canada's first Jewish senator.

de Gaulle, Charles André Joseph Marie (1890–1970) French general and statesman who opposed both the Nazi regime and French collaborationist Vichy government. De Gaulle, a World War I veteran and Brigadier General in World War II, escaped to London after the fall of France in 1940. In London, de Gaulle organized the Free French Forces, a partisan and resistance group comprised of French officers in exile. After the war, de Gaulle served as head of the French provisional government from 1944 to 1946, and as president of France from 1958 to 1969.

de Rothschild, Édouard Alphonse James (1868–1949) French businessman and investor from the prominent Rothschild banking family, an extensive and international family of German-Jewish origin who first established financial institutions in the late eighteenth century.

D-Day The well-known military term used to describe the Allied invasion of Normandy, France, on June 6, 1944, that marked the onset of the liberation of Western Europe during World War II.

Depression The term used to describe the aftermath of the worldwide economic collapse that started with the American stock market crash in October 1929. The Great Depression affected the economy of most countries up until the late-1930s. In Canada, the unemployment rate rose to 27 per cent by 1933.

Drancy A northeastern suburb of Paris that was the site of an internment and transit camp from which about 65,000 people, almost all Jews, were deported to concentration and death camps. Established in August 1941, the camp was run by the French police until it was taken over in July 1943 by the Nazi SS, who ran it until its liberation in August 1944.

electroshock therapy The former name for electroconvulsive therapy (ECT), a controversial psychiatric treatment developed in 1938, widely used in the 1940s and 1950s, and used to a lesser extent today. The treatment induces seizures in the patient through the administration of electric currents to the brain and is thought to help stabilize the moods of people suffering from anxiety or depression.

fifth column A term first used by the Nationalists in the Spanish Civil War of 1936–1939 to refer to their supporters within the territories controlled by the Republican side. Because these people were helping the four columns of the Nationalists' army, they were deemed to be their "fifth column." Since that time, the expression has been used to designate a group of people who are clandestinely collaborating with an invading enemy.

Four Questions Four questions that are recited at the start of the Passover seder, usually by the youngest child at the table. As much of the seder is designed to fulfill the biblical obligation to tell the Exodus story to children, the ritual of asking the Four Questions is one of the most important at the seder. The questions revolve around the theme of how this night of commemoration of the Exodus is different from other nights – e.g., Why do we eat unleavened bread? Why do we eat bitter herbs? The readings that follow answer the questions and in doing so tell the Exodus story. *See also* Passover.

Franco, Francisco (1892–1975) Spanish general, dictator and head of state of Spain from 1939 to 1975. Franco, who led the Nationalists in victory against the Republicans in the Spanish Civil War, at first remained officially neutral and then "non-belligerent" during World War II, but lent military support to the Axis powers. Paradoxically, his authoritarian, fascist regime did not follow an antisemitic policy of interning Jews unless they were stateless, instead allowing approximately 30,000 Jewish refugees who had documentation into Spain, often on their way through to neutral Portugal. *See also* Spanish Civil War.

French Communist Party (in French, *Parti communiste français*; PCF) A political party founded on communist principles in 1920. The party was led by Maurice Thorez in 1930 and supported the Popular Front government of 1936. The Jeunesses Communistes (Young Communists), a previously independent organization, became an auxiliary of the PCF by 1931 and was an essential element in the party, recruiting youth like Max Bornstein. *See also* Front Populaire; Thorez, Maurice.

French Foreign Legion A branch of the French army that was established in 1831 to bypass the restriction of foreigners serving in the French armed forces, allowing foreign nationals to serve in the military. The legion's headquarters were in Algeria and during the nineteenth century its members primarily fought to expand the French empire. During World War II, legionnaires served in Norway, Syria and North Africa. Currently, the Legion's headquarters are in Aubagne, France.

Front Populaire (French; Popular Front) A coalition of left-wing parties comprised of the French Communist Party (PCF), the French Section of the Workers' International (SFIO) and the Radical and Socialist Party. The Front Populaire governed France from June 1936 to June 1937 and briefly in the spring of 1938. The government initiated a variety of labour reforms while in power including the right to strike, collective bargaining, paid annual leaves, wage raises and a standard forty-hour work week. Although the Popular Front adopted a liberal stance toward France's refugee crisis and tried to establish refugees' rights to work visas, their policies were never firmly instituted. The party was dissolved in the fall of

MAX BORNSTEIN   257

1938. *See also* refugee and immigration policies (France).

Galitzianer Yid A Jewish person from the area of Galicia, a historical region in Eastern Europe that bordered western Ukraine and southeast Poland.

Gestapo (German) Abbreviation of Geheime Staatspolizei, the Secret State Police of Nazi Germany. The Gestapo was the brutal force that dealt with the perceived enemies of the Nazi regime and were responsible for rounding up European Jews for deportation to the death camps. They operated with very few legal constraints and were also responsible for issuing exit visas to the residents of German-occupied areas. A number of Gestapo members also joined the Einsatzgruppen, the mobile killing squads responsible for the roundup and murder of Jews in eastern Poland and the USSR through mass shooting operations.

Groupe Special de Securité (French; Special Security Group) The Vichy regime's secret police force. *See also* Gestapo, Vichy.

Haganah (Hebrew; The Defense) The Jewish paramilitary force in British Mandate Palestine that existed from 1920 to 1948 and later became the Israel Defense Forces. *See also* Irgun.

HICEM An organization that was established in 1927 to aid Jewish refugees. Its name is an acronym of three other aid organizations: the New York-based Hebrew Immigrant Aid Society (HIAS), the Jewish Colonization Association in Paris (ICA) and the United Committee for Jewish Migration (Emigdirect) in Berlin, which withdrew from the organization in 1934. During World War II, HICEM, in partnership with the American Jewish Joint Distribution Committee (JDC), helped between 25,000 and 40,000 European Jews immigrate to safe countries such as Canada, Argentina, Australia and China, while HIAS helped refugees immigrate to the United States. HICEM also helped prospective immigrants by disseminating information, acquiring visas, and through social services such as legal aid, financial and employment support, and language study. By 1937, HICEM had established relations with associated committees in thirty-two different countries to help Jewish refugees. *See also* Jewish Colonization Association.

insulin shock therapy A psychiatric treatment developed in 1933 in which insulin is administered in order to induce comas. Insulin shock therapy was generally used to treat schizophrenia, and lower insulin doses were often used to treat neurosis. Although some psychiatrists claimed a 50 per cent remission rate from the treatment, subsequent studies disproved any therapeutic benefit from the use of insulin. There was also risk of brain damage and death from insulin shock therapy, which was used widely in the 1940s and 1950s, and declined by the 1970s.

International Ladies' Garment Workers Union (ILGWU) A labour union formed in New York City in 1900 to represent workers in the clothing industry, which also had branches in Canada.

Irgun (abbreviated from Irgun Zvai Le'umi; Hebrew; National Military Organization) The Irgun (also known as the Etzel, its Hebrew acronym) was formed in 1937 after it separated from the Haganah, a military organization that operated in British Mandate Palestine between 1920 and 1948. Due to the increasing level of violence between Arab and Jewish citizens, the Irgun advocated active and armed resistance (in opposition to the policy of restraint that was advocated by the Haganah) as well as the establishment of a Jewish state in Palestine. The Irgun was responsible for numerous attacks in British Mandate Palestine and was also fundamental to the illegal transport and immigration of thousands of European Jews into the state. The activities of the Irgun were controversial – some viewed them as a terrorist organization, while others applauded their efforts as freedom fighters. *See also* Haganah; Stern Gang.

Jewish Board of Guardians Also known as the Board of Guardians for the Relief of the Jewish Poor. A British charitable organization in London founded by philanthropist Ephraim Alex in 1859 that provided social services to help impoverished Jews.

Jewish Colonization Association (J C A) A Paris-based philanthropic organization founded in 1891 by Baron Maurice de Hirsch that helped establish credit facilities and agricultural training centres internationally. During the 1920s the organization focused on helping Jews immigrate to Canada, Argentina and Brazil. In 1927, J C A merged with two other aid associations to create a successor agency, H I C E M , which continued to help Jewish refugees with immigration. *See also* H I C E M .

Jewish Refugee Committee (London) An organization that helped find employment and accommodation for Jewish refugees in England. The organization was located in Bloomsbury House along with more than thirty other associated organizations and committees that helped refugees in Britain, such as the Germany Emergency Committee (a Quaker-affiliated group later renamed The Friends Committee for Refugees and Aliens); the Church of England Committee for Non-Aryan Christians; the Catholic Committee for Refugees from Germany; and the Refugee Children's Movement. Due to the high number of refugees in Britain during the war (approximately 90,000), these organizations, and others, existed to help in all aspects of their settlement.

kiddush (Hebrew; literally, sanctification) The blessing over wine that is recited on Shabbat and other Jewish holidays. *See also* Shabbat.

Kindertransport (German; literally, children's transport) The organized attempts by British and American groups to get Jewish children out of Nazi Germany before 1939. Between December 1938 and September 3, 1939, the government-sanctioned but privately funded Kindertransport rescued nearly 10,000 children under the age of seventeen and placed them in British foster homes and hostels. There were also 1,400 children under the age of fourteen who went to the US between 1934 and 1945, through a program known as "One Thousand Children," which was initiated and run by private and communal organizations.

King George VI (1895–1952) Albert Frederick Arthur George was

260 IF HOME IS NOT HERE

king of the United Kingdom and the British Commonwealth countries (including Canada) from 1936 until his death in 1952. He remained in London throughout the war despite the constant threat from German bombing raids. By being willing to incur the same dangers as other Londoners, refusing to flee to safety, King George became an important symbol of wartime resistance for the British people. George's eldest daughter, Queen Elizabeth II, is the current reigning British monarch.

Kommandantur (German) Headquarters; commander's office.

kosher (Hebrew) Fit to eat according to Jewish dietary laws. Observant Jews follow a system of rules known as *kashruth* that regulates what can be eaten, how food is prepared and how meat and poultry are slaughtered. Food is kosher when it has been deemed fit for consumption according to this system of rules. There are several foods that are forbidden, most notably pork products and shellfish.

Leeds Jewish Refugee Committee An organization that helped arrange for Jewish refugees' admission to England and then assisted with job training and securing employment for them. It was founded in 1933 by Otto Schiff and was affiliated with the Central British Fund for Jewry in London, which later changed its name to the Central Council for Jewish Refugees. The branch in Leeds existed until 1971.

Mackenzie King, William Lyon (1874–1950) Prime minister of Canada from 1921 to 1930 and 1935 to 1948. Until 1947, his government followed an extremely restricted immigration policy and Frederick Charles Blair, director of immigration from 1936 to 1943, was also openly antisemitic. Between 1933 and 1939, Canada admitted 5,000 Jewish refugees, the lowest number out of any country during that time.

Maginot Line A line of massive border fortifications built by the French after World War I to prevent another German invasion. The defenses, named after Minister of War André Maginot, were thought to be virtually impregnable; however, in May 1940 the Germans invaded France through Belgium, bypassing the line, and then succeeded to defeat the French forces along various points of the Maginot Line.

Miranda de Ebro A city in northern Spain about 250 kilometres from Madrid that was the site of a concentration camp during and after the Spanish Civil War (1936–1939), until 1947. During World War II, the camp held both Spanish political prisoners and prisoners of various nationalities – many were Jewish refugees from both Western and Eastern Europe who had crossed into Spain illegally or were stateless; others were escaped British prisoners-of-war; and some were French soldiers or nationals who had fled their country after the German occupation in 1940. Conditions in the camp were grim in terms of sanitation, food and water supply, and prisoners were forced to work, but the death rate was very low. Prisoners who were protected by their national consulates received support such as extra food rations and fared better than stateless internees; they were also released from the camp much more quickly due to the interventions from their embassies, who guaranteed their care.

Mussolini, Benito (1883–1945) Prime minister of Italy from 1923 to 1943 and founder of the National Fascist Party. By 1925 Mussolini had adopted the title of "Il Duce" (leader), which referred both to his position as dictator and head of government. Mussolini gave military support to Franco's Nationalists during the Spanish Civil War and entered into an alliance with Germany in May 1939 known as the Pact of Steel. Italy officially became part of the Axis powers in September 1940. Mussolini was ousted from government in July 1943 and executed in April 1945. *See also* Axis; Franco, Francisco; Spanish Civil War.

Nansen Passport An identity card issued to stateless refugees by the League of Nations High Commission for Refugees that was named after its designer, the Norwegian explorer, scientist and diplomat, Fridtjof Nansen. The passport was created in 1922 and by 1942 was honoured by fifty-two countries. It was the first travel document for stateless refugees, and in 1938 the Nansen International Office for Refugees was awarded the Nobel Peace Prize for its pioneering work.

Nazi camps The Nazis established roughly 20,000 prison camps between 1933 and 1945. Although the term concentration camp is often used to refer generally to all these facilities, the various camps in fact served a wide variety of functions. They included concentration camps; forced labour camps; prisoner-of-war (POW) camps; transit camps; and death camps. Concentration camps were detention facilities first built in 1933 to imprison "enemies of the state," while forced labour camps held prisoners who had to do hard physical labour under brutal working conditions. POW camps were designated for captured prisoners of war and transit camps operated as holding facilities for Jews who were to be transported to main camps – often death camps in Poland. Death camps were killing centres where designated groups of people were murdered on a highly organized, mass scale. Some camps, such as Mauthausen, combined several of these functions into a huge complex of camps.

North African campaign World War II battles fought between Allied and Axis powers in Libya, Egypt, Morocco, Algeria and Tunisia between June 10, 1940, and May 13, 1943.

Nuremberg Trials A series of war crimes trials held in the city of Nuremberg between November 1945 and October 1946 that tried twenty-four key leaders of the Holocaust. A subsequent twelve trials, the Trials of War Criminals before the Nuremberg Military Tribunals, was held for lesser war criminals between December 1946 and April 1949.

Orthodox Judaism The set of beliefs and practices of Jews for whom the observance of Jewish law is closely connected to faith; it is characterized by strict religious observance of Jewish dietary laws, restrictions on work on the Sabbath and holidays, and a modest code of dress.

OSE (**Oeuvre de secours aux enfants**) (French; Society for Rescuing Children) A French-Jewish organization that helped rescue thousands of Jewish refugee children during World War II. The OSE was founded in Russia in 1912 and its offices were relocated to France in 1933, where it set up more than a dozen orphanages and homes; hid children from the Nazis; and, among other underground operations, arranged for their transfer to the US and Switzerland. Both Joseph Millner and Félix Chevrier, who Max Bornstein worked for, figured prominently in the OSE movement. By March 1942, the OSE, in order to continue its work, was forced under Vichy law to incorporate into the General Union of the Jews of France (UGIF), an organization that collaborated with the Nazis. While the OSE maintained its offices in places like Marseille, it moved its headquarters to Montpellier and then to Chambéry. Eventually, with the German occupation of the south of France in   · November 1942, and the increasing danger of arrests and deportation, much of OSE's work to rescue children went underground and it increased its efforts to both move children to safer homes in the Italian-occupied southeast and smuggle children across the Swiss border.

Passover One of the major festivals of the Jewish calendar, Passover takes place over eight days in the spring. One of the main observances of the holiday is to recount the story of Exodus, the Jews' flight from slavery in Egypt, at a ritual meal called a seder. The name itself refers to the fact that God "passed over" the houses of the Jews when he set about slaying the firstborn sons of Egypt as the last of the ten plagues aimed at convincing Pharaoh to free the Jews. *See also* Four Questions; seder.

Pearl Harbor A US naval base at Pearl Harbor on Oahu Island, Hawaii. Pearl Harbor usually refers to the December 7, 1941, surprise aerial attack on the base by Japanese forces. It is the event that led to the entrance of the US as a combatant in World War II.

Pétain, Philippe (1856–1951) French general and Maréchal (Marshal) of France who was the chief of state of the French government in Vichy from 1940 to 1944. After the war Pétain was tried for treason for his collaboration with the Nazis and sentenced to death, which was commuted to life imprisonment. *See also* Vichy.

rabbi A Jewish teacher, scholar or leader of a congregation.

refugee and immigration policies (France) France experienced a surge of immigration in the early 1930s of more than two million immigrants and by the end of 1938 of more than 100,000 refugees of various nationalities, and government policies toward foreigners fluctuated widely. In the years between 1933 and 1939, aside from a brief respite toward foreigners under the Popular Front government of 1936–1937, a range of restrictive laws were enacted against foreigners. A combination of the rise of antisemitism, along with France's economic depression, led to a general perspective on foreigners, especially Jewish refugees, as a "threat" to France's culture, even though, in comparison to other nationalities, the number of Jewish refugees was quite low. In the early and mid-1930s, there were quotas limiting the numbers of foreigners allowed to work in certain professions, and forcible expulsions or jail sentences for foreigners whose papers were not in order. Subsequently, the 1939 Statute of Foreigners included identification checks; supervision of foreigners; limits on where they could reside; internment or expulsion for various violations; and even included a provision whereby French citizenship could be revoked from those considered "undesirable."

Rommel, Erwin (1891–1944) German Field Marshal during World War II who led German and Italian forces in the North African campaign. *See also* North African campaign.

Roosevelt, Franklin Delano (1882–1945) President of the United States between 1933 and 1945. Roosevelt approved military support to Britain in 1940, but the US only officially entered into the war on the side of the Allies after Japan attacked Pearl Harbor in December 1941.

Rosh Hashanah (Hebrew) New Year. The autumn holiday that marks the beginning of the Jewish year and ushers in the High Holy Days. It is observed by a synagogue service that ends with blowing the *shofar* (ram's horn). The service is usually followed by a family dinner where sweet foods, such as apples and honey, are eaten to symbolize and celebrate a sweet new year. *See also* Yom Kippur.

seder (Hebrew; literally, order) A ritual family meal celebrated at the beginning of the festival of Passover. *See also* Four Questions; Passover.

Shabbat/Sabbath (Hebrew; in Yiddish, Shabbes, Shabbos) The weekly day of rest beginning Friday at sunset and ending Saturday at sundown ushered in by the lighting of candles on Friday night and the recitation of blessings over wine and challah (egg bread). A day of celebration as well as prayer, it is customary to eat three festive meals, attend synagogue services and refrain from doing any work or travelling.

shiva (Hebrew; literally, seven) In Judaism, the seven-day mourning period that is observed after the funeral of a close relative.

siddur (Hebrew) A Jewish prayer book.

Simchat Torah (Hebrew; literally, rejoicing in the Torah) The holiday that marks the end of the annual cycle of readings from the Torah and the beginning of a new one. The holiday is celebrated in synagogue by singing and dancing with the Torah scrolls.

Spanish Civil War (1936–1939) The war in Spain between the military – supported by Conservative, Catholic and fascist elements, together called the Nationalists – and the Republican government. Sparked by an initial coup that failed to win a decisive victory, the country was plunged into a bloody civil war. It ended when the Nationalists, under the leadership of General Francisco Franco, marched into Madrid. During the civil war, the Nationalists received aid from both Fascist Italy and Nazi Germany, and the Republicans received aid from volunteers worldwide. *See also* Franco, Francisco.

Stern Gang The British name for the radical Jewish paramilitary and Zionist group in British Mandate Palestine led by Avraham Stern called Lehi (in Hebrew, *Lohamei Herut Israel*, meaning Fighters for the Freedom of Israel). Lehi, which advocated for a Jewish state and open immigration for European Jewish refugees, split from the military organization Irgun in 1940 due to disagreement over armed conflict against the British, which Lehi supported and enacted. *See also* British Mandate Palestine; Irgun.

Sukkoth (also Sukkot; Hebrew; Feast of Tabernacles) Autumn harvest festival that recalls the forty years during which the ancient Israelites wandered the desert after their exodus from slavery in Egypt. The holiday lasts for seven days, and Jews traditionally eat meals during the holiday in a sukkah, a small structure covered with a roof made from leaves or branches.

tallis (Yiddish; in Hebrew, *tallit*) Jewish prayer shawl traditionally worn during morning prayers and on the Day of Atonement (Yom Kippur). One usually wears the *tallis* over one's shoulders but some choose to place it over their heads to express awe in the presence of God.

Talmud (Hebrew; literally, instruction or learning) An ancient rabbinic text that discusses and debates Jewish history, law and ethics; it is comprised of two sections: the Mishnah, which is further subdivided into six sections and focuses on legal issues, and the Gemara, which analyzes the legal issues.

tefillin (Hebrew) Phylacteries. Pair of black leather boxes containing scrolls of parchment inscribed with Bible verses and worn by Jews on the arm and forehead at prescribed times of prayer as a symbol of the covenantal relationship with God.

Thorez, Maurice (1900–1964) Leader of the French Communist Party (PCF) from 1930 to 1964 and vice premier of France from 1946 to 1947.

Torah (Hebrew) The Five Books of Moses (the first five books of the Bible), also called the Pentateuch. The Torah is the core of Jewish scripture, traditionally believed to have been given to Moses on Mount Sinai. In Christianity it is referred to as the "Old Testament."

tzedakah (charity; from the Hebrew word *tzadik*; righteousness) The act of charity, an important concept in Judaism.

Vichy A resort town in south-central France that was the seat of the government of Maréchal Pétain in unoccupied France. The Franco-German armistice of June 22, 1940, divided France into two zones: the northern three-fifths to be under German military occupation and the remaining southern region to be under nominal French sovereignty, also referred to as the *zone libre* ("free zone"). In October 1940 the administration in Vichy enacted antisemitic legislation, independently of Germany, and later collaborated with Nazi Germany by interning Jews in Drancy, which later led to their deportation to death camps. *See also* Drancy; Pétain, Philippe.

Women's Auxiliary Air Force (WAAF) The female auxiliary of the Royal Air Force that was established in 1939. The WAAFs were involved in aircraft control, communications and intelligence operations, among other duties, and were not involved in direct combat.

Wehrmacht (German) The Germany army during the Third Reich.

Yiddish A language derived from Middle High German with elements of Hebrew, Aramaic, Romance and Slavic languages, and written in Hebrew characters. Spoken by Jews in east-central Europe for roughly a thousand years from the tenth century to the mid-twentieth century, it was still the most common language among European Jews until the outbreak of World War II. There are similarities between Yiddish and contemporary German.

Yom Kippur (Hebrew; literally, day of atonement) A solemn day of fasting and repentance that comes eight days after Rosh Hashanah, the Jewish New Year, and marks the end of the high holidays. *See also* Rosh Hashanah.

Zionism A movement promoted by the Viennese Jewish journalist Theodor Herzl, who argued in his 1896 book *Der Judenstaat* (The Jewish State) that the best way to resolve the problem of antisemitism and persecution of Jews in Europe was to create an independent Jewish state in the historic Jewish homeland of biblical Israel. Zionists also promoted the revival of Hebrew as a Jewish national language.

Zone Libre (French; Free Zone) Southern region of France under nominal French sovereignty between June 1940 and November 1942, after which it was occupied by Germany. *See also* Vichy.

Photographs

1 Max's paternal grandmother with her second husband, date unknown.
2 Max's maternal grandparents, Chayala (née Kahnneman) and Mordechai Zalman
Korman, date unknown.

1   Max's aunt Jennie, left, standing beside an unknown relative. Max's maternal
    grandmother, Chayala, (centre) is seated beside his aunt Pola (right).
2   Aunt Pola and her husband, date unknown.
3   Max's aunt Sadie and her husband, Morris. 1920s.
4   Aunt Jennie and Max's mother, Liba, at Liba's wedding. Warsaw, Poland, 1920.

1 Max's relatives in France. His aunt Leah is seated in front (centre) beside Max's
  cousin Chai Liba (Luba); in the back row, left to right, are his cousin Philippe; his
  uncle Joseph; and his cousin Pierre. Paris, 1936.
2 Max's cousin Luba (left) and Aunt Leah in the late 1930s.
3 Philippe in his French army uniform, 1940.
4 Aunt Pola (left), Aunt Jennie (centre), and Pola's daughter, Hélène, 1937.

Max Bornstein, age 3. Winnipeg, 1924.

1 Left to right: Aunt Jennie; Max's sister, Clarice, age 2; and Max, age 5, standing in front of his mother, Liba. Winnipeg, circa 1926.

2 Max's cousin Max Kim, at about age 11. Winnipeg.

3 Max, age 10, at B'nai Brith summer camp. Gimli, Manitoba, 1932.

4 Max's cousin Jack, Aunt Pola's oldest son, in Canada, date unknown.

1

2

3

1 Max in Paris with his first bicycle, circa 1936.
2 The Bornstein family with Aunt Jennie when she came to visit Paris for the International Exposition dedicated to Art and Technology in Modern Life. Seated in front are Max and Clarice; standing behind, left to right, are Max's father, Chiel; Jennie (centre); and Liba. Paris, 1937.
3 Max at 16. Paris, 1937.

1

2

3

4

1 Chiel Bornstein's passport photo, 1938.
2 Favel and Sarah Silberstein, who sheltered Max, his mother and sister in Paris in August and September 1939. Paris, circa 1934.
3 Clarice (left), Liba and Chiel in Buenos Aires, Argentina, circa 1940. The purse Liba is holding was a goodbye present from Max.
4 Clarice (left) and Liba in Buenos Aires, Argentina, 1942.

Max (right), with his friends Jock (left) and Hershorn (centre) in the Miranda de Ebro camp. Spain, 1941.

1 Clarice in her Women's Auxiliary Air Force (WA A F) uniform. England, circa
  1944.
2 Max in early 1942, soon after arriving in England.
3 Max in front of the gates at Hyde Park, where he liked to walk. London.
4 Max's friends Irma and Eddy with their child. London, circa 1947.

1 Max (seated) and his cousin Pierre (right) during Max's first post-war visit to Paris, 1946.

2 Max's cousins Solomon and Hélène, Aunt Pola's son and daughter, (standing), with Aunt Jennie (centre) and Hélène's eldest daughter, Paulette. Paris, 1946.

3 Pierre (left), Aunt Jennie (centre) and Pierre's wife, Simone. Paris, 1946.

4 Max's relatives in Paris in the late 1960s. In the back row (left to right) are Uncle Joseph, his second wife, Esther, and Pierre's two daughters, Nadine and Lorette; seated in front (left to right) are Pierre; his son, Philippe; Aunt Sadie, and Simone.

1 Clarice and George Stein at their wedding. Toronto, early 1946.
2 Clarice (left) and Aunt Jennie at Clarice's wedding.

Max and Minnie's wedding, Toronto, July 4, 1948. Standing in the back row, left to right, are Solomon; his wife, Anne; a cousin, Dave Moskowitz; Aunt Sadie; Aunt Jennie; Clarice; and her husband, George Stein; seated in front, left to right, are Chiel, Minnie, Max and Liba.

1 Liba (left), Aunt Sadie (centre) and Aunt Jennie (right) at Max and Minnie's wedding. Toronto, July 4, 1948.

2 Max, Minnie and Aunt Sadie, who visited them while they were on their honeymoon. Toronto, 1948.

1 Max and Minnie with their daughter, Linda, at Queen's Park. Toronto, 1949.
2 Max and Clarice's families. Back row (left to right): Max, Chiel, Liba and Aunt Jennie. Front row (left to right): Minnie with their two children, Jeffrey and Linda; and Clarice with her two sons, Allen and Morris. Toronto, 1955.
3 Jeffrey and Linda, circa 1956.
4 The Bornstein family at Coronation Park in Burlington, 1957.

Jeffrey Bornstein's bar mitzvah, 1966. Left to right: Aunt Sadie, Minnie, Jeffrey, Linda, Max, and Liba.

Max's great-granddaughter's bat mitzvah. In the back row, left to right, are Max's granddaughter, Danielle Warman Toledano, her husband, Gilbert Toledano, Max's daughter, Linda Bornstein Warman, his great-granddaughter Samantha Warman, his grandson, Jordan Warman, and Jordan's wife, Lisa Menaker Warman. In the front row, left to right, are Max's great-granddaughter Jesse Toledano, Max Bornstein, and Max's great-grandson, Joshua Warman. Toronto, February 2012.

Index

The Azrieli Foundation was established in 1989 to realize and extend the philanthropic vision of David J. Azrieli, C.M., C.Q., M.Arch. The Foundation's mission is to support a wide spectrum of initiatives in education and research. The Azrieli Foundation is an active supporter of programs in the fields of Jewish education, the education of architects, scientific and medical research, and education in the arts. The Azrieli Foundation's many well-known initiatives include: the Holocaust Survivor Memoirs Program, which collects, preserves, publishes and distributes the written memoirs of survivors in Canada; the Azrieli Institute for Educational Empowerment, an innovative program successfully working to keep at-risk youth in school; and the Azrieli Fellows Program, which promotes academic excellence and leadership on the graduate level at Israeli universities.